TITANIC LIGHT

Texts and Contexts, volume 13

General Editor: Sander L. Gilman, *University of Chicago*

Editorial Board: David Bathrick, *Cornell University*

J. Edward Chamberlin, *University of Toronto*

Michael Fried, *Johns Hopkins University*

Anton Kaes, *University of California, Berkeley*

Robert Nye, *University of Oklahoma*

Nancy Stepan, *Columbia University*

ORTWIN DE GRAEF

Titanic Light

Paul de Man's Post-Romanticism, 1960-1969

UNIVERSITY OF NEBRASKA PRESS

LINCOLN & LONDON

Publication
of this book was assisted by a grant from
the Mellon Foundation.
© 1995 by the University of Nebraska Press
All rights reserved
Manufactured in the United States of America
The paper in this book meets
the minimum requirements of American National
Standard for Information
Sciences – Permanence of Paper for Printed Library
Materials, ANSI Z39.48-1984.
Library of Congress Cataloging in Publication Data
Graef, Ortwin de, 1963–
Titanic light: Paul de Man's post-romanticism,
1960–1969 / Ortwin de Graef.
p. cm. – (Texts and contexts)
Includes bibliographical references and index.
ISBN 0-8032-1695-5 (alkaline paper)
1. De Man, Paul. I. Title. II. Series.
PN75.D45G74 1995 801'.95'092–dc20
94-29809 CIP

For Mimi Wuyts
and
Herman de Graef

Contents

Preface, xi

A Note on Sources, xvii

List of Abbreviations, xix

PART ONE
Destiny

Chapter 1
Obstacle and *Aufhebung*, 3
Mountain Liberty, 5
The Stage, 11
The Sage, 20
Hypersensory Sensation, 29

Chapter 2
Anchorite Rhetoric, 33
Revolutions of Excessive Truth, 33
Stations of True Consciousness, 44
Terrible Maturity, 58

PART TWO
Source

Chapter 3
Recall, 77
Past Analogy, 83

Past Apocalypse, 93
Past Obsession, 101

Chapter 4
The Crisis of Contemporary
Romanticism, 114
Establish the Unbroken Link, 116
Naive, 121
Critical, 127
Barren, 141

PART THREE
Trope

Chapter 5
A Time of Total Form, 181
The Ontological Priority of the Circle, 184
Intimation of Totality, 190

Chapter 6
Resurrexi, 203

Notes, 217

Bibliography, 255

Index, 273

Paraphrase is the best way to distract the mind from genuine obstacles and to gain approval, replacing the burden of understanding with the mimicry of its performance. Its purpose is to blur, confound, and hide discontinuities and disruptions in the homogeneity of its own discourse. The precision of what is being said is not taken too seriously. Is it not, after all, the privilege of the arts, as opposed to sciences, to play freely with truth and falsehood for the sake of graceful effect? – Paul de Man

Nowadays, it is only the unreadable that occurs. – Oscar Wilde

Preface

Titanic Light continues an attempt to locate a persistent concern in Paul de Man's writing in terms of history and literature. The previous record of this project, *Serenity in Crisis*, started out with a reading of de Man's wartime journalism and ended up in a provisional reflection on the 1960 essay 'Structure intentionnelle de l'Image romantique,' read as a problematic modulation of de Man's thought in the 1950s. The present book tries to frame this modulation by placing it as a moment in a certain historical shift from symbolism to Romanticism in de Man's writing.

This change in perspective can be superficially illustrated by pointing to the compositional history of de Man's dissertation (which eventually contained a few pages from 'Intentional Structure'[1]): in 1951 de Man told Harry Levin that he was 'working on a book on poetical theory, taking French Symbolism as a starting point';[2] in the 1955 essay 'Le néant poétique,' he refers to a 'work in progress' called 'La Médiation poétique dans l'œuvre de Mallarmé, Stefan George et W.-B. Yeats';[3] but when he finally presented his thesis at Harvard in 1960, the title had been changed to 'Mallarmé, Yeats and the Post-Romantic Predicament.'[4] The shift, then, is one in which the initial starting point—French symbolism—is located in a wider European context and translated as the aftermath of its own starting point in Romanticism: Mallarmé, George, and Yeats become the heirs of Rousseau, Hölderlin, and Wordsworth.

This shift is not simply the momentous genealogical reversal this miniature narrative stages: 'already' around the middle of the 1950s, the 'postromantic' determination of symbolism and modern thought is a central *topos* for de Man (cf. 'DA' 149; 'YRT' 6–8), and there is no sudden change of mind in his 1958 declaration, 'However varied they may be, contemporary critical methods all originated within a poetic tradition which is that of romanticism—using the term in a sense wide enough to encompass Novalis as well as Rilke, Blake as well as Yeats, Nerval as well as Valéry' ('HRT' 128).[5] What *is* radical in this reversal is de Man's further translation, in the course of the 1960s, of the nature of this origination as a historical occurrence, and it is this translation of symbolism to its Romantic beyond that will be my primary concern here.[6]

Part of the justification of this approach can be derived from de Man's own concession, in the introduction to his dissertation, that his use of the term 'post-romantic' ('PHDI' i) largely depends on 'a few passing allusions to a persistence of certain themes and images' (ii) only, and that the 'nature of this continuity'—which in 1960 he 'merely state[s]' as '*a priori*'—'demands another study.' The task, therefore, is to 'establish the unbroken link' ('HB' 91) between the modern and the Romantic, to justify 'an a priori belief about romanticism illustrated by [a highly restricted] choice of texts.'[7] Yet my perspective on de Man's Romanticism is also dictated by a resistance to abandon this *a priori* in his own text. The name of this obstacle is the notion of 'intentional structure' itself—more particularly, de Man's intention to 'experiment' ('PHDI' iii) with this notion by, on Mallarmé's hand, treating it in terms of a 'thematic development in close parallel to that of a philosophical Idea (Hegel's conception of a "becoming" consciousness),' and, on Yeats's hand, following it through by way of a 'stylistic development in terms of an intentional theory of the poetic image.' The starkest formula for this double-handed discourse is that 'Mallarmé can be explicitated by means of internal exegesis and paraphrase,' while 'Yeats, in the fullest sense of the term, requires interpretation' ('PHDY' 3). The critical moment for de Man's thought is the possibility that instead of meeting somewhere in 'a synthesis between historical and stylistic approaches to literary problems' ('PHDI' iii), these two hands get stuck in the sterility of reciprocal indifference.

In hindsight—knowing, for instance, that toward the end of his life de Man decided not to 'resurrect' his writing on Mallarmé and on the 'more purely thematic aspects' of Yeats but recognized his stylistic interpretation of Yeats as 'already a rhetorical analysis of figural language *avant la lettre,* anticipating a mode that would later become predominant for me' ('PRR' vii–viii)—it is tempting to read the fate of this reciprocal indifference as the mutual undoing of philosophy and literature at the hands of reading, or as the final emergence of historical prose from the poetry that blindly contained it. I do not propose to offer such a reading here, though I intend to address its challenge in a third book on de Man. Instead, what I shall try to offer in these pages is an interpretive paraphrase of de Man's historical determination of the post-Romantic condition as a crisis whose resolution in the form of hermeneutic exegesis is a thing of the past. The pseudocryptic pathos of this program is perhaps a measure of my impatience with its self-imposed limitations, an attempt 'to recuperate on the level of style what is lost on the level of history' (ix). I can only hope that the program is not exhausted in the position of its original intent.

The earliest versions of some of the following chapters were written in 1990. Since then, a new collection of de Man's writing, *Romanticism and Contemporary Criticism,* has been published, comprising, among other papers, the previously unpublished (with one exception) lectures he delivered in his 1967 Gauss seminar at Princeton. From the perspective of the present book, the singular merit of this collection is that it decisively restores Romanticism as de Man's central historical concern in his reflections on contemporary criticism in the 1960s, lending new emphasis to his previously largely ignored acknowledgment that many of the essays published in the first edition of *Blindness and Insight* 'are by-products of a more extensive study of romantic and post-romantic literature' ('FBI 1970' vii). I am grateful to Andrzej Warminski, one of the editors of this collection, for the timely opportunity to read these papers before their publication. I am also indebted to Andrzej Warminski and, especially, Kevin Newmark for their willingness to share a number of unpublished graduate essays de Man wrote in 1953 and 1954 while studying at Harvard. Given the chronological straitjacket of my narrative, these papers should have been read in *Serenity in Crisis,* which, unfortunately, was about to be released when I received transcriptions of these texts. I have tried to turn this missed opportunity to the advantage of my argument by relocating some of these pieces in de Man's writing, turning back to and rehearsing in different detail my earlier paraphrase of its history.[8]

My debts continue to increase. I am very grateful for the valuable comments on earlier versions of this book by Jonathan Culler, Sander L. Gilman, Neil Hertz, Samuel IJsseling, Hendrik van Gorp, Ludo Verbeeck, Samuel Weber, and, especially, Herman Servotte. For their diverse remarks and contributions over the past years I am indebted to Evelyn Barish, Henri Bloemen, Michael Burri, Stefaan E. Cuypers, Patricia de Laet, Erik Derycke, Pierre Despiegeler, Lisa Dolling, David Herman, Filip Huyghe, Roger Janssens, Bradley Jordan, Géza Kàllay, Katalin Kàllay, Willem Lemmens, Dieter Lesage, Christopher Norris, Bart Philipsen, Jan Roelans, Stefano Rosso, Rei Terada, Tom Trezise, Dirk Vanderpoorten, Luc van Liedekerke, Georgi Verbeeck, Liliane Weissberg, Jeffrey Williams, and Peter V. Zima, and particularly to Dirk De Schutter and Hedwig Schwall. Koenraad Geldof's generous comments and trenchant disagreements have shaped my argument decisively, and Erik Leroy is a lasting presence in these pages. The members of the research group on 'Intentionality and Rationality in Contemporary Philosophy of Mind' of the Higher Institute of Philosophy of the Katholieke Universiteit Leuven and the participants in the seminars of the research association of the National Fund for Scientific Research, 'Letter & Zin,' will recognize traces of our discussions in what follows. Special thanks are also due to Neil Hertz and Thomas Keenan, and to Peter Brooks, Emory Elliot, Michael Holquist, Peter Hughes, Kris Humbeeck, José Lambert, Peter Steiner, Sanford Pinsker, and Gerald Prince for their generous invitations to speak on de Man at their various institutions.

To name everyone who has further helped my research would take up too much space, but I must mention Frida Vandervelden, de Man's daughter Patricia de Man, and Louis Dupré. If it had not been for the rare haven the Belgian National Fund for Scientific Research offers the humanities today, this book would never have been written; my debt to its scientific committee and to its permanent secretary, José Traest, is accordingly great. My colleagues at the Katholieke Universiteit Leuven know what I owe them, as do my friends. My gratitude to Caroline is first and last and without end, as is my different gratitude to my parents: to them this book is dedicated.

Nieuwrode, December 1993

A Note on Sources

A number of Paul de Man's texts considered in this study were not originally written in English. Whenever possible I have made use of published English translations of these texts for the purpose of quotation. In some cases I have modified these translations for the sake of consistency. In other cases I have emended translations that were inaccurate or simply wrong. Both types of alterations are indicated as such in the text. When no English translations were available (as in the case of de Man's wartime journalism) I have supplied translations myself. In the special case of texts that were revised or translated by de Man for publication in *Blindness and Insight*, I have always checked the original against the second version and have used the latter only when the differences were negligible or nonexistent; otherwise, I have quoted (and, when necessary, translated) the original and have marked this by adding the page reference for the original version (o.v.). When the only page number in a parenthetical reference is to the original version, this indicates that the relevant passage was deleted in de Man's later revision. Translations from other sources that were not available to me in English are also my own.

Abbreviations

References to de Man's wartime journalism identify the original source, the month and year of first publication (if not already specified), and the page number in the volume *Wartime Journalism*. References to de Man's later work are indicated by means of abbreviations for separate items as listed below. To facilitate cross-reference to the Bibliography, the year under which an item is listed is added after each entry. As a rule, the page number in each parenthetical reference is that of the collection in which the item was (re)published; the abbreviation for the relevant collection is added after each entry in the following list. An exception to this rule are references to the original version of an item whenever this differs significantly from its later republication in a collection (see the note on sources). Page references for items that have not yet been (re)published are to their first publication or to the transcript of the manuscript. For the texts originally written in French or German, the title of the English translation is added in parentheses.

WARTIME JOURNALISM

BD	*Bibliographie Dechenne*
C	*Les Cahiers du Libre Examen*
HVL	*Het Vlaamsche Land*
J	*Jeudi*
LS	*Le Soir*

BOOKS

AR	*Allegories of Reading*
BI	*Blindness and Insight*
CW	*Critical Writings, 1953–1978*
RCC	*Romanticism and Contemporary Criticism*
RR	*The Rhetoric of Romanticism*
RT	*The Resistance to Theory*
WJ	*Wartime Journalism*

ESSAYS AND ARTICLES

'AC'	'The Mask of Albert Camus' (1965) CW
'AD'	'Autobiography as De-Facement' (1979) RR
'AG'	'Whatever Happened to André Gide' (1965) CW
'AIB'	'Allegory and Irony in Baudelaire' (1967) RCC
'AT'	'Anthropomorphism and Trope in the Lyric' (1983) RR
'BB'	'Bachelard and Burke' (1954)
'C'	Comments (1966)
'CC'	'Criticism and Crisis' (1966) BI
'CCR'	'The Contemporary Criticism of Romanticism' (1967) RCC
'CJ'	Foreword to Carol Jacobs, *The Dissimulating Harmony* (1978) CW
'DA'	'The Double Aspect of Symbolism' (1955) RCC
'DD'	'Dialogue and Dialogism' (1983) RT
'DF'	'Impasse de la critique formaliste' ('The Dead-End of Formalist Criticism') (1956) BI
'F'	'La critique thématique devant le thème de Faust' ('Thematic Criticism and the Theme of Faust') (1957) CW
'FBI 1970'	'Foreword' to *Blindness and Insight* (1970) BI

'FBI 1983'	'Foreword' to *Blindness and Insight*, second edition (1983) *BI*
'FG'	Fragment of the Fifth Gauss Lecture (1967) *RCC*
'FI'	'New Criticism et nouvelle critique' ('Form and Intent in the American New Criticism') (1966) *BI*
'GL'	'Georg Lukács's *Theory of the Novel*' (1966) *BI*
'GP'	'Vérité et méthode dans l'œuvre de Georges Poulet' ('The Literary Self as Origin: The Work of Georges Poulet') (1969) *BI*
'HB'	'A New Vitalism' (1962) *CW*
'HE'	'Les exégèses de Hölderlin par Martin Heidegger' ('Heidegger's Exegeses of Hölderlin') (1955) *BI*
'HEW'	'Heaven and Earth in Wordsworth and Hölderlin' (1965) *RCC*
'HR'	'Heidegger Reconsidered' (1964) *CW*
'HRT'	'Hölderlin and the Romantic Tradition' (1958) *RCC*
'IG'	'The Inward Generation' (1955) *CW*
'INT 1980'	'Interview with Paul de Man' (1980)
'INT 1983'	'An Interview with Paul de Man' (1983) *RT*
'IR'	'L'Image de Rousseau dans la poésie de Hölderlin' ('The Image of Rousseau in the Poetry of Hölderlin') (1965) *RR*
'IS'	'Structure intentionnelle de l'Image romantique' ('Intentional Structure of the Romantic Image') (1960) *RR*
'JK'	Introduction to John Keats, *Selected Poetry* (1966) *CW*
'JPS'	'Sartre's Confessions' (1964) *CW*
'K'	'[Keats]' (1953)
'KH'	'Keats and Hölderlin' (1956) *CW*
'LB'	'Ludwig Binswanger et le problème du moi poétique' ('Ludwig Binswanger and the Sublimation of the Self') (1966) *BI*
'LH'	'Literary History and Literary Modernity' (1969) *BI*

'LM'	'Lyric and Modernity' (1969) *BI*
'LN'	'The Literature of Nihilism' (1966) *CW*
'MB'	'La circularité de l'interprétation dans l'œuvre de Maurice Blanchot' ('Impersonality in the Criticism of Maurice Blanchot') (1966)
'MK'	'Murray Krieger: A Commentary' (1981) *RCC*
'MP'	'Modern Poetics: French and German' (1965) *CW*
'MR'	'Hypogram and Inscription' (1981) *RT*
'MT'	'Montaigne et la transcendence' ('Montaigne and Transcendence') (1953) *CW*
'NG'	'Genesis and Genealogy (Nietzsche)' (1972) *AR*
'PAR'	'Preface' to *Allegories of Reading* (1979) *AR*
'PHDI'	Introduction to 'Mallarmé, Yeats and the Post-Romantic Predicament' (1960)
'PHDM'	Section on Mallarmé in 'Mallarmé . . .' (1960)
'PHDY'	Section on Yeats in 'Mallarmé . . .' (1960)
'PMK'	'Phenomenality and Materiality in Kant' (1983)
'PN'	'Le néant poétique' ('Poetic Nothingness') (1955) *CW*
'PP'	'Le devenir, la poésie' ('Process and Poetry') (1956) *CW*
'PRR'	'Preface' to *The Rhetoric of Romanticism* (1983) *RR*
'PT'	'Patterns of Temporality in Hölderlin . . .' (1967) *RCC*
'RB'	'Roland Barthes and the Limits of Structuralism' (1972) *RCC*
'RC'	'The Purloined Ribbon' (1977) *AR*
'RDS'	'Madame de Staël et Jean-Jacques Rousseau' ('Madame de Staël and Jean-Jacques Rousseau') (1966) *CW*
'RH'	'The Riddle of Hölderlin' (1970) *CW*
'RJ'	'Allegory *(Julie)*' (1979) *AR*
'RNP'	'Self *(Pygmalion)*' (1979) *AR*
'ROB'	'The Rhetoric of Blindness' (1971) *BI*

'ROT'	'The Rhetoric of Temporality' (1969) *BI*
'RSC'	'Political Allegory in Rousseau' (1976) *AR*
'RT'	'The Resistance to Theory' (1982) *RT*
'RTS'	'Rousseau and the Transcendence of the Self' (1967) *RCC*
'SC'	'Spacecritics' (1964) *CW*
'SD'	'Shelley Disfigured' (1979) *RR*
'SL'	'Symbolic Landscape in Wordsworth and Yeats' (1962) *RR*
'SR'	Introduction to *Studies in Romanticism* (1979)
'SS'	'Sign and Symbol in Hegel's *Aesthetics*' (1982)
'TB'	'Taine and Baudelaire' (1953)
'THW'	'Time and History in Wordsworth' (1967) *RCC*
'TP'	'Tentation de la permanence' ('The Temptation of Permanence') (1955) *CW*
'WB'	'"Conclusions": Walter Benjamin's *Task of the Translator*' (1983) *RT*
'WBY'	'Image and Emblem in Yeats' (1960) *RR*
'WM'	'What Is Modern?' (1965) *CW*
'WWH'	'Wordsworth und Hölderlin' ('Wordsworth and Hölderlin') (1966) *RR*
'YRT'	'Yeats and the German Romantic Tradition' (1954)

PART ONE

Destiny

CHAPTER ONE

Obstacle and Aufhebung

et que le trajet d'une rivière fait crime – Montaigne,
'Apologie de Raimond Sebond'

'Intentional Structure of the Romantic Image' reveals a lure in de Man's critique of reconciliatory readings of the tension between mind and nature. The name of this lure is the self-sufficient imagination, and in *Serenity in Crisis* I suggested that it risks foreclosing the concerted reflection on reading and history de Man's work continued to promise, ending up instead in an ontological absolute beyond dialogue and commitment. Arguably the one word in de Man's diction that could have most powerfully assumed a fall into this trap as a triumph is *serenity*. Such assumption would have espoused the movement of a superficial but highly effective redemptive dialectic. The serene frame of mind de Man had admired in his early models Jünger and Valéry (*LS*, January 1942, 182; *BD*, July 1942, 361), had then carried over into the 'tranquil irony' of Montaigne ('MT' 11), but had subsequently denounced as a false sentiment germane only to tired, conservative, nihilist minds ('IG' 15; 'PP' 65), would now, at the end of its negative labor as the badge of complacency, be allowed to ascend anew along the path traced in 'Intentional Structure' to the supreme realm of chastened awareness. Yet, the potentially crucial word *serenity* remained curiously muted, present only in a long passage from Rousseau's *Julie* quoted by de Man, alongside some lines from Hölderlin and Wordsworth, as an instance of the 'moment of peace' that 'determines the fate of the respective authors and marks it as being an essentially poetic destiny' ('IS' 15). De Man's description of the *telos* of this destiny, the self-sufficient imagination, takes its principal thrust from Wordsworth's apostrophe to the imagination in Book Six of *The Prelude,* and it stretches toward the point in the *Rêveries du promeneur solitaire (Reveries of the Solitary Walker)* where Rousseau 'declares himself "content d'être" [content to be] and "ne jouissant de rien d'extérieur à soi, de rien sinon de soi-même et de sa propre existence" [enjoying nothing external to himself, nothing if not himself and his own existence].' In this movement it sheds most of the weight of the pages from the *Nouvelle Héloïse,* but the terms of those pages continue to haunt de Man's argument.

Mountain Liberty

> ... *they are of the sky,*
> *And from our earthly memory fade away.*
> — Wordsworth, 'These words were
> uttered in a pensive mood'

The distinctive feature of the self-sufficient imagination is that it bespeaks an intent on the part of de Man's elected 'precursors of romanticism' ('IS' 9–10) to 'put into question, in the language of poetry, the ontological priority of the sensible object' (16; translation modified). The allegory of this question, as read by de Man, is the movement of ascent carried out in the three passages under consideration, a movement away 'from a terrestrial nature and . . . toward this "other nature" mentioned by Rousseau, associated with the diaphanous, limpid, and immaterial quality of a light that dwells nearer to the skies' (14). The lesson of this allegory is the transposition of ontological priority 'into an entity that could still, if one wishes, be called "nature," but could no longer be equated with matter, objects, earth, stones, or flowers . . . an entity that could never, by its very nature, become a particularized presence' (15). But no sooner has this movement of transposition been traced than it is frozen into the radical promise of 'a possibility for imagining and thinking consciousness to suffice unto itself, independently of all relationship with an exterior object, and without being moved by an intent aimed at such an object' (16; translation modified). And no sooner has this promise been made than it is, in its turn, set off against an admission of ignorance, cast as a recognition of the absence of concrete examples of 'the poetical language issuing from such an imagination' and supported by a qualification of the three chosen excerpts as, 'at most, *underway* toward such intuitions' (translation modified).¹ As far as Rousseau's text is concerned, this latter qualification is, to say the least, desirable.

The fragments from *La Nouvelle Héloïse* quoted by de Man are taken from an important letter to Julie written by Saint-Preux during his exile in the Valais. The first movements of the letter seem to lend themselves readily enough to the logic of ascent de Man seeks to demonstrate. Saint-Preux registers the 'astonishing mixture of wild nature and cultivated nature' as well as the heightening of this 'bizarre contrast' in the oppositional structure of 'wild nature' itself, and to this 'variety' (characterized in terms suggesting harmony [*agréments*] rather than, *pace* de Man, 'violen[t] turmoil' [16]) he then attributes the 'calm' he feels regenerating in his soul: 'I admired the sway the most insensible [*insensible*] beings hold over our most lively passions, and I despised philosophy for its inability to do even only as much for the soul as a sequence of inanimate objects could.'²

De Man omits this last sentence, but it could without too much difficulty be read in confirmation of his argument (which, it should be recalled, precisely denies such power to exterior objects): the stage in the text at which the sentence occurs is clearly located before the decisive ascent, and Saint-Preux immediately continues by judging this explanation insufficient and announcing 'some other cause' for his 'peaceful state,' a turn that could lead us to expect a further development along the lines suggested by de Man, where this 'other cause' would then be the 'other nature' that functions as the ethereal objective correlative of the self-sufficient imagination. Yet, as this phrasing already indicates, the possibility of such development is complicated by the inner contradiction of this function: insofar as the new, celestial imagination is in fact self-sufficient, its objective correlative must necessarily be wholly independent of an object other than itself, and hence no objective correlative at all— let alone a 'cause' for its self-sufficient existence.³ It is this contradiction that wrenches de Man's reading away from Saint-Preux's letter.

For de Man, the crucial point of the ascending movement is Rousseau's 'insisting on the fact that Saint-Preux's ecstasy has "rien de sensuel,"' a quality he reads as proof of this imagination's supreme independence 'of all relationship with an exterior object' (16; translation modified). Rousseau's 'rien de sensuel' is thereby effectively translated as a straightforward transcendence of sensory perception as such, but to judge from Saint-Preux's eventual identification of the 'true cause' of his 'inner peace,' the aesthetics of this movement are far less radically cut:

> In the high mountains, where the air is more pure and more subtle, one feels more ease in respiration, more lightness in the body, more serenity in the spirit; pleasures are less ardent there, passions more moderate. Meditations acquire a certain grand and sublime character there, in proportion to the objects that strike us, a certain tranquil delight [*volupté*] that has nothing of the acrid [*âcre*] or the sensual [*sensuel*]. It seems that in elevating oneself above the dwellings of man, one leaves behind all the lower and terrestrial sentiments, and that to the extent that one approaches the ethereal regions, the soul contracts something of their unchanging purity. One is serious there without being melancholic, peaceful without being indolent, content to be and to think.[4]

De Man is certainly right to underscore the movement away from the terrestrial regions in this passage, but it takes a good deal of countertextual pressure to further read this movement as a farewell to sensation. By highlighting the absence of the *sensuel* at the expense of the equally important absence of the *âcre*, de Man's commentary obscures not only the banality of the *aurea mediocritas* pervading Saint-Preux's sentiment but also the central role assigned to the sensation of specific proportions of the observable scene.[5] In this light, it is not surprising that de Man omits Saint-

Preux's immediate extension of this principle into the practice of medical and moral therapy:

> Thus a happy climate puts the passions that elsewhere form man's torment at the service of his bliss ... and I am surprised that exposure to the salutary and beneficent air of the mountains should not be one of the great remedies of medicine and morals.[6]

It would, however, be inaccurate to simply reduce Saint-Preux on the basis of this passage to a sage of the health resort, and to find de Man's suppression of these sensible precepts all too understandable. For if what de Man omits is hardly surprising, what he does quote is all the more puzzling, precisely because he only quotes it and fails to read it as what it appears to be: an index of Saint-Preux's truly undeluded understanding of the vanity of serenity, an understanding that might in fact approach the critique of sensation imposed on Rousseau in de Man's reading, but only as its negative, literally non-utopian face. The lines I am alluding to immediately precede Saint-Preux's praise of the salubrious air of his mountain retreat:

> I arrived that day at the least elevated mountains and, upon crossing this uneven terrain, at those among the highest that were within my reach. After having walked through the clouds for a while, I reached a more serene station, from which, during the season, one can see the thunder and the storm gathering below [*au-dessous de soi*]; all too vain an image for the soul of the sage, the example of which never existed, or only exists in the very places from which one has derived the emblem.

If Saint-Preux subsequently proceeds by apparently forgetting this cool appraisal of elevated superiority in order to recommend that one turn one's back on the dwellings of humans and take the moral medicine of the mountains, we should also register that he qualifies this recipe as precisely that—oblivion: 'One forgets everything, one forgets oneself, one no longer knows where one is'—*and* that he immediately turns away from this forgetfulness by recalling a delight 'even sweeter' than 'the charm of the landscape': 'the intercourse with its inhabitants.'[7] De Man's account once more fails to acknowledge both moments: Saint-Preux's praise of 'the simple, rustic, poor, primitive life'[8] is simply omitted, and his observation of self-oblivion is quoted but subsequently forgotten by way of the introduction of a phrase from the letter into the body of the Fifth *Rêverie,* where, according to de Man, 'Rousseau declares himself "content d'être" [a phrase lifted from Saint-Preux's letter] and "ne jouissant de rien d'extérieur à soi, de rien sinon de soi-même et de sa propre existence"' (16). Rather than being read, as is no doubt necessary, along the lines of another and finer connection than that of contrast, the difference between self-oblivion and auto-affection, or between Saint-Preux and Rousseau (or vice versa), is crossed out without comment, and through this erasure the tension of Rousseau's text is flattened into declaration.

The point of this exercise exceeds the mere observation of de Man's willful reading;[9] more significantly, it locates two crucial concerns of de Man's poetics on their way to dogma: the *Aufhebung* of sensory perception and the celebration of this process as the acquisition of serenity in the mode of historically effective wisdom. 'Intentional Structure of the Romantic Image' prepares the ground for this ideology but shies away from its own logic and nostalgically ends on a tentative note, balancing a return to the crisis (of poetry) de Man had been documenting since the mid-fifties with a quasireligious suggestion of the hope for resurrection that poetry nonetheless contains. Some five years later, however, 'the serenity of . . . ideal knowledge' is finally given its full historical voice:

> There was a man who, in reaffirming the ontological priority of consciousness over the sensible object, put the thought and the destiny of the West back onto its authentic path; the same man had the wisdom and the patience to remain faithful to the limi-

tations that this knowledge, in accordance with its own laws, imposes upon the human spirit. He was thus able to safeguard the future of mankind. This man is called Rousseau. ('IR' 44, 45; translation modified)

It remains for us to begin reading this name.

The Stage

> ... they are of the sky,
> And from our earthly memory fade away.
> – Wordsworth, 'Composed after a Journey
> across the Hamilton Hills, Yorkshire'

De Man's most obstinate elaboration of the imagination projected into the sky of early Romanticism occurs in the course of the dense 1965 essay 'The Image of Rousseau in the Poetry of Hölderlin,' and this is one of the reasons why I shall worry this text at what may seem a disproportionate length. A good deal of the essay's impetus is derived from a conventional reaction to the state of the art: the extant exegeses addressing the presence of Rousseau in Hölderlin's writing, de Man asserts, invariably come up against and founder on 'a kind of obstacle to thought,' and it is this obstacle he here proposes 'to name,' 'in the hope of thus transforming it into a point of departure' ('IR' 21). In fact, this is not the first time de Man took this specific task to heart: in 'Hölderlin and the Romantic Tradition,' an essay probably written around 1958 but never published during his lifetime, he had already set out to understand precisely what 'The Image of Rousseau' eventually claims to name—'what Rousseau signifies for Hölderlin' ('HRT' 132)—and, through such understanding, to arrive at a different reading of Romanticism and, eventually, of 'the history of the Western mind' (135).

The manuscript suggests that this reading would have included a critique of the natural image similar to that sketched in 'Intentional Structure' (see especially 'HRT' 130), but we can only guess at its precise historical impact, for the text breaks off at the bottom of a page in midsentence (207 n. 14). If, that is, this promised impact was given voice at all, for although it seems likely that the remaining pages of the essay (ostensibly intended for a lecture) were lost rather than never written, the resulting abrupt cut does graphically capture the resistance of the obstacle about to be named in 'The Image of Rousseau.'[10] Our question will therefore have to be how this name can overcome this resistance.

After a sustained interpretation primarily drawing on 'Hymne an die Menschheit' ('Hymn to Humanity'), *Hyperion*, 'An die Stille' ('To Stillness'), and the ode 'Rousseau,' de Man suggests (as he had already done in 'Hölderlin and the Romantic Tradition') that this enabling naming can best be performed in a reading of 'Der Rhein,' 'the veritable keystone of Hölderlin interpretation' (19). Obeying 'das Gesetz dieses Gesanges' [the law of this song] as Hölderlin himself had laid it down in a prefatory note, he divides the hymn into three major parts, which he aligns to the tripartite generic hermeneutics developed in Hölderlin's theoretical essays.[11] The first part deals with the river Rhine itself, as a natural entity fulfilling the destiny of 'a "being" *("étant")* devoid of consciousness' (34)—fulfilling destiny, that is, as it is in itself, *'en soi,'* in a 'naïve' mode. The second part is itself subdivided into two sections, devoted respectively to the *Heros* (the Promethean hero) and to the *sterblicher Mann* (the mortal, Rousseau), both of whom are said to accomplish the destinies of the conscious and historical beings they are for themselves, *'pour elles,'* in a heroic mode—that is, 'from the point of view of the consciousness that experiences it.' Part three, finally, is no longer concerned with particular beings but instead names the knowledge *(savoir)* of this experience from the most general level conceivable, that of cognition *(connaissance)* itself, a level Hölderlin characterizes as *idealisch*.[12] The position of Rousseau in this narrative, then, is such that he and the Promethean hero preceding him represent 'two distinct experiences of consciousness on the way to its fulfillment, which follow one another chronologically.' De Man then goes on to interpret this sequence more closely, but before we can follow his reading we must circle back to an earlier stage in the argument, where the notions here deployed—destiny, the sacred, the source, and the demigod—are explicitated in almost catechetical detail.

'Der Rhein' owes its status as a crucial moment in Hölderlin's poetics to the fact that its tight structure allows for a reading of the poet's conception of 'the full and exemplary "destiny" of every earthly entity' (31). This destiny is what is possible within what is allowed: 'the way [in which every earthly entity] completely fulfills its possibilities of being yet without overstepping the temporal and spatial limits assigned to it.' The Rhine, as a natural entity, is the 'natural prototype' of all entities obeying this law, including the conscious and historical figures of the Promethean hero and Rousseau. And all such 'creatures that fulfill completely their destiny on earth'—creatures that obey 'the word of Goethe, quoted by Heidegger, "*werde, was du bist*"'[13]—deserve to be called demigods *(Halbgötter)*. It would be wrong, de Man contends, to read this term as designating a (quantitative) degree of presence of the sacred in a natural or conscious entity: for Hölderlin, the sacred is essentially parousia; it is everywhere at all times as that which envelops and supports everything that is to the same degree, and there can consequently be no question of the semidivine being a mixture of sacred and nonsacred 'essences.' However, this omnipresence does not entail that the *mode* of presence of the sacred is unchanging: for earthly beings, the sacred is always present, but it is necessarily present through mediation only, which is to say that it is present as the hidden and the secret: as absence.

> Demi-gods are those entities which either through their natural and objective behavior or through their internal consciousness (there is no distinction on this level) show that they conform to this fundamental law of the earthly creature; being is always present for them, even if in the mediated mode of absence. Such is the source. (32)

The source is the point of intersection between the sacred and the earth (the latter, quite literally, being the surface 'inhabited' by nature and man). As a point of intersection, the source marks the moment where the supratemporal realm of the sacred suspends itself and where earthly being commences its falling unfolding in time as becoming. The source, then, is 'the place where time is engendered.'

> The demi-gods are therefore those who act in conformity with the source; they realize themselves fully as entities whose origin is simultaneously downfall and becoming: the falling of the sacred into time. They remember the source, not the sacred—for Hölderlin, in contrast to Plato, it is not possible for us to remember that which we, as sons of the earth, have never known; on the other hand, it is possible for us to recall the source and consequently also to forget it. Most entities, both men and things, forget, but not the demi-gods. (32)

It is impossible, then, to remember what has never been known—the best we/the demigods can do is to remember the source. But the source is precisely that point where the rememberable and the immemorial (the sacred) meet, and the danger is thus that in remembering the source, the demigod may be tempted to transgress his earthly limits and aspire to know what cannot be recalled, to remember what is necessarily unmembered in the mediating time of memory. The true demigod, true to the law of the source, recoils from this temptation and pursues (that is, obeys) the proper destiny.

Such is the fundamental pattern set by Being. In response to the demands of (the) narrative, this ontological pattern subsequently has to be instantiated in the careers of the various demigods, on what could be called the ontic level. As far as the prototypical natural entity is concerned, this transposition apparently poses no particular problems: the Rhine, in Hölderlin's reading of its course and especially of its turn from the East (the sacred) to the West (its destiny) in the stretch between its source and the lake of Konstanz, is a true demigod in that it has avoided this danger.[14] But for the hero and for Rousseau, this felicitous fit between narrative demand and geographical trajectory is not available, and the pattern has to be complicated.

The hero and Rousseau are distinguished from the Rhine in that they are endowed with consciousness. As such, they represent 'two distinct experiences of consciousness on the way to its fulfillment' (35). This way is the destiny of consciousness, as distinct from that of the natural entity epitomized in the Rhine but similar (or even, as de Man writes, 'perfectly equal') to that destiny in its conformity to the source (295 n.31). For this equality to obtain, the moment of transition between the hero and mortals is of the utmost importance: on this moment hinges the very movement of destiny and it must thus mark a turning point analogous to the saving bend in the course of the Rhine near Chur. Just like the Rhine recoiled from its aspiration to actually enter the sacred, so consciousness must renounce this temptation, without, however, thereby forgetting the source. In order to obey this postulate of an ontological identity between natural being and consciousness on the level of their respective (identical) destinies, the narrative is forced once more to impose itself on the ontic level and to cast the hero as an actual type of individual (equal in onticity to the Rhine as an actual river): the man of action, 'the very type of a man who acts as though he were the equal of the gods' (35), a type whose prototype has to be located subsequently in a certain past so as to keep up the developmental rule of the road, which requires a strict parallel between the course of this action and the course of the Rhine before its turn to destiny.

Both demands are predictably met in the 'experience' of Ancient Greece, whose typical hero (Prometheus) engaged in an act designed to 'directly confront the sacred in suppressing all intermediary mediation,' and who thus brought catastrophe upon himself and upon 'the nation that accept[ed] such an individual as leader.' The story of this destiny is one of apocalyptic accomplishment: in their all 'too direct confrontation with being,' the Greeks have 'experienced [the greatest ultimate danger] in the heroic mode of historical action; the rise and fall of their civilization existed in reality and have thus concretely inscribed in human memory the absolute law of temporality' (35–36). The letter of this law is 'the necessary moment of the defeat of action': 'because heroic action (that is, in conformity with the source) makes us too much the equal of the gods, it signifies our destruction' (36). It is in this defeat that 'Greece realized herself completely and thus became semi-divine' (35).

Compelling though this narrative is, it does raise an odd problem: if Greece is to be seen as truly semidivine, like the Rhine, it is not clear how at the same time it can be said to have transgressed, in a moment of *hubris,* the limitations set to it insofar as it is an earthly entity. The Rhine corrected its destructive thrust to the East, where the sacred resides, and *therefore* deserves the title of demigod; Greece did not effect this saving swerve and 'call[ed] down upon [itself] the sacred lightning which reduced [it] to ashes' (36), yet it is still called semidivine. The most likely ground for this ostensible inconsistency is the developmental pattern itself: the narrative demands an ontological analogy—though de Man prefers to speak of an 'identity' here, for reasons we shall discuss later on—between natural being and the being of consciousness, and in order to meet this requirement it is forced to devise an incarnation for both types of being by means of 'real' entities. But whereas the line of the Rhine on the map (its ontic course) readily supports the developmental unity demanded on the ontological level, the destiny of 'man' as the *hypokeimenon* of consciousness can be enlisted in such narrative only through the introduction of historical catastrophe and diachronic continuity (as opposed to the spatial swerve in synchronic continuity of an entity like the Rhine). The point being that in the terminological framework set up by de Man (through Hölderlin), Greece (itself already synecdochically figured as the man of action) can only be called semidivine insofar as it partakes of the development of human consciousness on the ontological level; not insofar as it has actually, 'historically,' trespassed against its destined course by aspiring to, and foundering in, the divine or the sacred as such.

Such as it is, this point may seem trivial, reducible to a terminological rather than a logical or cognitive inconsistency (if such a distinction can be upheld), but it deserves to be signaled inasmuch as the inconsistency involves precisely the notions of action and analogy that will prove to be central obstacles in de Man's historical thought. For the moment, we can suffice by underscoring that if the story recounted here proposes to account for the conception of history as destiny, there is some cause for concern when it then turns out that the story in fact presupposes (this) history as its own narrative and (thus) legitimating principle, and this on the basis of a spatial analogy that, adding vertigo to tautology, it claims to be neither spatial, nor an analogy. The further aspect of this incongruity we shall have to return to is the extent to which, despite de Man's express protestations to the contrary, the dice are decisively loaded against the 'man of action':[15] if heroic action is indeed 'in conformity with the source,' the question remains why it necessarily has to lead to destruction—destruction being, after all, the divine punishment inflicted upon those who do not follow their destiny, who do not, strictly speaking, honor the source, even while they do remember it (all too vividly, in fact). If, on a first level, these inconsistencies may merely indicate the degree to which de Man is still uncomfortably stuck in a muddled dialectic, this is not to say that his implication in this predicament is merely naive, or merely repeats earlier and unresolved complications. But before we can labor this point, we must get on with the story.

The destiny of Greek civilization has concretely inscribed 'the absolute law of temporality' in human memory. De Man specifies the point (leaving aside, for the time being, the notion of time itself):

> This experience is far from being in vain. In revealing the danger to us, it makes us more experienced *(erfahren)* like the Rhine at the end of its course. And, again like the Rhine, the Greeks are for us who come after them precursors, pioneers who, in danger, traced the first paths. The wisdom they bequeathed us

is summarized in the eighth strophe, which contains the 'ideal' lesson drawn from the 'heroic' experience of the preceding strophe: that is, the understanding of the structure of consciousness from an already semi-ontological point of view. (36)

This 'pre-ontology of consciousness' is the lesson that reads that consciousness—as self-consciousness, de Man's reading of Rousseau's 'sentiment (de soi)' and of Hölderlin's 'fühlen von selbst' at this stage of his argument—is like *(comme)* an obstacle that keeps humans from swerving into the sacred and retains them on earth. The reason why this lesson—itself no more than a rehearsal of the notion of destiny—is only pre- or semi-ontological is that the imposition of the obstacle is still understood as an 'ontic' act of the gods.[16] An important consequence of this ontic impurity is that in the absence of a full (ontological) understanding of consciousness, the lesson contained in the Greek experience is not yet properly spelled out and available primarily as the gods' *Gericht*, 'the negative law that is its corollary: the impossibility of avoiding the defeat of heroic action' (the action of what Hölderlin calls the 'Schwärmer' that would be God) and 'the necessity of recognizing what Goethe . . . called *Grenzen der Menschheit*' (36–37). Enter Rousseau.

For it is in the figure of Rousseau that the ontology of consciousness receives its purest articulation. Rousseau is indeed a true demigod in that, unlike his Greek predecessor, he did observe the law of the earth. Rather than to aspire to the source in the sky, this avatar of the 'Söhne der Erde' sought to obey the source on earth. This, then, is the 'obstacle' to be named: how to read this earth? Most interpreters of Hölderlin, de Man contends, have read it as a conventionally pastoral,[17] idyllic realm of reverie, but in doing so they miss the essence of Hölderlin's Rousseau:

> For how can one explain the absolutely central role assigned to Rousseau in the development of the hymn—it is a question of him who not only in his own way goes beyond the grandeur of the Greeks but also guides the destiny of the West towards a

new marriage of men and gods—if this is nothing but an idyllic interlude? (37; translation modified)

With this question, the stage has been set and the obstacles have been defined. The stage is the surface on which the destiny of consciousness is (to be) traced, around, by means of, and in reading at least three obstacles. The first obstacle is consciousness as that which keeps humans gracefully locked to earth in obstructing their 'rush' toward the sacred, in guiding them back into the channels of their proper, earthly destiny. The second obstacle is the ontic impurity that blocks the true reading of this obstacle from sight. The third and decisive obstacle is the figure of Rousseau as the demigod who, for the first time, has rightly read the first obstacle and has thus successfully negotiated the second, but whose affiliation with what appears to be a celebration of idyllic repose clashes with this pioneering function. It is this third obstacle de Man, in reading Rousseau, now has to confront, and it will not come as a surprise that this confrontation will essentially take shape in a rethinking of the obstacle he himself had repeatedly run into before.

The Sage

> Give me but one firm spot on which to stand . . .
> — Archimedes

The centrepiece of de Man's reading of Rousseau develops around Hölderlin's reception of the 'Cinquième promenade' in the *Rêveries du promeneur solitaire*. As is only natural, not only because Hölderlin quite explicitly singles this text out, but also because from its opening lines onward, Rousseau's report on his sojourn on the Isle de Saint Pierre declares itself a pioneering report on destiny, the natural, the lawful, and the limit:

> This small island . . . is little known, even in Switzerland. As far as I know, no traveller makes mention of it. Nonetheless, it is very agreeable and singularly well-situated for the happiness of a man who likes to define himself [*se circonscrire*]; for even if I may be the only one in the world whose destiny has made this into a law, I cannot believe that I am the only one with so natural a taste, even though up to this point I have not yet found it in someone else.[18]

The body of the Fifth *Rêverie* lives up to this promising isotopy and—telescoping two passages from the text (§§ 9 and 15)—de Man swiftly establishes the point:

> The famous pages of Rousseau deal most of all—in the form of an inner experience of temporality—with the priority of what he calls 'le sentiment d'existence' over sense perception. When the senses are 'fixed' by the waves' steady rocking of the boat carrying Rousseau, another perception appears, one which 'does not come from outside (but) arises within us.' One cannot

insist enough on how much these lines deepen the experience of sense perception ('sensation') to the point where one could speak of a devaluation, a going beyond sense perception [*sensation*]. The sensation [*sensation*] that appears here no longer emanates in any way from objects but rather proceeds entirely from within ourselves. ('IR' *RR* 37–38; translation modified)

We are back on familiar ground: the hierarchical shift in the initial inside/outside polarity (the essential separation as read in 'The Double Aspect of Symbolism') that governed the concept of the self-sufficient imagination returns in full force. But whereas the Hegelian substratum of this notion in 'Intentional Structure' was textually alluded to only in the resonances of the loaded phrase 'lifting itself up,' lifted from *The Prelude*, a footnote to the present passage clearly establishes the point: 'The movement in Rousseau's text seems to me . . . to go dialectically from "pure sensation" to "sentiment intime," so that it is a matter of going beyond mere sense perception [*sensation*] in a Hegelian sense *(Aufhebung)* here' (295 n.41). And it is this movement, 'Rousseau's turning away from sense perception toward the "sentiment of existence" that [Hölderlin] sees as the crucial moment in the development of Western thought' (38).

De Man begins to specify this moment by turning to the eighth stanza of 'Der Rhein,' and more precisely to the term 'fühlen' in the following lines:

> Es haben aber an eigner
> Unsterblichkeit die Götter genug, und bedürfen
> Die Himmlischen eines Dings,
> So sind's Heroën und Menschen
> Und sterbliche sonst. Denn weil
> Die Seeligsten nichts fühlen von selbst,
> Muß wohl, wenn solches zu sagen
> Erlaubt ist, in der Götter Nahmen
> Theilnehmend fühlen ein Andrer,
> Den brauchen sie;[19]

> [Yet their own
> Immortality is enough for the gods, and if
> The celestials need one thing,
> Then it is heroes and humans
> And further mortals. For since
> The most blessed ones do not feel on their own,
> There must be an other who, if it is
> Allowed to say this, feels participatingly
> In the gods' name,
> That one they need;]

This 'fühlen,' which was previously collapsed with a 'sentiment de soi,' is now read with more respect for its ambiguity—as 'sentiment' and as 'sensation'—and in this ambiguity, de Man declares, 'the destiny of thought is at stake' (38; translation modified). It is this double construct that figures as 'the obstacle that restrains the earthly creature in its rush [*élan*] toward being,' and the product of this restraint is consciousness, which 'founds itself [*se fonde*] by colliding with sensible things which keep us at a distance from being' (translation modified).[20] Rather than being an obstacle imposed by the gods, consciousness now becomes that which develops in an encounter with sensible objects, and with this notion de Man begins to explicitate the critical turn against his earlier ontological presuppositions that was adumbrated in 'Intentional Structure':

> From an ontological point of view, sensible things are therefore those that are the farthest from being, even though they play an essential role in the dialectic that preserves the earthly entities in the mode of existence proper to them. Hence there is a temptation to grant them an ontological priority over nonsensible entities, and to make sense perception [*sensation*] (the immediate encounter with the object) into the ontological experience par excellence. (38–39; translation modified)

This temptation (of permanence, of substance, of natural being, of the sensible object),[21] de Man continues, is a recurrent feature in the history of thought, and

In giving in to this temptation, we commit a fundamental error, for we grant being to the entity that is most devoid of it. We put a screen of objects which have become opaque and static between being and ourselves, and thus cut ourselves off from the source forever; it is the forgetting of the source (often called incorrectly the forgetting of Being) that characterizes our present civilization (39).[22]

But as we know, Rousseau did not make this mistake (or error): being a true demigod, he never forgets the source and thus never puts inauthentic obstacles between himself and being. In more positive terms, this means that Rousseau holds the answer to the following demand:

> There has to be [*il faut*] an entity other than the object, an experience other than sensation, in which our mediated relation to being can establish itself without separating us from the origin. It must be possible to apprehend things in such a way that they appear as secondary in relation to a more fundamental entity that supports them and subtends them and which nevertheless is not being itself, which always remains inaccessible. (translation modified)

The pivotal importance of this categorical imperative deserves to be underscored: it states, quite explicitly, not only the necessity of abandoning the attribution of ontological priority to sensible objects (that much is familiar), but also (and more crucially) the concomitant necessity of preserving mediation and the 'apprehension' of things. De Man's imperative 'il faut,' in other words, is leveled as much against his own earlier hypostasis of the celestial imagination as against the victims (and the challengers as initially portrayed) of the various temptations inventoried in his essays of the mid-fifties. What is needed, emphatically, is an entity that simultaneously dislodges sensible objects from their illegitimate position of ontological superiority and avoids the total expulsion of these entities from an imagination divested of 'all relationship with an exterior object' ('IS' 16; translation modified): 'This is precisely what happens in Rousseau's Fifth Rêverie' ('IR' 39)—and more specifically in the following passage from that reverie as read by Hölderlin as read by de Man.[23]

> When the evening approached I would descend from the peaks of the Isle and gladly sit down at the side of the lake in some hidden retreat on its shore; there, the sound of the waves and the agitation of the water, fixing my senses and chasing from my soul all other agitation, submerged my soul in a delicious reverie in which the night often surprised me without my having noticed it. The flux and the reflux of this water, its continuous but intermittently swelling sound striking [*frappant*] my ear and my eyes without cease, substituted for [*suppléoient*] the inner movements the reverie extinguished in me and sufficed to make me feel [*sentir*] my existence with pleasure, without taking the trouble to think. Now and again some weak and brief reflection on the instability of the things of this world, of which the surface of the waters offered me the image, would arise in me [*naissoit*]: but soon these impressions effaced themselves in the uniformity of the continuous movement that rocked me, and which, without any active assistance from my soul, did not fail to capture me [*m'attacher*] to the point that, called by the hour and by the agreed signal, I could not tear myself away from the spot without effort.[24]

It seems difficult not to construe this passage as yet another instance of capitulation to the temptation to submerge consciousness in the permanent continuity of an analogy-inviting nature, but de Man sees the matter differently: in a typical sweeping move, he posits that the 'sound of the water that Rousseau perceived (or, it would be better to say, of which he has the "sentiment") is the sound caused by the water which strives to plunge in the absolute depth of being but is prevented from doing so by the protective intercession of the earth' (39). As such, it is the sound of the source itself, a sound Rousseau, in Hölderlin's phrase, has the 'sicherer Sinn / Und süße Gabe zu hören' [the sure sense / And the sweet talent to hear]. To 'hear' this source, then, is to be pervaded with 'the power that permits us to see objects in their true dependency in relation to being and in their authentic dialectical role as a protective but nevertheless transparent obstacle.' In keeping with the initial demand, the objects are no longer simply perceived—for then they would block Being from sight—but are instead apprehended as being contained in a larger entity that itself is lodged between Being and the furniture of the sensible world: this entity is earth.

With this earth, de Man can name and sublate the obstacle: far from being a realm of idyllic reverie, the earth introduced here is just what it should be in the narrative of 'Der Rhein':

> Earth is precisely the going beyond the obstacle of sense perception [*sensation*] toward being, a going beyond which remains all the same rigorously enclosed within the limits of the mediated. The 'earth' of Hölderlin is the Heideggerian Being-in-the-world [*être-dans-le-monde*], the sentiment of existence [*sentiment de l'existence*] of Rousseau; let us say, to remain within Hölderlin's own vocabulary, that it designates the ontological priority of *consciousness* over the object. (40; translation modified)

The equation is formidable: consciousness, now at last explicitly granted ontological priority, is 'the discursive equivalent of the poetic term "earth."' Where *phusis* was (to be rejected), there *khthoon* (perhaps) shall be. This earth can evidently no longer be the earth opposed to the sky of 'Intentional Structure of the Romantic Image': it is no longer the realm in which consciousness seeks refuge from its own constitutive instability—rather, it is the space in which this instability has been generalized (and this to the extent that it becomes doubtful whether it can still be called unstable at all). The previous positioning of the celestial imagination was predicated on a subject/object relationship qualified as a tension between the permanent and the becoming and realized in the opposition between solid earth and unparticularizable sky, an opposition that itself still uneasily functioned as a check on the unmistakable tendency to transpose ontological priority onto consciousness itself. The present consciousness, and with it earth, can no longer be construed according to this model, and de Man is quite explicit about this: the 'earth thought of as consciousness' is itself the possibility condition for the 'mediated apprehension of being in inwardness,' and it is for this reason that consciousness can confidently be granted ontological priority. This means that the notion of mediation is now refined as the process that honors both the sky as 'being itself' (which is necessarily inaccessible) and the world of sensible objects. These latter are now 'apprehended' in their true relation to earth and thus to Being: not as privileged manifestations of or means of access to this Being, but as obstacles that precisely forbid such access, even while they are necessarily taken up in Being through their dependence on the earth thought as consciousness. This earth, then, becomes the authentic obstacle to Being as the entity in which sensible objects—inauthentic only insofar as they are credited with ontological priority—are sublated and preserved. Or so de Man would have us believe.

For there are some serious fault lines in this earth rethought as consciousness. De Man himself admits that the notion 'may appear paradoxical to us,' but he immediately goes on to pull the carpet from under this admission by accusing 'us' of having produced this appearance of paradox in the first place, 'used as we are to thinking of consciousness in terms of the duality or the analogy of the subject/object relation.' And he continues that 'it is precisely this duality founded on the ontological priority of the sensible object that Hölderlin [following Rousseau] would go beyond,' thus authoritatively banishing the paradox to the mists of pre-Rousseauist/pre-Hölderlinian thought. Which is not quite good enough.[25]

It is in fact from within this 'apparent paradox' that the potential destruction of the principle of intentionality encountered in 'Intentional Structure' can be addressed more systematically. This betrayal of intentionality took shape as the solipsistic imagination's short-circuiting of the noetic *visée* on the ultimately unattainable world of intended objects. In the guise under which the principle of intentionality had first made its appearance in de Man's work, this unattainability of the real intended object—the real cat—was processed as proof of the ontological superiority of that object over the intentional object (and thus over consciousness itself), and it was thus only 'natural'—though hardly inevitable—that the reversal in ontological priority eventually announced in 'Intentional Structure' should also entail an implicit rejection of the principle the initial hierarchy had been paired to. In other words: if the exteriority of the real object to consciousness was read as inexorably commensurate with its ontological priority over and against the inwardness of consciousness, the postulate of the ontological priority of consciousness quasi-automatically invited a rejection both of exteriority as such and of the principle of intentionality designed to think that exteriority through.

The present case tries to be importantly different. In a sense, the chiasm is undone: the postulate of the ontological priority of consciousness is retained (or, more accurately, positively spelled out), but it is no longer seen as requiring a rejection of exteriority, since what is outside now also figures inside by virtue of the equation of consciousness and earth. The epochal importance of Rousseau (for de Man's Hölderlin) is precisely that he pioneered the attempt to escape from the dualist stalemate (de Man himself got stuck in) of the inside/outside polarity—that, after him, Hölderlin, and Western thought, 'no longer needs analogical thinking,' which conceived of consciousness according to the paradigm of the subject/object relation. But the question remains to what extent this attempt can be called successful, since it is not clear whether the very notion of ontological priority can in fact be made consistent with the claim that the inside/outside duality is (being) superseded—*a fortiori* when this advance is qualified as the 'mediated apprehension of being in *inwardness*.' Put differently: we must ask whether this new model does not actually presuppose the duality it pretends to leave behind, albeit that it presupposes it in the modified form of the interiorized, mediated duality proper to a 'sentiment de l'existence' that contains the exterior through its posited coincidence with the earth in which this exterior itself is contained.[26]

The question takes us back to the terms that haunted de Man's thought in the fifties: Is it this pioneering turn, then, that heralds the ultimate victory over the 'essential separation' ('DA' 150); is this the 'new synthesis that Hegel had the audacity to name' ('PN' 28); is it in/as this rethought earth-as-consciousness that the ultimate 'new true object' projected in Hegel's dialectics of experience finally arises?[27] Is the advent of this 'new true object' what is announced in de Man's suggestion that 'the word "water" is closer to the ontological essence of water than the sense perception of this element' ('IR' 40–41)? Is it here that the *noema* and the *noumenon* finally coincide in their essence—in which case the principle of intentionality would be subverted (or rewritten) along lines diametrically opposed to those followed by the solipsistic imagination; in which case the 'sentiment de l'existence' would itself become a solipsistic imagination now, through its rewriting of mediation as totalization, in possession of what it deliberately alienated itself from before?

In order to confront these questions—and so as to read more accurately the far-reaching historical impact of this moment—we must first reread de Man's production of this earth in its difference (emphatically marked by one of the very few exclamation marks in de Man's writing) from 'the world that engenders sense perception!' (39).[28]

Hypersensory Sensation

The round earth rolls;
I cannot hear it hum—
The stars are dumb—
The voices of the world are in my ear
A sensuous murmur. Nothing speaks
But man, my fellow—him I hear,
And understand; but beasts and birds
And winds and waves are destitute of words
What is the alphabet
The gods have set?
– T. E. Brown,
'Dartmoor: Sunset at Chagford'

The sound of the water that Rousseau perceives (or, it would be better to say, of which he has the "sentiment") is the sound caused by the water which strives to plunge in the absolute depth of being but is prevented from doing so by the protective intercession of the earth' ('IS' 39). A prosaic question: Why would it be better to say that Rousseau 'has the "sentiment"' of the sound of the water? De Man's poetic answer: because 'the attributes proper to the world that engenders sense perception' must be filtered out for the object to be named in its 'authentic dialectical role'—as the 'transparent obstacle' whose recognition functions as a 'point of departure' in the itinerary of Western thought toward the ontological priority of consciousness-as-earth. But this poetic demand comes up against the resistance of Rousseau's rêverie. For the subject of the passage from the Fifth *Rêverie* de Man proposes to read is, emphatically, hearing and seeing; what 'fixes' his 'senses' is 'le bruit des vagues et l'agitation de l'eau'; what makes him 'sense' his existence with pleasure is the water's 'bruit continu mais renflé par intervalles frappant sans relâche mon oreille et mes yeux,'[29] much as Saint-Preux's meditations in the Valais acquired a distinctive character 'proportionné aux objets qui nous frappent.'[30]

De Man's leveling of this resistance—as a property of matter and/in the text[31]—deserves to be read carefully. What can it mean to have one's senses fixed? In a footnote we have already referred to, and which is sketched as a response to Georges Poulet's reading of the passage in terms of a 'conjunction of two original elements: inner feeling and pure sense perception [*sentiment intime et pure sensation*],' de Man proposes the following answer:

> The movement in Rousseau's text seems to me nevertheless to go dialectically from 'pure sensation' to 'sentiment intime,' so that it is a matter of going beyond mere sense perception in a Hegelian sense *(Aufhebung)* here. This is certainly the movement in the Fifth *Rêverie,* where Rousseau speaks at first of a joint action of sense perception ('le bruit continu [de l'eau] frappant sans relâche mon oreille et mes yeux') and the internal movements of the reverie. But the more the text develops, the more clearly it indicates that what reveals itself in this way is precisely not the object, the cause of sense perception, but 'nothing that is outside oneself *(rien d'extérieur à soi).*' It seems then, that the expression 'to fix my senses' must be read as a going beyond sense perception. (295–96 n.41; translation modified)

In the shift from how the text 'seems' to move to what is 'certainly' its movement—a shift repeated in the imperative coloring of the concluding hypothesis—de Man hammers the *Rêverie* in place. On the one hand he concedes that the experience described in the passage marks a 'joining' of sensation and sentiment; on the other hand he asserts that the key expression in that passage 'must' be understood as a 'going beyond' sensation, but for this assertion to be grounded he has to go six paragraphs beyond the 'here' of the passage in order to return to it with the required exclusion of exteriority ('rien d'extérieur à soi')[32]—and this while the whole point of the passage is supposed to be that it transcends the inside/outside polarity.

A similar move can be detected in de Man's statement, 'When the senses are "fixed" by the waves' steady rocking of the boat carrying Rousseau, another perception appears, one which "does not come from outside (but) arises within us"' (37–38): the point is not merely that Rousseau is not sitting in a boat when he has his senses fixed,[33] but rather that the 'movement that does not come from outside' appears in a later reflection and figures explicitly as an alternative to appropriate sensory impressions—such as the exterior movements of the waves—when these latter are not available.[34] Reading this 'movement that does not come from outside' as a 'devaluation of sense perception' (38) is making Rousseau too straightforwardly intelligible by half.

To return to the footnote, it is furthermore not quite true that 'Rousseau speaks at first of a joint action of sense perception . . . and the internal movements of the reverie': what he does write is that the sounds of the water reaching *(frappant)* his ear and eyes 'substituted for [*suppléoient*] the inner movements the reverie extinguished in me and sufficed to make me feel my existence with pleasure, without taking the trouble to think.' Rousseau is submerged in his delicious reverie through the sound of the water lapping on the lakeshore, 'fixing my senses and chasing from my soul all other agitation.' Rather than being beyond sensation, he is beyond thinking: at the moment in the text under consideration here, the reverie is described as being wholly induced by sensory perception and is said in so many words to actually extinguish the inner movements that are supplanted by this perception. In the words of Jean Wahl:

> There is no philosopher closer to the pure sentiment of existence than Rousseau. . . . I think, therefore I am, Descartes said. But in the states Rousseau describes for us, I am because I hardly think, one could say: because I do not think. . . . There

is no active assistance from my soul anymore. There is nothing but the uniformity of the continuous exterior movement that awakens in me an interior continuum.[35]

Thus, for Wahl it is not so much a question of a 'joint action' of consciousness and exterior movement as of a wholesale homologization of the former to the latter. Certainly, Wahl's reading of Rousseau's 'existential mysticism' can be said to err in the opposite direction, but the point remains that de Man's reading, too, is an untenable disambiguation of the text: it is one thing to note Rousseau's subtle paradoxes of perception and the striking rereading of fixed catachreses in his reverie;[36] it is another to claim that the sensation given voice to here, at this particular point, 'no longer emanates in any way from objects but rather proceeds entirely from within ourselves' ('IR' 38; translation modified). As we already indicated, de Man goes on to qualify the exclusionary nature of this new sensation by reading it as earth itself, but this abrupt imposition of a new name cannot erase the effacement of the senses it is founded on. The continuation of Hölderlin's saga of Rousseau as read by de Man suggests that this complication is more than the matter of philological pedantry it also, necessarily, remains.

CHAPTER TWO

Anchorite Rhetoric

> Yet the play must find releasement [*Erlösung*], and for the play of mourning [*Trauerspiel*] the releasing mystery is music; the rebirth of feelings in a super-sensible nature [*übersinnliche Natur*].
> — Walter Benjamin, 'Die Bedeutung der Sprache im Trauerspiel und Tragödie'

Revolutions of Excessive Truth

Rousseau is the name of an epochal turn in the history of (Western) consciousness under way to a new dispensation under the sign of 'the ontological priority of *consciousness* over the object' ('IR' 40). Having rounded this obstacle, de Man accelerates his dialectics to the point of history.

The central thesis is swiftly established: Hölderlin's Rousseau 'appears above all as the man of language'; he 'also appears as the creature of temporality'; this 'union of language and temporality constitutes poetry'; and an alternative name for this union is 'a term like "history," however corrupted by misuse it may be':

> It is as a creature of earth, as a creature pivoting on language and on time, that Rousseau profoundly has an effect on history. Like Mnemosyne, he engenders time as the noematic correlative of consciousness. History, so to speak [*si l'on peut dire*], becomes the music of humanity, the 'still, sad music of humanity' Wordsworth speaks of in 'Tintern Abbey.'[1] (41; translation modified)

The hesitation voiced in the conditional 'si l'on peut dire' is quickly overcome in a return to 'the dialectic of repose and action,' an issue de Man had already considered at earlier stages of the essay but which he had bracketed, 'in order to simplify things,' in the first movements of his reading of 'Der Rhein.' The task faced in this dialectic is the integration of interiority in history; its truth is the 'dialectical necessity' following which 'the repose of inwardness is a way of putting oneself into a relation to being, thereby transposing the action that preceded it and that will follow it onto a higher level' (28). In Rousseau, this necessity is admirably enacted: rather than seeing history as a succession of 'spectacular actions'—as was the case in the 'dangerous Greek activism'—Rousseau rethinks it as 'a solitary meditation that can only be produced in repose' (42).

The question remains how this retreat into interiority relates to the actual reality of history, or, put differently, just how history as the 'noematic correlative'[2] of consciousness translates as the real history Rousseau is said to have a profound effect on. De Man imperiously dismisses the potential objection registered in this question:

> But this initial inwardness does not at all exclude a later transposition onto the plane of reality. Only a philosophy imbued with the ontological priority of the sensible object could confuse to this degree ideality with irreality; it is not because a thought is no longer centered on sensible objects that it loses all possibility of practical efficacy, and it is not because it emanates from inside that a thought becomes incapable of attaining generality. On the contrary, to the extent that it reestablishes an authentic relation to being, it extends itself to the entire human community, and its particular will becomes general will. (41; translation modified)

It does not require a great deal of critical unpacking to realise that the doctrine sported in this passage courts a crude(ly) Hegelian ideology of history. That the future of humanity here announced should be described in a phrase echoing the 'new synthesis that

Hegel had the audacity to name' ('PN' 28) as 'the perfect world whose possibility Rousseau had the audacity to affirm' ('IR' 23) is entirely appropriate. For de Man, the pertinence of this echo is a matter of course—once again, the point is reserved for a footnote:

> This [the possibility of practical efficacity in Rousseau's thought] is so obvious for Hölderlin that he has no difficulty in fusing the figures of Rousseau and Bonaparte. Like his friends Hegel and Schelling, he sees Bonaparte (in any case until the peace of Lunéville) as the culmination of the French Revolution. He is like the practical side of Rousseau's ideality. With this aspect of his thought, which he shares with a number of his contemporaries, Hölderlin appears as one of the founders of the ideological conception of history, which, since Romanticism, holds sway in the world. (296 n.47)

The ideology that is the possibility condition for Rousseau's daring affirmation is nothing less than ideology itself: in the spirit of de Man's argument, ideology is the proper name for the power of interiority in its profound and practical effects on the actual history of the human community.

We do not need puns to appreciate the consistency of this conception with the *Aufhebung* of sensory perception that paved the way for it, but we may as well abuse one for our purpose. The point of the ideology 'is so obvious' that it requires no argument: 'La chose est tellement évidente pour Hölderlin qu'il n'éprouve aucune difficulté à amalgamer les figures de Rousseau et de Bonaparte.' A perverse but pertinent German translation of this 'chose' would have to be 'die Sache' rather than 'das Ding,' and in the 'transposition onto the plane of reality' of the 'initial interiority' that is at stake here, such is precisely the Hegelian point. Consider Jean Hyppolite's prefiguration of the conclusion to this chapter on 'The Human Work and the Dialectic of Action' in *Genesis and Structure of Hegel's 'Phenomenology of Spirit'*:

> At the end of this chapter reality will appear as the work of self-consciousness, but of a universal self-consciousness which

transcends individuality. This work of all and of each, this world engendered by self-consciousness, in which the notion of the opaque and impenetrable object *(Ding)* will vanish and be replaced by a new notion of objectivity *(Sache)* corresponding to the Greek $\rho\tau\alpha\gamma\mu\alpha$, will open up for us the 'world of realized reason' which is the spirit.[3]

This 'world engendered by self-consciousness' in which the 'opaque object' is supplanted by the new objectivity of the spirit is the 'perfect world' audaciously envisaged by Rousseau in his turn away from the screen of 'opaque' ('IR' 39) objects toward a true apprehension through which he 'engenders history as the noematic correlative of consciousness' (42). Such is the dialectic of the 'authentic path' of consciousness (45): the universality of the conception of history as the correlative of ideology produces the external world as the project of solitary meditation. The particular will becomes the general will of a consciousness beyond individuality: interiority put back onto its true track engenders a will that demands a particular general politics: 'It necessarily has an aspect not merely political but revolutionary. It is completely consistent that the author of *Julie* should also be the author of the *Social Contract*' (41).

It is because of this consistency that we need to emphasize the affirmative nature of de Man's apology for the historical spirit of 'radically revolutionary' general politics at this stage in his argument. It is 'simply *not* the case'[4] that—as Christopher Norris has suggested—the 'wisdom' of de Man's Rousseau 'has a limit at precisely those points in Rousseau's more "political" texts (like the *Social Contract*) where thought oversteps the bounds of an "authentic relation to being" and seeks to legislate in terms of an "entire human community" or "general will."'[5] We need only repeat the text to show up the simple error of this parataxis: 'On the contrary, to the extent that it [thought] reestablishes an authentic relation to being, it extends itself to the entire human community, and its particular will becomes general will' (41). Rousseau's wisdom does come up against a limit—we shall turn to that presently—but this limit is not the cautionary sign severing inwardness from historical action and its historical lesson is emphatically *not* that 'consciousness must choose between stark alternatives: *either* the life of unthinking spontaneous action (with all its dangerous consequences) *or* the kind of inward, contemplative life that can never bring itself to act in any way.'[6] Insofar as Rousseau's wisdom is conceived as the dialectical development of the Greek experience of excessive action, it must do more than simply reject this experience. The political aspect of Rousseau's thought is not a 'fall[ing] back into the Greek or Promethean way of thinking'[7] as in a past error: it is precisely a lifting up of this error to the truth of historical efficacity the error itself betrayed by embracing it all too immediately. The claim to historical impact is a necessary extension of inward reflection, not a regressive transgression of 'the bounds of an "authentic relation to being."'

Nor is de Man's insistence on this necessary extension merely 'a temporary positive moment' soon to be erased in an 'otherwise permanent strategy of dismantling.'[8] Far from being a reactionary warning call issuing from a chastened awareness, de Man's thought on the politics of Romanticism repeatedly directs an affirmative historical charge through his work. Thus, reading Rousseau in his 1966 introduction to Keats, he identifies as one of the principal strengths of Romanticism its ability to 'encompass the greatest degree of generality in an experience that never loses contact with the individual self in which it originates' ('JK' 197) and specifies that it is Rousseau's 'universal moral sense' and his 'generalized passion' that 'make it possible for him to be at the same time the poet who wrote *Julie* and the moral philosopher who wrote the *Social Contract*. . . . For the great romantics, consciousness of self was the first and necessary step toward moral judgment.'[9] Elsewhere, in a contrastive passage in his dismissive 1964 review of Sartre's *The Words*, he asserts that 'Rousseau's *Confessions* support Montaigne's claim that "all men carry within themselves the entire human condition"' ('JPS' 121)[10] and argues that it is in this claim that the key to the Romantics' commitment to literature must be sought:

> They realized that literature, in spite of its inherent distortions, remains a privileged way of access to reality, not because it reflects this reality, but because it reveals degrees of authenticity that no other activity is able to reach. For them, too, political action and social reform were part of this process of self-knowledge, and they found it far less difficult than we do now to reconcile the demands of history with those of the self. (122)

Such was also Mallarmé's 'admirably uncompromising' answer to the question 'whether political action should not take precedence over poetical speculation' as de Man understood it in 1960: 'The way to be present to one's own time begins in total inwardness, certainly not out of indifference towards history, but because the urgency of one's concern demands lucid self-insight; action will follow from itself, when this insight has been gained' ('PHDM' 102 n.1). And this insight is to be gained, not surprisingly, in thought conceived as the faculty that '*engenders* time as the mediating entity between consciousness and the chaos of immediate reality. The language of thought contains time as a substance in which consciousness can remain suspended. Within this temporal substance can take place the "legs à quelqu'un" which . . . characterize the historicity of a universal consciousness' (116).

Yet, it is not enough to underscore the extent to which de Man's understanding of a lucid commitment to literature cannot simply be read, *pace* Norris, as 'an allegory of political disenchantment.'[11] If it is simply not the case that de Man's thought 'would divorce "poetry" from "active political involvement,"'[12] the opposite is not simply the case either. The suggestion of a marriage between inwardness and universal efficacity must be qualified on at least two counts.

First, the above combination of the fragments from de Man's

Mallarmé study and from his Sartre review betrays a retrospective sentiment of some complexity: Mallarmé's thought is the legacy of Rousseau's in that it, too, 'engenders time' as 'the substance' for 'the historicity of universal consciousness'; but as an attempt to engage 'the post-romantic predicament,' it also partakes of the 'decline' of 'romantic historical consciousness' diagnosed in the Sartre review ('JPS' 122). In 1960, contemporary poetry is 'the depository of hopes of resurrection that no other activity of the spirit seems able to offer' ('IS' 17; translation modified); in 1964, the literature that 'reveals degrees of authenticity that no other activity is able to offer' ('JPS' 122) has (almost) become a thing of the (Romantic) past. Indeed, the ability to wed the 'process of self-knowledge' unfolding in literature to 'the demands of history . . . seems to have been lost in the course of the nineteenth century.'

The decisive factor in this loss, which engenders a 'threatening paralysis' ('IS' 9), is, as we know, the erroneous commitment to the priority of the sensible object, but the specific purport of the very notion of this wrong turn in de Man's thought is as yet not sufficiently accounted for. For the moment (and only for the moment) we can understand it as a symptom of nostalgia for a pre-lapsarian future of literary efficacity—the effect of such an understanding being that the divorce of action and lucid insight is a matter of unfortunate historical possibility, not one of necessity. The regression from the rigor of Rousseau's turn in post-Romantic literature is lamented by de Man precisely because it entails an inability to generalize thought into action, while such generalization—or totalization—itself remains the regulative principle, however remote, for his conception of authentic poetry, that is, thought. In short: de Man's disenchantment results from a recognition of historical error, not from a recognition of this error as historically inevitable. The lesson this recognition imposes will be the burden of this book.

The second qualification of the political thrust of pure inwardness concerns us more immediately at this stage, because it takes us back to the original path of Rousseau—or, rather, to the conceptual interruption of that path from within the logic of its own historical development. For instead of further pursuing the implementation of a revolutionary politics this dialectic announces, de Man appears to take off on a tangent. Having remarked that it is 'entirely consistent' that 'this radically revolutionary spirit should be persecuted by those who refuse to follow him on his path,' he suddenly seems to shift the grounds of the debate:

> But this is not the worst danger. It comes rather from an excess of truth which risks a forgetting of the mediated limits of the human. Whereas the Greeks were destroyed by an action that was almost too splendid, we risk being destroyed by the very risk of a thought all too lucid. ('IR' 41–42; translation modified)

For Rousseau, this danger takes on the two complementary aspects of an interior self-sufficiency ('se suffire à soi-même comme Dieu' [to suffice unto oneself like God]) and the exteriorized 'excessive hopes' engendered by the French Revolution, the 'revolutionary community that takes its origin from his solitary thinking,' 'its ideological aspirations so legitimate that it risks creating a belief in the possibility of a definitive and meta-temporal political order' ('IR' 42). Both these states, interior and exterior, court 'destruction by a direct confrontation with the sacred' (42), but Rousseau succeeds in warding off this apocalypse by effecting a retreat into the repose of a contemplative interiority, sheltered from the withering force of unmediated Being. In Hölderlin's poem, this moment occurs when the 'mortal man' is described as he who, after having carried the heavens in his arms, recoils in the oblivion of the shady woods on the shores of the lac de Bienne, where he 'sorglosarm an Tönen / Anfängern gleich, bei Nachtigallen . . . lern[t]' [carefree and poor in tunes / Like beginners, learns from nightingales]:

> This retreat, this recollection of being onto his own consciousness, this return to the originary I at the moment when this I,

although saved from the temptation of the object, risks losing itself in the infinity of the divine parousia—this is Rousseau's profound fidelity to his nature as a human being (for whom access to the divine is prohibited) and as demi-god (who cannot forget the presence of being in consciousness). (43; translation modified)

But it is only when consciousness awakens from this refuge—when Hölderlin's Rousseau enters 'the unforgettable Hölderlinian landscape of interiority,' where he who has built the mountains and traced the paths of the streams now also rests and where 'Zur heutigen Erde der Tag sich neiget' [the day bends itself toward the present Earth]—that we finally reach the prefiguration of 'the highest experience possible for the historical man of the present day, the culmination of Western destiny.' (44) The collective equivalent of this moment, 'its extension to the general will,' is, 'naturally,' the 'Brautfest' of men and gods. This 'perfect world' is now transposed onto the level of ideality—'the very sign of a truly complete thought'—which entails that for us,[13] conscious historical men in the post-Rousseau era, the real moment of this 'fulfillment' is inaccessible and can be retained only as an ideality to be prepared in, but necessarily absent from, 'our destiny as essentially temporal.'

For, creatures of the earth and of language that we are, it is our duty (our *Pflicht*, perhaps also our plight) to observe the rules by recollecting ourselves, and by forgetting—not the source (which must be obeyed), nor Being (which 'was never known in the first place'), but 'the fullness of our thought itself when it has been put back on the path of truth' (44–45). For this thought is dangerous precisely in 'its almost uncanny understanding of the past and its concrete anticipation of the future':

At the moment when the Western spirit reaches maturity (when, as the hymn 'Mnemosyne' says, 'Reif sind, in Feuer getaucht, gekochet / Die Frücht . . .') it permits a knowledge of its own genesis—one thinks of Hegel's *Phenomenology of Spirit,* for example—but such that the power of its clarity threatens to blind like lightning. (45)

It is to shelter us from this imminent danger that there is the 'divine will,' reflected, according to de Man, in 'Mnemosyne,' which does not look kindly upon he who has not 'die Seele schonend sich / Zusammengenommen' [protecting the soul / Recollected himself]: 'er muß doch' [yet he must]. And Rousseau did:

> There was a man who, in reaffirming the ontological priority of consciousness over the sensible object, put the thought and the destiny of the West back onto its authentic path; the same man had the wisdom and the patience to remain faithful to the limitations that this knowledge, in accordance with its own laws, imposes upon the human spirit. He was thus able to safeguard the future of mankind. This man is called Rousseau. His act is called: to recollect oneself. ('IR' 45; translation modified)

The dramatic force and pathos of this closure seduce and invite resistance. The story ends up by informing us that if it were to end up by revealing the whole truth, its narrator—and, presumably, its narratee—would be struck with blindness—even while it presupposes that very truth. What takes place in this enticing less-is-more road story is the unfolding of consciousness along a dialectical route fixed by Being in such a way that consciousness can only be true to this route to the extent that it recoils from the truth of this self-same route. Yet, if consciousness is only true to the road as it forgets the truth of the road (such forgetting being itself the truth of the road), from which position can this true story then be told, if not from within a knowledge of precisely this (unforgotten) truth? That is: from a position that assumes as true that there is indeed a road in the first place, from a position that claims lucidity for a conceptualization of history—as the history of consciousness—as a road, but that abstains from actually arguing (let alone questioning) this conceptualization in any consistent critical way.

We should be careful not to fix this question as itself a critical answer—not in any special deference to de Man (he needs none), but because the challenge of the question is better responded to in a rereading of Rousseau's road more single-mindedly intent on (and resistant to) the stations that grant it the coherence of intelligibility.

Stations of True Consciousness

> From here I will descend to the fields of physics.
> – 'The Oldest System-Program of German Idealism'

The first explicitly circumscribed point in the course of the destiny of consciousness following Rousseau's epochal turn is the moment of danger, where Rousseau is depicted as facing the risk of being destroyed by the excessive lucidity of his own thought. De Man identifies this moment quite precisely in Rousseau's text: 'This danger can be seen in Rousseau when he allows himself to be carried away by the intoxication of his own lucidity and declares himself capable of being "sufficient unto himself, like God"' ('IR' 42). The specificity of this reference invites us to turn to the passage in question. Toward the end of the Fifth *Rêverie,* Rousseau proposes to recapitulate his analysis of the 'state' he frequently found himself in during his sojourn on the Isle de Saint Pierre:

> What does one enjoy in such a situation? Nothing outside oneself, nothing but oneself and one's own existence, as long as this state lasts, one is sufficient unto oneself, like God. The sentiment of existence, stripped of all other affection, is by itself a precious sentiment of contentment and peace that would alone suffice to render this existence dear and sweet to those who are able to push away from themselves all the sensible and terrestrial impressions that ceaselessly come to distract us from it and to disturb its sweetness down here.[14]

The difficulty this passage raises in the light of de Man's reading should be clear: 'se suffire à soi-même comme Dieu' is presented here as being fully commensurate with 'jouir de rien d'extérieur à soi,' with being wholly free from 'les impressions sensuelles et terrestres'—like Wordsworth's 'Moralist,' who 'has neither eyes nor ears; / Himself his world, and his own God':

> One to whose smooth-rubbed soul can cling
> Nor form nor feeling great nor small,
> A reasoning, self-sufficing thing,
> An intellectual All in All![15]

And since it is precisely the second term of this equation ('jouir de rien d'extérieur à soi') that de Man singles out as the clinching evidence of Rousseau's truth to Being in sublating exterior sensation, his subsequent rejection of the first term as signaling a supreme moment of blindness and transgression is necessarily arresting. To argue that such is precisely the rule of the dialectic is merely to restate the *a priori* to be interrogated, since the question remains where this dialectic comes from, or, more accurately, how it is to be accounted for without taking recourse to the developmental road-story it presupposes rather than rigorously reflects upon.

We recall that the principal explanation initially offered for the necessity to overcome sensation was that only in this way the ontological priority of consciousness could be established. Ostensibly the motive for this move was the need to escape from the temptation of permanence attendant upon the attribution of ontological priority to the object, but this does not constitute a sufficient legitimation: if the ontological priority of the object is the problem, one could with equal (if not superior) justice propose to engage in a critique of the notion of ontological priority itself, instead of mounting an attempt to reverse (and thus maintain) the hierarchical conceptual framework it participates in. This is arguably one of the hearts of the matter: it is the very (precritical) notion of ontological priority that brings with it, imperiously but not therefore legitimately, the demand to trace a growth of consciousness in a way that is still tributary to the natural model allegedly abandoned. The idea of an emancipation of consciousness from the sway of natural being is realized in a developmental drive conceived of precisely in terms of the intuited evolution of natural being—the question whether a 'development' *can* be conceived of independently of this natural model remains fundamentally unanswered, and this, only seemingly paradoxically, as a result of the confident assumption of an affirmative answer. The starting point of the growth of consciousness may very well be an attempt to renounce the temptation of unity with natural being, but since such a rejection of nature is still effected under the aegis of a fundamentally uncritical notion of growth, the movement it generates leads with imperious logic to precisely the kind of wholeness and self-sufficiency that was deemed alien to consciousness and typical of nature as understood by the capitulating spirit at the outset. It is thus wholly natural that the product of the initial intention should be the postulate of a situation formally identical to that which this intention set out to abolish.

The point returns us to the earlier suggestion that there seemed to be more than an apparent similarity between the conception of consciousness-as-earth and that of the self-contained imagination in 'Intentional Structure' (as indeed the use of the same phrase—'jouir de rien d'extérieur à soi'—to characterize 'both' constructs would indicate ['IS' 16; 'IR' 296 n.41]). In the final analysis, the question whether there is or is not (said to be) a relation to exteriority is less important than the qualification of the consciousness that does or does not entertain such a relation as being whole, and wholly intelligible. As intelligible, in fact, as nature is thought to be—be it only in a wishful projection into the future of such intelligibility—in the deluded doctrines of those who shun true consciousness and confer ontological priority upon the object. It is the absolute self-sufficiency that is the (natural) fruit of the demand to grow away from the ontological (or, rather, ontic) enthrallment to the object that is incompatible with the opposition to permanence that engendered this same demand, irrespective of whether this self-sufficiency is asserted to contain the world of natural objects or no.

The only difference between the self-sufficient imagination and the notion of consciousness proposed as an alternative to it here is that whereas the first negatively maintained the unattainability of the intended object by renouncing all intentional relations to that object, the second goes one further and actually claims privileged access to the ontological reality of the sensible object. Both, however, converge insofar as they borrow for their self-definition the (illusion of) unity and wholeness whose projection in the realm of natural being they propose to oppose. The contradictions in Rousseau's own text—which on the one hand locates the source of the 'sentiment de l'existence' in the 'continuous noise' of the waves, but on the other hand pretends that this sentiment marks a state wherein one enjoys nothing outside the self—confirm this suggestion: the burden of the sentiment is its wholeness, not the phenomenological account of its interactional structure, and this wholeness is irreconcilable with a temporality that would not be dependent on the permanence and solidity 'elsewhere' and 'previously' desired from a unity with nature.

If this be the case, it is no wonder that the next landmark alongside the road should be a point of retreat from this state of 'danger.' However, given the suppressed undecidability of the difference between the state of danger and the allegedly authentic *démarche* preceding it, it is not to be expected that the anatomy of this retreat will be as unproblematic as is suggested by the commonsensicality of de Man's narrative (as read through Hölderlin)—'a movement of surprised retraction, the gesture of someone who has just incautiously touched a live flame' ('IR' 42).

The key term in de Man's description of the retreat is 'rassemblement,' recollection. This 'recollection of being onto his own consciousness,' this 'return to the originary I,' is what would make possible the further awakening to 'the comprehension of our destiny as essentially temporal' and would thus prepare the final turn of the dialectic, the 'passage to ideality' (43–44). Yet, to judge from

Anchorite Rhetoric | 47

Rousseau's text, this retreat is not only a retreat from a state that coincides with the truth that, in de Man's reading, it endangers: rather, it, too, is itself that same state.

We recall that Rousseau, in the fragment de Man read as stating the ontological priority of consciousness conceived as earth, described the 'flux and reflux' of the water in the lake as the source of his 'sentiment de l'existence.' The same water, however, also furnished him intermittently with images triggering 'some weak and brief reflection on the instability of the things of this world,' but these annoying impressions fortunately soon dissolved in 'the uniformity of the continuous movement that rocked me.'[16] Three paragraphs later, this continuous movement or flux makes a second appearance in the text, but this time Rousseau has a different reading. Having just asserted that the happiness he desires 'is not composed of fugitive instants but [is] a simple and permanent state that has nothing lively in itself but whose duration increases the charm to the point that in it supreme bliss can fully be found,' he continues his diagnosis in the following terms:

> All is in a continual flux on earth: nothing retains a constant and firm form, and our affections that attach themselves [*s'attachent*] to exterior things necessarily pass away and change like them. Always in advance of us or behind us, they recall the past that is no more or anticipate the future that often should not be at all: there is nothing solid there to which the heart could attach [*attacher*] itself.[17]

Instead of being the movement 'which, without any active assistance from [his] soul did not fail to capture [*attacher*]' Rousseau in the previous passage, dispelling all disturbing thoughts about 'the instability of the things of this world' as it did so, the continuous flux is now identified as the very source of the transitoriness of everything earthly and is consequently condemned as being detrimental to the true happiness it was previously said to be conducive to: 'How can we call happiness a fugitive state that leaves our heart restless and empty, that makes us regret something in advance, or desire something afterwards?'[18] True happiness must therefore be sought elsewhere, and Rousseau duly elaborates this demand:

> But if there is a state in which the soul finds a seat sufficiently solid to repose in it in its entirety and to recollect all its being there, without needing to recall the past nor to stride towards the future: where time would be nothing for the soul, where the present would last forever yet without marking its duration and without any trace of succession, without any other sentiment of loss or joy, of pleasure or trouble, of desire or fear other than that of our existence, and where this sentiment alone would suffice to fill the soul in its entirety; as long as this state lasts, he who finds himself in it can call himself happy, not in the sense of an imperfect, poor and relative happiness such as one finds in the pleasures of life, but in the sense of a sufficient, perfect and full happiness that does not leave in the soul any emptiness which it feels the need to fill. Such is the state I often found myself in on the Isle de Saint Pierre in my solitary reveries, be it lying down in my boat which I allowed to drift at the will of the water, be it seated on the shores of the agitated lake, or elsewhere on the bank of a beautiful river or a stream murmuring over the gravel.
>
> What does one enjoy in such a situation? Nothing that is outside oneself, nothing except oneself and one's own existence, as long as this state lasts, one is sufficient unto oneself, like God.[19]

The terms of this passage suggest some of the reasons why de Man refrains from actually quoting Rousseau's eulogy of the 'rassemblement.' Apart even from the fact that in the textual disposition of the narrative, the 'recollection' precedes the moment de Man identifies as the encounter with imminent destruction it is supposed to ward off, and even if we ignore for a moment that in the conceptual logic of Rousseau's diagnosis the 'recollection' is figured as being identical to this same moment of danger ('on se suffit à soi-même comme Dieu'), the very anatomy of this recollection threatens to wreak havoc on de Man's interpretation of its thrust as opening up to a true conception of temporality.

Reading through the movement of the paragraphs from the Fifth *Rêverie* singled out here, a movement culminating in Rousseau's praise of recollection, we note that the initial moment de Man selected as the point of departure for his argument—the sound of the water that Rousseau's 'süße Gabe / Zu hören' processed as 'the fundamental rhythm, the musical measure of time' (40)—becomes intricate to the point of incomprehensibility. Either it is the 'continual flux' of all things earthly, or it is indeed completely distinct from this 'continual flux'—from anything 'outside' Rousseau—but it can hardly be both at the same time. Or if it can be both at once (and of these neither), the mode of this divided being stands in need of a reflection more rigorous than de Man's argument here allows for.

We should, no doubt, once more refrain from reducing Rousseau's text to nothing but the opposite of what de Man claims it to be, though it is tempting to classify his misreading as a case in point for his own verdict that '[c]ritical statements about Rousseau have a recurrent, obsessive way of stating the precise opposite of what he himself asserted with a minimum of ambivalence' ('RTS' 31). The Fifth *Rêverie* is not a discourse given to minimal ambivalence, and it is hard to imagine what its 'precise opposite' might be, but the point remains that the writing does turn against de Man's reading, and that it does so in a highly significant way. For what appears to happen is that, wholly in keeping with the dialectic of the road, Rousseau's argument almost imperceptibly transforms the stability of natural time as heard in the 'flux and reflux' of the water into a stability and permanence outside of time and in interiority, forgetting the very source these features were borrowed from as it completes this transformation.[20]

The 'temporality' de Man sees Rousseau celebrating is explicitly defined in the text as being wholly indifferent to time ('time would be nothing' for the soul in this state), but this indifference effectively quotes the initial tribute to the permanence and stability in the continuous flux of nature, even while it brackets this flux, now divested of these saving features, as being, in the end, the eroding movement of time itself. Far from being an expression of allegiance to what de Man envisages as authentic temporality, Rousseau's retreat is more properly a panegyric upon the eternal present of interior contemplation, where 'the heart could truly say: "*I wish this moment would last forever*,"'[21] and where the inauthentic temporality of nature is fully recuperated for the self.

In abandoning nature to the 'trace of succession,' Rousseau's self sets out to clear a space divorced from past and future and seeks a 'seat [*assiete*]' for its existence splendidly removed from 'the difficult, unresolved realm of time, where everything is always still ahead of us, at once threateningly imminent and elusively beyond our grasp'—but this 'seat' is itself still founded on spatial coordinates animated by the flow of natural presence: 'Such is the state in which I often found myself on the Isle de Saint Pierre, be it lying down in my boat which I allowed to drift at the will of the water, be it seated [*assis*] on the shores of the agitated lake, or elsewhere on the bank of a beautiful river or a stream murmuring over the gravel.'[22] Rousseau's eternal present does not 'mark its duration'— which is why it is, ultimately, pure duration, a timeless coincidence without the blemish of a mark, undisturbed by the cesura of notation, yet dependent for its constitution on the exterior imprint it cannot sublate in a second's thought. As an excellent reader of Rousseau has put it:

> Duration is indeed the privileged temporal mode for a system in quest of its own authority and striving for a state in which events are no longer changes but the confirmation of an identity no longer threatened by an exterior force. . . . Duration, the coincidence of an entity with its own present, requires the vocabulary of an inwardness detached from anything that is other or elsewhere, containing nothing desirable that is not already possessed. . . . Duration appears as self-enclosed and autonomous, yet it borrows 'jouissance' and 'volupté' from a restless outside world. . . . It remains linked to this world by sensations and memories. . . and it is by way of this metonymical link that the metaphorical illusion of duration is achieved. ('RJ' 214–15)

But in the present interpretation, this illusion is hardened into a dialectical truth beyond argument and inimical to reading, imposing 'narrative developments and transitions that conceal incompatible affirmations' ('RSC' 252), blind to the damaging nondialectical repetition of the stations on a road that can only be a road if this repetition is energized as an *Aufhebung*. The fascinating inconsistency of Rousseau's text is rendered intelligible by dint of its being plotted into a dialectical allegory—or, more accurately, an allegory mastered by the dialectic (as opposed to an allegorical reading of this dialectical mastery). Rousseau's reverie is read (not read) as an extended metaphor, a narrativized symbol that restructures its primary matter—Rousseau's writing—according to the phenomenological precepts of a movement of growth that, paradoxically, imitates the negation of a noneternalist temporality explicitly worked out in the 'original' narrative, even while it pretends to describe the acquisition of such a noneternalist temporality over and against the mystifications of permanence and stability. The stubborn refusal of de Man's narrative to acknowledge the defiant praise of just these 'mystified' features in the text it purports to read is the imperious imprint of the road of understanding as it begins to be beset with history—the history that must still be kept waiting here.

But perhaps this road was already read by Hölderlin: if de Man, instead of reading the Fifth *Rêverie,* so imperiously understands the text, this may well be because his reader's guide is Hölderlin's 'poetically transfigured' Rousseau.[23] How, then, does Hölderlin render the retreat? De Man quotes the following lines:

>Dann scheint ihm oft das beste
>Fast ganz vergessen da,
>Wo der Stral nicht brennt,
>Im Schatten des Walds
>Am Bielersee in frischer Grüne zu seyn,

Und sorglosarm an Tönen,
Anfängern gleich, bei Nachtigallen zu lernen.

[Then it often seems best to him
To be almost completely forgotten there,
Where the ray does not burn,
In the shade of the wood
Near the lac de Bienne in fresh verdure,
And, carefree and poor in tunes,
Like beginners, to learn from the nightingales.]

It is more properly this 'poetically transfigured' moment de Man understands as the 'return to the originary I,' and our brief comments on Rousseau's text clarify why de Man feels the need to point out that the allusion to Rousseau in these lines is now no longer to a specific passage from the Fifth *Rêverie* (as was the case with the 'süße Gabe') but rather to the text as a whole—that is, as a reflection upon the narrative of Rousseau's retreat after having been chased from Môtiers. The retreat thus figures more properly in 'the context of Rousseau's life' and functions as a moment in the 'alternation of violence, necessary defeat, and recovered inwardness' that serves to illustrate 'the exemplary wisdom of Rousseau who, in the confusion of suffering and ideological activity, was able to recover the tranquil, rhythmic language of inwardness' ('IR' 43, 44).

The apparently casual relocation of this moment as a biographical index pointing to Rousseau's refuge from personal persecution and ideological upheaval into a renewed inwardness comes as a surprise, but for de Man's larger argument it has considerable advantages. It allows him to cover up the disturbing similarity of the state of *hubris* Rousseau, in his exemplary semidivine wisdom, was initially said to take refuge *from* to the state he is said to take refuge *in*. The notion that the return to interiority is a retreat from the violence and suffering of the world outside the island smooths out the problematic suggestion that as an escape from excessive truth, the retreat is (also) an escape from interiority. Put differently, the shift in de Man's argument masks the faulty (indeterminate) negation that (fails to) connect(s) the stations of consciousness on the track of interiorizing destiny.

The further effect of this shift is that it prepares the reintroduction of the notion of temporality via the dialectic of action and repose through which the concept of history is being developed. For if the recollection is now a retreat not only from the excessive interiority of the illegitimately apotheosized self-sufficient consciousness, but also—and in fact, at the present stage of the narrative, primarily—from the excessive violence of historical action, it follows that the lesson of the nightingales Hölderlin's verse reads as the reward for the retreat can be aligned without too much difficulty to an intimation of temporality. At least at the surface level of the argument. For once again de Man refrains from clarifying why exactly the song of the nightingales as a lesson for consciousness would be different from the deluded readings of analogies of consciousness in (superior) natural being he criticizes elsewhere (most insistently in his comments on Wordsworth's self-figuration as the Winander Boy, to which we shall turn below), and this oversight seriously compromises the concept of temporality allegedly derived from the ('warnend ängstiges'?) song for the inexperienced (the *Anfängern*). The eventual expression of this concept is not of a nature to counter this impression: the lesson Rousseau experiences in his retreat among the nightingales is nothing other than 'the very moment of rebirth [*palingénésie*]' (43), and de Man's argument fails to prevent the always already imminent collapse of this notion into the eternal regenerative cycles of natural time.

In order to determine this collapse more specifically, we can once again follow de Man's footnote, which identifies the nightingale as the 'symbol of this rebirth' and refers to its previous occurrence at the close of *Hyperion* (297 n.52). The reference points us back to de Man's earlier commentary on this novel, from which we can suffice to retain that it, too, characterizes both a belief in 'immediate external action' and a certain inward repose as 'errors' insofar as they testify to 'the illusory hope of being able to escape time,' and further argues that it is 'the defeat of the reverie of repose [that] marks the obligation to think of human destiny as an essentially temporal unfolding, within which cyclical repetitions are no longer possible and which knows only transitory rebirths [*palingénésies*]' (27–28). The point is not just that in *Hyperion* the palingenesis is read as a result of 'the defeat of the reverie' whereas in 'Der Rhein' it is figured as the outcome of the 'alternation of violence, necessary defeat, and recovered inwardness' (43) (an inconsistency that mirrors the shift we traced within de Man's reading of 'Der Rhein'). Rather, what must interest us here is de Man's candid emphasis on the recurrence of the natural figure of the nightingale even while he dismisses any suggestion that the palingenesis it symbolizes (and which he also qualifies as 'otherwise quite relative' [28]) would have anything in common with the permanent 'cyclical repetitions' of natural temporality. In order to establish that the nightingale's song is not the deluded projection of the natural-analogical imagination, at least some argument is necessary—de Man, however, clips his quotations instead. In the footnote linking 'Der Rhein' to *Hyperion,* he cites a few lines from the beginning of the final letter of the novel (which I here translate):

> 'Bellarmin! I have never experienced it so fully, that old firm saying of destiny [*Schiksaalswort*] that a new bliss dawns on the heart when it endures, and bears out the midnight of sorrow, and that, like the song of the nightingale in the darkness, it is only in deep suffering that the world's song of life divinely resounds for us. For, as with genii, I now lived with the blossoming trees, and the clear brooks that flow under them murmured [*säußelten*], like voices of gods, my grief out of my bosom. . . etc.' (297 n.52)

The anticlimactic 'etc.' is de Man's, and he completes the suspension by adding, 'One should quote almost the entire final letter of the novel.'[24] 'Almost': not, presumably, the apostrophe to Nature that occurs a few paragraphs later:

> Human beings fall from you like lazy fruit, O let them perish, so they may return to your roots, and I, O tree of life, may I blossom with you again and may I embreathe [*umathme*] your peaks with all your budding twigs, peacefully and intensely [*innig*], for we all grow upward from the same golden grain of seed![25]

Stirb und werde, si le grain ne meurt, etc.: is not this an expression of precisely the cyclical eternalism de Man would have us believe the palingenesis to be splendidly untainted with? How can we know Hölderlin's 'Baum des Lebens' from Malraux's walnut trees ('IG' 16; 'TP' 31–32)? What is learned from this rebirth if not that no matter how 'relative' or 'transitory' it may be, it is always already relayed on the smooth and soothing track of natural temporality? Is this 'the comprehension of our destiny as essentially temporal,' or is it a desire for wholesale participation in the 'pastoral palingenesis,' the 'circle that is as reassuring as the circular pattern of the weather' ('PT' 60)?

In the spirit of de Man's argument, it could be objected that this suggestion misses the main point, which consists in understanding that the retreat/rebirth marks only the preparation for the completion of thought and the foundation of the perfect world in the ideality and generality of a 'not yet,' and that consciousness 'now' can only be true to the temporality of this destiny to the extent that it serenely accepts the distance that separates it from this 'fulfillment,' thus returning to history and 'forgetting' the plenitude of its own thought. But what is this history—insofar as it can actually be said to be thought here at all—if not precisely the comforting flow, the road, the permanent and stable march in the direction of just this unmistakable grand finale whose allegedly 'ephemeral' nature is wholly neutralized in the conviction that it will be, and is, reached and repeated again and again? Is not the very introduction of a state of ideality a foreclosure of the attempt to think history as a question rather than as a response on the road to completion? In short, how can we not recall here, in reading the 'serenity of ideal knowledge' Rousseau is credited with, de Man's own warning a decade earlier that systems claiming the ability to solve the problem of the historical 'are in fact appealing to a temptation that exists in all of us: a desire for serenity that tries to forget the original anxiety' ('IG' 15)? In order to remember and refine this question so as to restore its historical impact, we must turn to language.

Terrible Maturity

> For there no longer exists any philosophy, any history, poetry alone shall survive all other sciences and arts.
> – 'The Oldest System-Program of German Idealism'

De Man's attempt to refocus the perception of Romanticism—through Hölderlin's Rousseau—should be credited to the full. Yet, the attractive iconoclasm of this ambition tends to burn itself out in a stubborn thetic repetition of its saving intent—to redress the interpretation of Romanticism as (laudably or deplorably) implicated in an organico-analogical doctrine—in the face of the resistance encountered in the texts it proposes to restore. The argument developed against the analogical reading of nature and consciousness is itself overdetermined by a concept of growth or development tributary to this analogical reading, and this largely as a result of the uncritical attempt to salvage the notion of ontological priority and harness it to the cause of consciousness. Rather than marking an escape from the analogies of nature, de Man's repeated explicit refusals to acknowledge the convergence of the road he traces, in his own argument and in the texts he reads, with that of the permanent and stable growth inauthentically envied in nature figure as countertextual instances of embarrassment—the very obstinacy of these refusals suggesting a fundamental unease instead of the genuine confidence they try to enact. In its present gross format, this state of affairs can mean two things: either de Man is fatally wrong about Romanticism (in which case his attempt to acclaim its representative poets for their authentic notion of temporality is doomed to misfire, and to undercut this very notion in the process), or he does have a point but fails to argue it satisfactorily. The evidence would appear to favor the first possibility, and a recuperative reading of both de Man's work and Romantic thought might even construe this as a triumph. If de Man does indeed remain implicated in an uncritical and tellingly denegated analogical doctrine that maps out (the) history (of consciousness) along the lines of nature, this might figure as an indication of the extent to which his understanding of Romanticism is ultimately accurate (be it blind). De Man would then be right about Romanticism insofar as he fails to argue his (perverse) case. For the possibility exists that the analogy of the *via naturaliter* is inherent in Romanticism, at the very core of its thought: 'Since the assertion of a radical priority of the subject over objective nature is not easily compatible with the poetic praxis of the romantic poets, who all gave a great deal of importance to the presence of nature, a certain degree of confusion ensues' ('ROT' 196).

The following famous passage, taken from the 'Thalia-Fragment,' the second of the six extant 'versions' of Hölderlin's *Hyperion,* is a case in point:

> There are [*Es giebt*] two ideals for our existence: a state of supreme simplicity [*Einfalt*], in which our needs are in mutual agreement [*zusammenstimmen*] with themselves, with our capacities [*Kräfte*], and with everything we are connected to, and this *through the mere organisation of Nature* [*die bloße Organisation der Natur*], without our assistance; and a state of supreme formation [*Bildung*], where *the same would take place* [*wo dasselbe stattfinden würde*], relative to infinitely multiplied and strengthened needs and capacities, *through the organisation we are able to give to ourselves. The eccentric road,* which human beings, in general and as individuals, travel from one point (more or less pure simplicity) to the other (more or less accomplished formation [*vollendeten Bildung*]), seems, *in its essential directions* [*nach ihrer wesentlichen Richtungen*], to be *always the same* [*immer gleich*].[26]

Anchorite Rhetoric | 59

As an affirmation of the fundamental homology of natural *Einfalt* and human *Bildung,* this seems about as straightforward as one can get. The difference between both states is not so much a real distinction as it is a remnant of the postulate of a dichotomy the homology itself is intended to fully contain in the qualification of both states as 'Ideale unseres Daseyns' and in the assertion that, again in both states, connected as they are by an ideally unidirectional road, 'the same' takes place. And yet. We should not fail to notice that the passage also contains elements of a certain indecision (as in the use of the verb 'scheint,' in the repeated qualification 'mehr oder weniger,' or in the tension between the assertive expression of availability 'es giebt' and the hypothetical 'würde') that threatens the composure of the system. And this especially as this hesitation is replicated and heightened, on a different level, in a following paragraph of Hölderlin's manifesto. It is no accident that this paragraph should touch upon the notion of excess we have identified as one of the major cruxes in de Man's reading of this eccentric road:

> The human being would like to be *in* everything and *above* everything, and the sentence in Loyola's epitaph:
>
> non coerceri maximo, contineri tamen a minimo
>
> can designate the all-desiring, all-subjugating dangerous side of human beings as well as the highest and most beautiful state he can attain. Which of these senses is valid must be decided by the free will of each.[27]

The point hardly needs to be italicized: the question that crops up here, ostensibly concerning only the end-point of the 'eccentric road,' in fact affects the notion of the road itself in such a way that the text can no longer contain the destabilization of this notion. For what is here released or disseminated is the possibility of an indecision at the heart of the very process of conceptualization, and thus also at the heart of the interpretation of conceptualization (i.e. dialectics). The 'free will' Hölderlin here abruptly appeals to dislodges the earlier *Schein* of the homogeneity of the road with itself and consequently also of its homology with the *bloße Organisation der Natur*. This free will, summoned almost desperately as a final measure, in effect points to an interpretive task that can no longer take for granted the *wesentliche Richtungen* of the road, a task that can no longer rest assured that it is able to read the directive of the road in the opaque language of the epitaph—or in that of the poet, for that matter. The dromology, too, is structured as (a) language, and we cannot assume knowing what that means. We are made aware of (what we were looking for:) the nature of language as the solvent of which it is never clear whether it resolves obstacles on the road to meaning or dissolves (the) meaning (of the road) itself. What must interest us now is the strategy de Man's argument adopts in order to contain this awareness.

One of the principal attributes of the figure of Rousseau in Hölderlin is its association 'with modes of behavior that properly belong to language,' an association itself related to 'the internalized consciousness that contains time *within* itself' (29). Reading Hölderlin's ode 'Rousseau,' de Man glosses this double association as follows: 'The God within us exists in the form of language, a mediate form of contact with being,' and the product of this contact is that 'despite their apparent defeat . . . creatures of language like Rousseau and the poets possess the future perhaps more fully than others.' Hölderlin's image for this superior possession is striking:

> Klanglos ist's, armer Mann, in der Halle dir,
>   Und gleich den Unbegrabenen, irrest du
>   Unstet und suchest Ruh und niemand
>   Weiß den beschiedenen Weg zu weisen.
>
> Sei denn zufrieden!   der Baum entwächst
>   Dem heimatlichen Boden, aber es sinken ihm
>   Die liebenden, die jugendlichen
>   Arme, und trauernd neigt er sein Haupt.

Anchorite Rhetoric | 61

>   Des Lebens Überfluß, das Unendliche,
>   Das um ihn   und dämmert, er faßt es nie.
>   Doch lebt's in ihm und gegenwärtig,
>   Wärmend und wirkend, die Frucht
>   entquillt ihm.²⁸

> [Soundless, poor man, is it for you in the hall,
>   And like the unburied one, you err
>   Restless and seek rest and no-one
>   Can show you the modest way.
> So be contented!   the tree grows out of
>   The native soil, but his
>   Loving, youthful arms sink away from him
>   And in mourning he inclines his head.
> The abundance of life, the infinite,
>   Which and dawns/fades around him, he never grasps it.
>   Yet it lives within him and present,
>   Warming and working, the fruit springs
>   forth from him.]

For de Man, the point of the passage is that Rousseau, and the poets in general, 'bear [the future] within themselves like the tree bears its ripening fruit,' and having read his critique of the delusion in the figure 'Worte, wie Blumen' in 'Intentional Structure,' we can appreciate why this trope must immediately be turned against its vehicle: 'They bear [the future] within themselves like the tree bears its ripening fruit, that is, in a potential and mediated form for protection, a gestation—for the tree here is not the triumphant organic tree of eternal cycles but the fragile mindfulness of nascent thought' (29). There is no argument here: the logic of de Man's qualification is entirely spent in the unwarranted assertion of 'for' and 'that is.' The generous exemption of Hölderlin from the damaging verdict on Malraux's self-destructive self-projection into 'the unassailable and solid security of the walnut tree,' where 'time is eliminated by a grounded future' allowing us 'to rise splendidly toward a sky that [we] will not be long in reaching' ('TP' 32), is an interpretive imposition that, especially on de Man's own terms, cannot even be grounded in the mournful diction preparing the substitution of fruit for thought. For—and this *is* an argumentative for—'it is in experiencing the material presence of the particular flower [which we can here read as 'fruit'—OdG] that the desire arises to be reborn in the manner of a natural creation' ('IS' 6), and when this desire turns into an article of faith, it can articulate, in Shelley's words, the poet's vision of 'the future in the present' and his 'thoughts' as 'the germ of the flower and the fruit of the present time.'[29]

The point is not that Hölderlin's image (or Shelley's, for that matter) should in fact be diagnosed as a symptom of nostalgic delusion—rather, it should be read in the intensity of its tension, instead of being understood as an established thesis crossing out the complicating crossover from natural 'gestation' to 'nascent thought.' Just as, contrary to de Man's strictly perverse judgment, Hölderlin's Rhine does bear more than a 'trace of anthropomorphism' ('IR' 295 n.31) and as a result of this facilitates the inverted feedback conferring a deceptive intelligibility upon the notion of human historical destiny, so his fruitful Rousseau is granted a degree of comforting coherence in the natural image through which he is figured. De Man's resistance to this natural plot is radical and, in fact, helpful, but in missing the root of the image it is also in danger of becoming all too helpful, and of ending up with an ideal understanding that, insofar as it does understand and thereby replicates the accessibility of the natural plot, is not nearly radical enough. Such ideal resistance in the name of understanding must be interrupted, especially if it turns out that, as we shall see, understanding—and more specifically the understanding of history as destiny—is itself the issue.

Rousseau's thought of the future, de Man continues, should be recognized as signaling a distance from the sacred, or from being, and as such it can be justified as an attribute of the poet rather than of the man of action. This distinction is translated into linguistic terms as a difference in (degree of) mediation: 'Whereas for the men of action, the gods signify *(zeigen),* for the poets they are a sign *(ein Zeichen)* . . . that [they] must try with great difficulty to decipher' (30). But despite this suggestion of a greater intimacy between the men of action and the gods, it is the poets who are favored, in 'Rousseau,' with the 'supreme word' of the earlier 'Hymne an die Menschheit': *Vollendung,* the notion de Man had already glossed as 'the perfect world whose possibility Rousseau had the audacity to affirm': the 'ultimate fulfillment of human destiny [which] has to be realized by revolutionary and violent political action' (23), and which one would consequently have expected to be the province of the men of action rather than of the poets. As evidence for this important redistribution of merits in the later poem ('Rousseau'), de Man then quotes the following lines:

> Und wunderbar, als hätte von Anbeginn
> > Des Menschen Geist das Werden und Wirken all,
> > > Des Lebens Weise schon erfahren
> Kennt er im ersten Zeichen Vollendetes schon, . . .

> [And wonderful, as if from the very beginning
> > The spirit of the human being had already experienced
> > > All the becoming and the working, the way of life,
> He already knows the accomplished in the first sign.]

A footnote immediately qualifies the point:

> This fulfillment is now distinguished very precisely from the eternal harmony of 'Hymne an die Menschheit.' It is immediately compared to storms *('Gewittern')* in the plural; this *Vollendung* indicates the moments, the articulations of consciously comprehended historical becoming, not even the 'end of history' in the Hegelian sense. (294 n.28; translation modified)

The poet's interpretive task, then, is once again defined as the production of history as the noematic correlative of consciousness, while the disjunction from the homecoming of Hegel's Spirit (prefiguring the withdrawal from the blinding clarity of Hegel's 'maturity' suggested toward the end of the essay) is the almost compulsive modulation of this process we have become accustomed to—but have not yet adequately translated—in de Man's thought. Back in the main text, an extensive gloss specifies the point:

> The temporal alienation that separates Hölderlin from his time and imposes on him the solitary suffering of always falling short of its fullness, everything that lends this thought the tension towards the future expressed by verbs like *ahnen* and *sehnen*, thus properly belongs to his poetic nature, to the fact that he is a creature of language whose function is to interpret, and not to represent immediately, the manifestations of being. (30; translation modified)

The point is indeed more than familiar—but here, too, de Man adds a note, which, in contrast to the previous one, opens a different and challenging perspective that will furnish us with a more appropriate framework from within which to readdress the poet's interpretive task as it is outlined here. The remark concerns the circle of understanding:

> This premonition *('Ahnen')* linked to the notion of interpretation amounts to a poetic definition of what Heidegger, since *Sein und Zeit*, 1(5):§32, calls the hermeneutic circle. His own commentaries on Hölderlin are nothing but a demonstration of this notion. (294 n.28)

Thus, Hölderlin's poetical project prefigures the understanding of understanding Heidegger developed as the hermeneutic circle and subsequently 'demonstrated' in his readings of Hölderlin. Which, coming from de Man, is a curious suggestion. For were not Heidegger's exegeses of Hölderlin demonstrably wrong precisely insofar as they 'violently' and 'blindly' ignored the optative, praying mode of premonition in this poetry by casting it as the (immediate) naming of Being ('HE' 258)? The suspicion this incongruence raises is predictable but enlightening: Given the presupposition of completion *(Vollendung)* governing any interpretation, is it possible to avoid succumbing to the temptation to actually state this completion, to name it as already attained in the future of the present rather than preserve its absence in the mode of premonition? Can the notion of interpretation spatialized as a road, or path, or circle suspend the interpretive desire to actually claim immediate access to the completion that, as a potentiality, is a constitutive feature of this road, path, or circle? Or to put this more naively: is not the circle precisely the (eminently analogical) symbol of the eternal cyclical repetition de Man peremptorily bans from (his reading of) Hölderlin's account of the poet's interpretive task, and is not Heidegger's misreading of Hölderlin (previously challenged by de Man but oddly forgotten here) precisely the unwarranted performance of this circle?[30]

It is in response to these questions (for questions they should remain, despite the temptation to let them come to rest in the negativity their rhetorical position here invites) that we can better delineate the fundamental deficiency of de Man's thought at this stage. The hypothesis—the *Vollendung* of our interpretation in its present nonhistorical format—would be that it is because these questions are not rigorously faced here that de Man's writing falls short of the demands it has set itself. That is to say: because interpretation (the poet's crucial task) as the interference of language and temporality (the poet's central concerns) is reduced to the status of a problem already resolved in the text that is interpreted (Hölderlin's) through the introduction of the hypostasis of ontologically prior consciousness, de Man's interpretation remains blind to the necessary extension of the questioning in the interpreted text to his own interpretive act. The problem of interpretation is interpreted without this interpretation itself being sufficiently affected by its own alleged 'object.' And it is because of this incompleteness that de Man's interpretation fails to accurately register the incompleteness of the notion of completion *(Vollendung)* in Hölderlin's reading of interpretation, regularizing it instead into the notion of a comprehended or contained incompleteness, mastered by a dialectic of interpretation wherein it is rewritten as, precisely, ideal *(idealisch)* completion. What is a crux in Hölderlin—the question as to just how language and temporality can be understood as constitutive of the (poet's) interpretive production of history—is read as the resolution of that crux in de Man's critical account.

The image of Rousseau in the poetry of Hölderlin is the category in which the various components of this resolution are gathered, but what does not take place in this rhetorical recollection is the indispensable reflection on the very status of 'Rousseau' *as* an image.[31] De Man's presentation of the four lines from 'Rousseau' quoted above is an instructive index of this nonreading in that it effaces a crucial absence from Hölderlin's original:

> Vernommen hast du sie, verstanden die Sprache der Fremdlinge!
>   Gedeutet ihre Seele! Dem Sehnenden war
>   Der Wink genug, und Winke sind
>   Von alters her die Sprache der Götter.
>
> Und wunderbar, als hätte von Anbeginn
>   Des Menschen Geist das Werden und Wirken all,
>   Des Lebens Weise schon erfahren,
>
> Kennt er im ersten Zeichen Vollendetes schon,
>   Und fliegt der kühne Geist, wie Adler den
>   Gewittern, weissagend seinen
>   Kommenden Göttern voraus,[32]

[You have heard it, understood the language of the strangers!
    Interpreted its soul! To the yearning
        The hint was enough, and hints are
            The language of the Gods from the days of old.

And wonderful, as if from the very beginning
    The spirit of the human being had already experienced
        All the becoming and the working, the way of life,

He already knows the accomplished in the first sign,
And the bold Spirit flies, like eagles ahead of
Storms, prophetically in advance of
His coming Gods,]

Thus, what is rendered by de Man as a fully voiced thesis is in Hölderlin's writing the failure to complete a gloss (and with it the poem) that would explain and found the thesis preceding it by means of a legitimating comparative hypothesis ('als hätte'), which, moreover, spills over into a natural image. The thesis to be developed, and which de Man takes as read, is in Hölderlin's poem left hanging in the suspense of analogies and images that fail to be wrought home and thus dislodge exactly that which they propose to define: interpretation.

To be fair, de Man does explicitly acknowledge the actual incompleteness of the text, but he does so only to announce the completion of its thought in its later development, thereby negating this incompleteness as an intelligible prefiguration of its determinate *Bestimmung* in auto-negation. For de Man, the poem's understandable and hence excusable lack of finish is the corollary of the 'apologetic tone' indicating the poet's inability to 'grasp the dialectic of action and poetry in its totality or, more precisely, within the formal unity of a single poem' (30). But if in 'Rousseau' Hölderlin still seems to feel 'inferior to those who directly take part in action and who appear to be privileged over him,' the mature hymn 'Der Rhein' allows his thought to 'fully unfold' (31), and thus to effect the *Aufhebung* of the earlier ode's fractures.

In 1970 de Man would chide Michael Hamburger for his translation of the line 'Kennt er im ersten Zeichen Vollendetes schon' as 'In seed grains he can measure the full-grown plant,' and instead of this 'metaphor of Mr. Hamburger's own invention [which is] out of place at this point in the poem,' he would suggest his own 'literal' reading: 'In the earliest sign he can already read fulfillment' ('RH' 210). In 'The Image of Rousseau,' however, de Man is closer to Hamburger's botany than to Hölderlin's reading/recognition:

his reading of 'kennt' is marked by the growth toward full unfolding rather than by the possibility of reading that must always recognize its noncoincidence with the understanding that is its figure. This is not only a matter of registering, or failing to register, obvious blanks, such as occur in 'Rousseau.' The recognition of reading must also leave its mark on 'Der Rhein,' and on Rousseau, in a thorough reflection on the very act of reading the hymn bears traces of, in a sustained attempt to acknowledge the emphatic presence of natural models in both the hymn and the Fifth *Rêverie*, in a nondogmatic confrontation with the explicit rejection of time (especially) in this latter text, and in a critical opposition to the quasi-inevitability of the completion of interpretation. But none of this happens.

What does happen is that after having sketched his reading of the 'rassemblement' supposedly readable in (Hölderlin's reading of) Rousseau, de Man brings his argument quite literally full circle by singling out some two lines and a half from the third version of 'Mnemosyne' that contain the verb he was looking for. Again:

Such is indeed the divine will:

Himmlische nemlich sind
Unwillig, wenn einer nicht die Seele schonend sich
Zusammengenommen, aber er muß doch; . . .

Nothing summarizes better what Rousseau signifies for Hölderlin than the conclusion that imposes itself as a result of this preparatory examination: the 'one' *('einer')* designated here can be none other than Rousseau. There was a man who in reaffirming the ontological priority of consciousness over the sensible object put the thought and the destiny of the West back onto its authentic path; the same man had the wisdom and the patience to remain faithful to the limitations that this knowledge, in accordance with its own laws, imposes upon the human spirit. He was thus able to safeguard the future of mankind. This man is called Rousseau. His act is called: to recollect oneself. With the reappearance of this word in 'Mnemosyne' *('sich zusammen-*

nehmen'), the circle opened in the youthful poem 'An die Stille' closes.³³ ('IR' 45; translation modified)

As if we knew what 'Mnemosyne' means. As if, to paraphrase Hölderlin's 'wenn solches zu sagen / Erlaubt ist,' we can presume to speak the will of the gods in their name, which would effectively resolve the tension betrayed in the brusque appeal to the 'free will' in the 'Thalia-Fragment.' The resolution of this tension is what lifts the 'pre-ontology of consciousness, which is still seen in its ontic form as an "act" of the gods' (36), up to the ideal level of pure ontology, where we see 'the divine will' as the corollary of our own understanding. Unconditionally, and without irony. The faculty that can assume this 'as if' as a fulfilled condition in the received idea of hermeneutics is the leap toward understanding over obstacles of reading. Hearing a God's tremendous voice, the poet is consulted and retires. The name of this gift of hearing: 'Divination.'³⁴ But, to jump backward and forward to two other places: such a leap risks landing us in the company of deluded archetypal critics who conceive of 'poetry as the language in which the divine is preserved and to which, therefore . . . one returns . . . to be reborn' ('F' 87); while—second jump—the task is precisely, ironically, 'to take the divine out of reading.'³⁵ Which is not what happens here.

De Man's stated concern is with the articulation of language and temporality that would, 'if one can say this [*si l'on peut dire*],' allow poetry to speak the production of history consciously comprehended. It is because he assumes the right to effectively say this that he can conceive of this articulation as already accomplished and recollected in the ideality of Hölderlin's interpretations (of Rousseau): the balance of his reading decisively shifts, through divination, to a thematic stabilization of temporality as a notion effectively mastered in the language of those interpretations. This language itself is consequently cast as a medium whose understandability is never—or, more accurately, no longer—at stake, and it is in this divine assumption that de Man's argument invites a new perspective that is of a nature to put an end to the particular necessity of his entire undertaking. What is moving toward a damaging certainty here is nothing other than a certain understanding of Hegel's terrible verdict on the pastness of art, and it is this understanding that 'threatens to blind' reading, not through 'the power of its clarity' ('IR' 45), not through the excessive lucidity of its truth, but through the mindless, nonhistorical and entirely irresponsible imposition of its constitutive para-historical logic.

The fundamental readability of Hölderlin's and Rousseau's language is what allows de Man to read this language as the assertion of the *Aufhebung* of sensory perception, which, in turn, spells the authentic destiny of the human spirit. This *Aufhebung* is *itself* the readability of writing and the pastness of art—the pastness of what has passed away, what has been passed by on the road to *Vollendung*, 'ein Vergangenes.'[36] To the extent that Hölderlin's language prepares the way for the 'necessary transcend[ence] of the real [historical] moment of fulfillment,' and thus teaches us 'to think this moment in the ideal temporality that contains it' (44), this language points to the Idea as the Absolute in which language itself obeys a certain reading of Hegel's law and becomes a superfluous objectivity. For when Hegel writes, 'The tough rinds of nature and the ordinary world make it harder for the Spirit to penetrate towards the Idea than works of art do,'[37] this implies that art, too, remains an obstacle to this penetration, be it a less resistant one. The resistance of art is its lingering determination toward the sensible; the reaction formation of this determination is its premonition of the *Vollendung* that will put an end to it:

> In this way the *after* of art consists in this, that within the Spirit there dwells the need to satisfy itself only in its own interior as the true form for truth. Art in its first stages still displays a measure of mystery, a mysterious premonition [*Ahnen*] and a sense of yearning [*Sehnsucht*], since its constructs [*Gebilde*] have not yet fully exposed [*vollendet herausgestellt*] their full content [*vollen Gehalt*] to the figurative intuition [*Bildliche Anschauung*].

> However, when the complete content [*vollkommene Inhalt*] has completely stepped forward [*vollkommen hervorgetreten*] in the shapes of art [*Kunstgestalten*], then the further-looking Spirit [*weiterblickende Geist*] turns away from this objectivity into his interiority [*Inneres*] and pushes this objectivity away from him.[38]

The truth of Hölderlin's 'ahnen' and 'sehnen'—'the premonition linked to the notion of interpretation' (294 n.29), which is the proper name of his hypersensible 'poetic nature' (30)—finally comes into its own as the end of art in (as *after*) poetry, 'the most disembodied of all the arts, the furthest removed from the object' ('PP' 75). But this end of interpretation—'the comprehension of our destiny,' Hegel's *begriffne Geschichte*, can only be spelled out at the expense of reading. Actual reading: a reading that does not dialectically 'progress beyond local difficulties of interpretation' ('PAR' ix), that does not obfuscate the obstacles it runs into (and in fact does not run at all) by projecting their fully articulated name in the ideality of an excessive truth whose absence is recuperated by the Infernal-Proverbial panacea of apotropaic recollection: 'The road of excess leads to the palace of wisdom.'

Such reading cannot occur as a mere rejection of natural analogism, for that way the terrible maturity of the unreading Absolute Spirit lies. Neither can it occur as a recollection in the face of this fulfilment, posited as different from 'the "end of history" in a Hegelian sense' (294 n.28), for this face is precisely irresistibly readable, and thus *a priori* beyond reading resistance. Rousseau's wisdom is his faithfulness to the limits his knowledge of the authentic path of Western destiny imposes upon the human spirit, but this patience is the limitless and timeless serenity engendered by the prefigurative acquisition of the future of mankind. Hegel has the audacity to name this acquisition:

> Freedom has found the lever to realize its concept as well as its truth. This is the goal of world history, and we must follow the long road that has just been given in the form of a survey. But

length of time is something wholly relative, and the Spirit belongs to eternity. There is no such thing as actual length for it.[39]

In de Man's recollection, Rousseau follows the same path, only blindfolded: understanding retreats into interiority to propose a mask with which to hide what it has already understood, not read. And yet there must be reading.

> Himmlische nämlich sind
> Unwillig, wenn einer nicht die Seele schonend sich
> Zusammengenommen, aber er muß doch; dem
> Gleich fehlet die Trauer.

As if we knew what Mnemosyne means. 'Nächstens mehr.'[40]

PART TWO

Source

CHAPTER THREE

Recall

Mit der Sonne sehn' ich mich oft von Aufgang bis zum
  Niedergang
den weiten Bogen schnell hineilend zu wandeln, oft mit
  Gesang zu
folgen dem Großen, dem Vollendungsgang der Alten Natur,
Und, wie der Feldherr auf dem Helme den Adler trägt in
  Kampf und
Triumph, so möcht ich, daß sie mich trüge
Mächtig das Sehnen der Sterblichen.
Aber es wohnet auch ein Gott in dem Menschen daß er
  Vergangenes
Und Zukünftiges sieht und wie vom Strom ins Gebirg
  hinauf an die
Quelle lustwandelt er durch Zeiten
Aus ihrer Thaten stillem Buch ist Vergangenem bekannt
  er durch—die goldenes beut
        – Hölderlin, 'Palingenesie'

I crossed (a blank and empty area then)
The Square of the Carousel, few weeks back
Heaped up with dead and dying, upon these
And other sights looking as doth a man
Upon a volume whose contents he knows
Are memorable, but from him locked up,
Being written in a tongue he cannot read,

> So that he questions the mute leaves with pain
> And half upbraids their silence.
> — Wordsworth, 1805 *Prelude,* Book Ten, 46–54.

The Image of Rousseau in the Poetry of Hölderlin' appears to terminate the oscillation between 'crisis' and 'resurrection' that sent poetry spinning at the close of 'Intentional Structure of the Romantic Image.'[1] The destiny of the poetic imagination names itself as the sublation of sensory perception into the ontological priority of consciousness, and this oracular name imposes itself as a moment of singular historical power. This power takes shape as the ideal knowledge that recognizes the limits that must separate 'particular consciousness' and its 'necessary extension to the generalized will' ('IR' 44) from the fulfilled 'future of mankind' (45), which it prepares as the realization of its noematic correlative. This separation is emphatically not a condition consciousness fails to overcome: rather, consciousness succeeds in gathering the terms of the separation within itself, and its triumph is its ability to sustain them in their lawful tension. In its recollection of this tension—its recognition of the limits that save it from being resolved in the end of history—consciousness achieves the total historical understanding proper to pure ideology. The ideology is pure to the extent that it succeeds in containing—or domesticating—the unthinkable end of history as an unactualized term of its thought. It recognizes the counterpoetic nature of definitive fulfillment and purifies it, 'comme de juste,' as 'the generalized ideality of fiction' (44), assigning it a properly delimited function in (that is, beyond) the unfolding of history—the history it itself produces as pure understanding, pure ideology. The ideology is pure in that it speaks the end of history as the pure ideal whose absence cannot disturb ideological composure, for the ideology has itself composed the ideal in the mode of lawful absence. The ideology is pure because it understands its structure as the structure of Being itself.

Yet this ideology is also a thing of the past: the structure of Being has a history—*is* history—our history. In the present chapter we shall follow a first reading of this recognition in de Man's further reenactment of Romantic thought; in the next chapter we shall relocate this reenactment as the truth of the post-Romantic predicament, which will allow us to trace an as yet unargued historical sense through de Man's writing.

Being has not come to an end—therefore, the end of interpretation must figure as a recognition of this absent ending within the language that reenacts this ending in a concentrated commitment to itself as language. In this act, language fulfills the recollection of fulfillment as a promise and as a warning. The warning concerns the apocalypse brought about by 'the substitution of ontological for what could well be called formal dimensions of language'; the promise concerns the 'ontological . . . principle of totalization [which] has to be sought in the discontinuous structure of being itself' ('PT' 71, 72). The name of the apocalypse is the substitution of ontology for form; the name of the authentic principle is the total form of language in its ontological orientation. And the task of the ideology is to decisively purify this difference into an understanding of destiny: the intentional structure of the ideology prepares the articulation of its form as the very form of Being; it must name the formal dimensions of language *as* the only lawful ontological concern. A central moment in de Man's performance of this thought can be brought out in the encounter between Hölderlin and the third voice of de Man's Romanticism, Wordsworth.

The juxtaposition of Rousseau, Hölderlin, and Wordsworth in 'Intentional Structure' figured as a statement of intent in de Man's poetics to identify the common concern that 'determines [their] fate and marks it as being an essentially poetic destiny' ('IS' 15). The same intent is repeated in a footnote to his reading of Rousseau's and Hölderlin's water in 'Image of Rousseau,' where he 'indicate[s] in passing that in Wordsworth's central passages on the imagination (especially in *The Prelude*) the sound of water has exactly the same poetic function': 'Wordsworth's "Imagination" is in all points similar to Rousseau's sentiment of existence, to Hölderlin's "sweet talent to hear"—but of course this cannot be demonstrated quickly' ('IR' 296 n.44; translation modified). Two of de Man's most focused attempts to engage in the demonstration prefigured here occur in the paper he read for the 1965 *MLA* panel on 'Romanticism and Religion,' 'Heaven and Earth in Wordsworth and Hölderlin,' and in his January 1966 inaugural lecture at the University of Zürich, 'Wordsworth und Hölderlin.'

Here is the promise concluding the first of these attempts:

> Yet, in the long run, both Wordsworth and Hölderlin are equally poets of the earthly soul, of consciousness, and of historical time—and not poets of nature, of eternity, or of transcendental vision. As such they make of romanticism a crucial articulation in the history of human consciousness. With Rousseau, they stand at the threshold of a posthellenic, post-Christian, new dispensation. ('HEW' 146)

The 'yet' introducing this summation marks the typical *volta* in de Man's thought as it takes the long view and redirects it through the liminal prism of the revisionary promise. To counter this hypermetropy is not to make a virtue of myopia, but lest we do counter it, we cut ourselves off from the source of its insight, which resists the proleptic turn of the promise. Our focus must therefore be the difference between (or, more accurately, within) Wordsworth and Hölderlin left behind in the promise of Romanticism. The terms in which this difference is registered in order to be sublated are analogy and apocalypse: analogy is the natural shelter for history, apocalypse is the transcendental leap beyond history, and the historical face of poetry is its articulation of this tension as sheltering understanding. The logic of this understanding consists of the confident accomplishment of the pattern that structured de Man's reading of Mallarmé and Baudelaire in the 1950s: it moves from the naive opposition of distinct poetic practices to the ideal self-identity of essential poetry. In 1956, the articulate conclusion of this pattern remained in suspension:

> Thus, we are led to distinguish two kinds of poetic attitude: the first would be that of a poetry of becoming [Mallarmé], maintaining itself as consciousness at the expense of the sensible object, whereas the other would be a poetry of substance [Baudelaire], maintaining the sensible object at the expense of consciousness.
> Quite clearly, though, this schema is oversimplistic. The problem of poetry and becoming does not present itself in the form of a choice between two equally possible directions. ('PP' 71)

In 1965, the essential identity of these two directions figures as the resolution of a similar, although less simplistic scheme:

> Being a truly dialectical mind, Hölderlin escaped the tendency toward analogical thought easily, but the apocalyptic always remained a strong temptation for him. Wordsworth's truly Kantian rationality, on the other hand, shelters him from the apocalyptic mood that is certainly present in other English romantics, but he had to disengage himself gradually from the trappings of analogical thought. ('HEW' 146)

The truth of Romanticism is decided in the in-between of a truly Kantian rationality and a truly dialectical—to all intents and purposes Hegelian—mind, and we know that, for de Man, the form of this intuition goes back at least to his earlier intention to engage in a 'critical dialogue' with Heidegger by considering his 'effort' as 'an attempt to sublate *(aufheben)* the antinomy between Hegelian historicism and Kantian eternalism by conserving what is essential in each' ('TP' 39).[2] The substantial point of the present project, however, is precisely the historical relocation of this antinomy as a Romantic interruption of the history of consciousness: as Alexandre Kojève has dictated, 'But between Kant and Hegel Romanticism interposes itself,'[3] and de Man's reading retrospectively focuses on this interphilosophical point of suspension as itself an extra-Kantian and extra-Hegelian 'new dispensation' ('HEW' 146). For, 'in the long run,' Romantic poetry formulates its adherence to 'the earthly soul,' to 'consciousness,' and to 'historical time' in its own terms. In the course of this long run, Wordsworth takes leave of his senses and Hölderlin turns his back on transcendence: the faculty in which both are finally, but provisionally, suspended is memory—the origination of this memory and its further formalization is our focal point in what follows.

Past Analogy

> Here is a cottage to be moved, if not a mountain, and a waterfall to be silent, if it is not to hang listening: but with what difference to the mind that contemplates them!
> – John Ruskin, 'Of the Pathetic Fallacy'

De Man's 'avowedly somewhat sinister purpose' in reading Wordsworth is to question the reconciliatory role assigned to nature in the prevalent readings of his poetry ('HEW' 138). This involves demonstrating that—contrary to the famous thesis of reciprocal adaptation in the 1802 Preface to the *Lyrical Ballads* (which de Man quotes)—the truth of poetry is not mediated through analogies of mind and nature but instead occurs in 'a passing alliance between the self and time' (146). An exemplary test for this demonstration is the case of the Winander Boy, whose mimic hootings at the side of the lake respond to the analogical program and, upon being answered by the owls, are promptly taken up in an 'idyllic world' of 'gentle constancy' in which 'nature and consciousness correspond with the reassuring symmetry of voice and echo' ('WWH' 51).[4] However—and unsurprisingly—the poem, in its turn, promptly responds to the test: 'the unity filled with analogy' is recognized as an illusion when 'pauses of deep silence' intervene and the Boy—in Wordsworth's queer phrase—'hung listening' in that silence. It is this queer phrase de Man latches on to by pointing out, in the best philological tradition, that 'hung' also occurs in the 1815 Preface to *Poems,* where it designates 'the precise moment where fancy, dependent on kinship between mind and nature, is superseded by imagination,' a shift involving 'a higher pitch of audacity in the language'

('HEW' 142).[5] The continuation of the poem, in which the churchyard where the Boy is now buried also 'hangs,' allows de Man to round off his argument against analogy by identifying the truth gained in the passage through uncertainty and anxiety: the loss of analogy invites the 'experience of mortality' and contributes to the 'growth' of consciousness away from illusion and toward 'the true language of the imagination,' which can state 'the frailty of our condition' and allows us to hope that 'by fully understanding the contingency of [this] condition, the fall into death will be . . . gentle' (143).

According to de Man, this 'thematic sequence—from analogical echo to imagination, by way of a consciousness of mortality—is a recurrent figure in Wordsworth' (143), and its pursuit offers access to Wordsworth's 'feeling of existence' (144), which teaches us that 'the analogy between mind and nature is an inauthentic covering up of the barrenness of our condition.' Only by blowing this cover can poetic language become 'authentic,' that is, 'essentially temporal': it then stakes out 'a spot of *time,* authentic time disrupting for an instance the false texture of everyday existence,' and dispels 'the false image of time as mere succession—an illusion of physical continuity borrowed from the geometrical world of space' (145). The 'act of consciousness' that thus opens up 'authentic time' is 'memory,' at once the assertion of the mind's 'priority over nature' and the assertion of its 'unbreachable separation from Being' (146). Before we can turn to the further development of this memory, we must double back and investigate its complicated and contradictory genesis in response to and as a rejection of the 'actual order' of 'fact.'

To the extent that the rejection of analogy is the true dynamic of Wordsworth's thought, he rejoins Hölderlin, whom de Man, as he puts it, 'uses' in order 'to throw light on Wordsworth' (138). Hölderlin's light reveals that 'the analogy between nature and consciousness is not . . . a part of the actual order of things' but rather 'a creation of the human mind, an illusion invented by us to hide the fact that we are forever fallen away from Being' (140). De Man admits that 'the early Hölderlin' (138) sometimes does appear to honor an analogical ontology, but immediately adds that this appearance, even in the 1794 project for the 'Metrical Version' of *Hyperion*, already functions as a strategical-pedagogical point of transition only, as a 'naïve statement of pantheistic unity' to be replaced by 'a statement of the (ontological) priority of consciousness over nature, dismissing the analogy between mind and nature as illusory and inauthentic' (141).

A case in point here is the 'higher truth' revealed to Hyperion by his tutor in recognition of his 'advanced state of maturity':

> I know that only an inner shortcoming [*Bedürfnis*] forces us to give nature an affinity with whatever immortal element we carry within ourselves and makes us believe that a spirit inhabits matter. . . . I know that, when the beautiful forms of nature seem to announce the very presence of the divine, it is we ourselves who inspire the world with our own soul [*wir Selbst beseelen die Welt mit unserer Seele*]. Is there anything in the world that does not receive its attributes from us? [*Was ist dann, das nicht durch uns so wäre wie es ist?*][6] (140)

The passage functions as a classical prefiguration of the analytics of the pathetic fallacy.[7] In de Man's argument, its evident use—the light it throws on Wordsworth—is that it clears the way for the critique of the analogical imagination that inspires the first movements of the Winander Boy poem and the thesis on the mutual fit in the 1802 Preface to the *Lyrical Ballads*. Leaving aside, for the moment, the question whether this use does justice to Hölderlin's text (it does not), what must interest us is the specific elaboration of this critique de Man traces to Wordsworth's 'sentiment of existence' along the lines of the sublation of sensation supposedly attained in Rousseau's sentiment of the same name.

De Man's reading of Wordsworth's imagination hinges on his claim that Wordsworth's true language 'is opposed to the sensory and mimetic language' de Man sees as the exclusive and distinctive feature of 'organicist analogy' ('HEW' 143). For Wordsworth, as de Man reads him, the difference between Fancy, 'dependent on kinship between mind and nature,' and Imagination is precisely that the latter is 'defined by its power *not* to remain analogically or mimetically faithful to sensory perception,' a bold betrayal that grants it the ability 'to create appearances "for the gratification of the mind in contemplating the image itself"' (142). But Wordsworth's distinction follows a finer logic: his Imagination does not 'create appearances' out of the blue: it emphatically uses those that are 'present[ed] to the senses' and then 'represents' them to its own advantage. Speaking of the use of 'hung' in Virgil and Shakespeare, in the passage from the 1815 'Preface' de Man quotes, Wordsworth observes:

> In these instances is a slight exertion of the faculty which I denominate imagination, in the use of one word: neither the goat nor the samphire-gatherer do literally hang, as does the parrot or the monkey; but, presenting to the senses something of such an appearance, the mind in its activity, for its own gratification, contemplates them as hanging.[8]

It would require some strain to move this thought in de Man's direction by emphasizing the syntactic ambiguity as to the agency of the presentation involved in this operation (either, commonsensically, the visible scene, or, in line with de Man's judgment, the mind itself), but even then the marked presence of, specifically, the senses as the recipient of the image would obstruct de Man's reading. And similarly, Wordsworth's further commentary on Milton's 'flying Fiend' compared to a fleet descried far off at sea as hanging in the clouds complicates de Man's point by stressing the poet's 'taking advantage of its appearance to the senses' in his 'dar[ing] represent[ation]' of the fleet, 'both for the gratification of the mind in contemplating the image itself, and in reference to the motion and appearance of the sublime object to which it is compared.'

Again, as was the case for our objections to de Man's reception of Rousseau, these remarks do not intend to champion the true Wordsworth as the inverted image of what de Man has made of him: the relation of Wordsworth's imagination to the senses is neither a matter of opposition nor a question of the simple mimetic representation (if there is such a thing) of available appearances.[9] De Man is right to insist that the 1815 Preface does not move 'back to a mechanical concept of association' (143), but if the recognition of a dependence on moments of sensory perception in language necessarily signals 'the trappings of analogical thought' (146), the Preface's true move 'beyond the concept of analogy' (143) remains to be demonstrated.

Similarly, de Man is right to question the celebration of the 'charm' of Wordsworth's world as primarily and ultimately one of 'gentle constancy' ('WWH' 51), in which 'nature and consciousness are "interwoven"' (52) through the echoes of analogical correspondence, and to highlight the moments of uncertain suspension in a 'reflective and silent world' (55) marked by mutability, but if the mute reflection of the speaker at the end of the Winander Boy poem is read as the full understanding of these moments, it must also be recognized as itself retrospectively rehearsed in a speech act deeply implicated in the analogical figure *par excellence:* 'There was a Boy, ye knew him well, ye Cliffs / And Islands of Winander!' To argue, as de Man might, that the presence of sensible traces and unrepudiated anthropomorphism merely 'indicates the hold that an analogical ontology has over our minds and vocabulary' ('HEW' 146) and thus does not affect the true insight of Wordsworth's language is to transform a challenging difficulty into unproblematic residue duly to be processed by a massively indifferent system.

For, as in the case of Rousseau, there is a system here, a systematic and countertextual rejection of the sensory and (but it appears to be the same thing) the analogical in the name of 'authentic time.' The law of Wordsworth's language is that 'contact' with this true temporality only 'occurs as an act of consciousness and not as a natural sensation' (145), and in speaking this law *The Prelude* 'strives toward establishing the distinction between Nature and Being.' Before we turn to de Man's extension of this law to the world of history, we must first circle back to the rejection of analogical thought he diagnoses in Hölderlin.

*

In 'The Image of Rousseau' de Man tells us that Hölderlin's Rhine 'is not at all to be taken as a metaphor or an analogical symbol' and that his poetry shows 'no trace of anthropomorphism' ('IR' 295–96 n.31). 'Heaven and Earth in Wordsworth and Hölderlin,' however, is more cautious in admitting that in 'the early Hölderlin, one is able to find many examples of a nature experience that could be called pantheistic' ('HEW' 138), where pantheism designates a celebration of 'the analogy between mind and nature' (141). By way of illustration, de Man quotes a few lines from Hölderlin's project for the so-called 'Metrical Version' of *Hyperion*, in which 'an elderly sage whose word is supposed to be true wisdom' insists that ' "something in us expects and hopes for assistance from nature, even when we are fighting against it," ' and that ' "our Spirit . . . encounter[s] a kindred Spirit in all that exists" ' (138–39).[10] De Man acknowledges that this 'kindred Spirit suggests the conciliatory mood, the mutual attraction founded on affinity which is to be the basis of a true marriage,' but immediately goes on to say that 'the same text, or other fragments closely related to it and from the same period, puts this possibility radically into question; the movement toward unity has to be counterbalanced by the repeated assurance that it can never succeed' (139)—an assurance such as appears, for instance, in the slightly later preface to the so-called 'Penultimate Version' of the novel, where the 'Editor' stresses that 'the possibility of "uniting ourselves with Nature in one infinite totality" ' cannot 'exist for us as an actual, unmediated experience': 'Hölderlin's statements,' de Man writes, 'are remarkable for the stress they put on the prevalence of the division, which lasts for the entire duration of our conscious existence, and not on the unity, which is relegated to a remote and fictional past or to an unreachable future.' This is not to say that unity is not 'present to us': it is present to us, but 'only in a mediated form called Beauty [which] is not to be equated with unmediated Being' and moreover should not be understood as 'the discovery of an affinity or correspondence between mind and nature . . . that would allow us to ascend gradually, as in a Neoplatonic processive scheme, to Schelling's ultimate Identity, by ways of a series of increasingly transcendentalized marriages' (140). For such an 'analogy between nature and consciousness is not for Hölderlin a part of the actual order of things,' but rather 'an illusion invented by us to hide the fact that we are forever fallen away from Being.'

De Man then presents as 'a crucial statement to this effect' the passage from the project for the 'Metrical Version' on the 'inner shortcoming' which we have already quoted—the double effect being that Hölderlin's emphasis on *Bedürfnis* identifies our 'earthly condition' as one of 'barrenness,' the result of our 'separat[ion] from divine origin,' and that our 'invention' of an 'affinity with nature, which in fact does not exist,' is only a means of 'giving ourselves the illusion of an eternity which we do not possess.' Hölderlin is free from such delusions: he knows that this 'form of analogical thought' is 'a flight into inauthenticity' and that the 'true way is the way of love, Eros (the son of poverty and wealth), which sustains the knowledge of the discrepancy between divine origin and earthly predicament' (140–41). A final quotation from the same project establishes this knowledge as 'the very essence of all consciousness' and as 'linked with the full awareness of our temporal finitude': 'At the moment when the beautiful world began for us, when we gained consciousness, then we became finite.'[11] De Man concludes: 'Without leaving the same group of texts, we have moved from the naive statement of pantheistic unity to a statement of the (ontological) priority of consciousness over nature, dismissing the analogy between mind and nature as illusory and inauthentic' (141).

We have done no such thing—de Man's demonstration is yet again dependent on doctored quotations. More in particular, while he presents the passage on the *Bedürfnis* as a sequence of two cognitions ('I know . . . I know') leading to lucidity voiced in a rhetorical question, the original has a balanced structure of two pairs of statements (the last statement a rhetorical question) revolving around two 'buts' that turn the text toward another insight:

> I know that only need [*Bedürfnis*] forces us to give nature an affinity with the immortal element in us and to believe that a spirit inhabits matter, *but I know that this need gives us the right to do so* [*daß dieses Bedürfnis uns dazu berechtigt*], I know that when the beautiful forms of nature announce the presence of the divine to us [*uns die gegenwärtige Gottheit verkundigen*], it is we ourselves that animate the world with *our* soul, but what is there that is not the way it is through us?[12]

Thus, our *Bedürfnis* gives us *the right* to confer an affinity with ourselves upon nature; and the beautiful forms of Nature do not merely '*seem to* announce the very presence of the divine' (as de Man has it), they *do* announce this presence, because we make use of our right to animate the world with our soul. To read this as a dismissal of analogy as 'illusory and inauthentic' requires more renunciation than the text is ready to profess. Nor is the 'true way of love' the sublation of inauthentic analogy into an authentic 'awareness of our temporal finitude': rather, love is the mediating spirit that 'unifies [*vereinigt*]' our anti-animal 'drive [*Trieb*]' to 'free' our 'originally infinite essence [*ursprünglich unendliches Wesen*]' from its 'confinement [*Beschränkung*],' with our 'human' drive 'to be determined, to receive [*bestimmt zu werden, zu empfangen*],' to 'retain the chains [*die Fesseln behalten*]' that lock us in finitude. If 'the divine in us would be hemmed in by no resistance, then we would know of nothing outside ourselves, and thus we would know nothing of ourselves either, and not to know anything of oneself, not to feel oneself, and to be annihilated is one and the same for us [*denn würde das Göttliche in uns von keinem Widerstande beschränkt, so wüßten wir von nichts außer uns, und so auch von uns selbst nichts, und von sich nichts wissen, sich nicht zu fühlen, und vernichtet sein, ist für uns eines*].'[13] Yet, if we would not strive to 'ennoble [*veredlen*]' ourselves and to 'march into infinity [*fortzuschreiten ins Unendliche*],' we would be mere animals *(tierisch)*. We recognize this structure as the source of Rousseau's semidivine recollection, but the crucial point in our reading of de Man's perception of this source is that the unifying power of love as it is here analyzed *is* the exertion of the analogical imagination. Here are the sage's last words:

> To love in this way is human. That highest need of our being [*jenes höchste Bedürfnis unseres Wesens*] which forces us to confer upon [*beizulegen*] Nature an affinity with the immortal in us [*dem Unsterblichen in uns*], and to believe that a spirit inhabits matter, it is this love.[14]

What de Man reads as inauthentic naiveté *is* authentic love, what he presents as deluded analogism *is* the superior truth and legitimacy of analogical vision. Analogy does not apotropaically concoct an affinity between Nature and 'whatever immortal element we carry within ourselves' (de Man's translation); it exerts the right to give Nature the affinity with the immortal that *is* in us and it is in the recognition of this affinity that we are faithful to what we are.

If de Man rightly insists that the final *Vollendung* in Hölderlin's thought is systematically and consciously deferred, his refusal to recognize that the law of this deferral is itself the province of the analogical imagination radically refracts the light that Hölderlin is supposed to throw on Wordsworth. De Man's Wordsworth has to train himself not to perceive but to imagine, to 'create appearances "for the gratification of the mind in contemplating the image itself"' ('HEW' 142); his Hölderlin has to abandon the 'illusions' we 'invent' in order to face the truth that this invention 'does not in fact exist' and is not 'a part of the actual order of things' (140). But for Hölderlin the actual order of things is precisely to be reinvented by the love of analogy, and for Wordsworth the imagination cannot do without 'the appearance to the senses.' Hölderlin's Rhine has a distinctive voice ('Die Stimme wars des edelsten der Ströme, des freigeborenen Rheins'),[15] as do Wordsworth's 'mountain torrents': their language hears and modulates the sound of the water as voice, and this vision is not one they can abandon at will—

Recall | 91

which is not to say they uncritically celebrate it. The difference they do mark can neither be recuperated for nor be abandoned by the dialectic: it is not a thing of the past and it cannot assert itself as the future of such a past.

In the undecidable difference between 'inventing affinities' and 'creating appearances,' or between sensory perception and the actual order of fact, de Man tries to create and to reinvent Romanticism as a memory stretched between analogy and apocalypse. The rejection of analogy is, as yet, unreadable; we can now turn to the warning of the apocalypse.

Past Apocalypse

> The Terrorists are those who, desiring absolute freedom, know that by the same token they desire their death, who are conscious of this freedom they affirm as of their death which they realize, and who consequently, while they are alive, act, not as living men, but as beings deprived of being, as universal thoughts, pure abstractions judging and deciding, beyond history, in the name of the entirety of history.
>
> – Maurice Blanchot, 'La littérature et le droit à la mort'

Wordsworth's 'access to the world of history' ('WWH' 55) is opened in de Man's reading of the poet's encounter with the revolutionary 'Delegates returning / From the great Spousals'[16] in the Champ de Mars of 14 July 1790. The elation of this 'blithe Company' does not fail to infect Wordsworth and his companion, who 'feel themselves carried away by the joy of a rejuvenating historical act,' a joy that is 'spontaneous and sincere, as had been the corresponding joy of the boy who stood in evening conversation with the invisible birds. It is the joy in an active world in which the movement of our wishes appears to correspond to that of (the) time(s).'[17]

The analogy with the Winander Boy bodes little good for the revolutionary company, and a passage interposed by Wordsworth at an early stage of composition confirms this premonition: 'Despite its doubtless healthy character, this joy conceals a danger which the continuation of the poem embodies in the threat posed to the cloister of the Grande Chartreuse in the wake of the revolutionary enthusiasm.' This imminent desecration of the convent is a threat to 'something much more worthy than a particular religious symbol,' for the cloister 'signifies an entity [*Wesenheit*] that is so capacious as to take in faith and reason, but also nature in its most universal form' (55–56; translation modified):

> This is not that nature which docilely fits our will and puts itself at the disposal of the play of our faculty of understanding. Rather, it is nature as the principle in which time finds itself preserved, without losing the movement of passing away which makes it real *(eignet)* for those who are submitted to it. . . .
>
> Thus, what the insurgents threaten to destroy in their enthusiasm is the temporal nature of our existence. Their joy expresses itself with such self-assurance and lack of measure that it believes itself capable of reconciling the instant with eternity. They mean to possess something that remains [*ein Bleibendes*] which they fashion according to the intoxication of the act, even while this remaining only exists in a nature that has duration because it negates the instant, just as reflection must negate the act that nonetheless constitutes its origin. (56; translation modified)

At first sight, this close affiliation between universal nature and true temporality appears to rehearse the advent of a true conception of temporality in Hölderlin's rethinking of Rousseau's earth-as-consciousness. Yet, there is a significant shift in perspective. We get a first intimation of this shift in de Man's comments, before he identifies the principle governing the nature of the revolutionary threat, on some of the memorably quotable figures from Book Six of *The Prelude* he had already lined up in 'Intentional Structure' ('forests unapproachable by death,' 'woods decaying, never to be decayed,' 'workings of one mind,' 'features of the same face,' 'blossoms upon one tree,' 'characters of the great Apocalypse,' 'types and symbols of eternity,' 'first and last, and midst, and without end'—though not this time the 'bodily eyes' that formed a glaring incongruity in the antisensory doctrine under construction in the earlier essay). 'Wordsworth's language,' de Man writes, 'exerts itself to grasp this apparently contradictory nature in paradoxes, in which the movement of passing away curiously joins with a condition of remaining and allows a unity to arise that lies at the very limit of comprehensible language' (56; translation modified).

It is not clear whether Wordsworth's paradoxes actually succeed in this attempt, nor is it clear whether the limits of intelligible language are effectively mastered in these paradoxes. What is clear, however, is that this nature is not identified with consciousness itself as Hölderlin's earth was, and that, with parallel caution, Wordsworth's consciousness is not favored with the confident acquisition of ontological superiority claimed for Rousseau. The point is tenuous but it may help us toward a better understanding of the marked disappearance of the euphoric chords that underscored 'Image of Rousseau' and still resonated in the conclusion to 'Heaven and Earth.' For whereas Rousseau was praised for having secured the future of humanity, the merits ascribed to Wordsworth's vision are substantially less sanguine.

The insurgents threatening the Grande Chartreuse deploy a historical activity in danger of going astray and of thus destroying time—much as, in the anecdote recounted by Walter Benjamin, their heirs in the 1830 July Revolution, 'irritated at the hour,' shot at the clocks on the church towers 'to stop the day.'[18] Their action participates in and turns against history, a paradox reminiscent of the dialectic of action and reflection in Hölderlin and Rousseau: 'History is, to the extent that it is a deed, a dangerous and destructive act, a kind of hubris of the will that rebels against the grasp of time. But on the other hand it also engenders time [*zeiterzeugend*], since it allows the language of reflection to constitute itself' (57; translation modified). Wordsworth's celebrated account of the missed crossing on the Simplon Pass figures as a 'symbolical narrative, a kind of comparison' demonstrating this 'complex comprehension of history' and articulating its relation to the Imagination, famously addressed against the flow of the story. The enthusiastic ascent of a mountain that lies already beyond the peak to be scaled is read in line with the equally naive movement toward the destruction of the cloister and this reading reveals the shared intent of the travelers and the insurgents: all are 'driven by the same, almost divine wish,' and all 'stand under the influence of the poetic faculty' (58).

The difference between Wordsworth's historical vision and Rousseau's ideal and generalized knowledge of the future of humanity gradually emerges: what Wordsworth's 'Hymn to the Imagination' teaches us is that our 'striving for action [*Tatstreben*]' —a drive which is itself a function of 'poetic enthusiasm'—bespeaks 'a need [*Bedürfnis*] for a future,' a '*maladie d'idéalité* (as Mallarmé put it), that throws us out of the everyday present into the future' (57; translation modified; cf. also 'PHDM' 41). Instead of preparing the ideality of a perfect future whose possibility Rousseau had the audacity to affirm, Wordsworth's imagination, in the 'interpretive stage' in which it recognizes true temporality, can only look back upon the violent and unwarranted requisition of such a future in the unleashed acts and thoughts of those infected with the sickness of ideality. This emphatically includes the poets: they, too, are necessarily subject to the 'excess of interiority [*Übermaß der Innigkeit*],'[19] to what de Man has later called 'the temptation of immediacy . . . constitutive of a literary consciousness' ('LH' 152)—as in fact was Rousseau.

But whereas Rousseau was said to recoil from this excess in order to prepare the future, Wordsworth is seen as retreating into a reflection upon the past in which this future was thought. Wordsworth's reflection is essentially retrospective: his road (for a road it still is) only runs backward. The apotropaic retreat is preserved, but it is divested—*as* reflection—of its prospective potential. The history that is thought in this recollection is now no longer to be understood as the interpretation of a preordained course of destiny toward the future of an ideality beyond questioning, but rather as the imperfect product of an attempt to interpret the events and thoughts effected in the name of such an ideality. As de Man puts it, in one of the richest samples of his prose:

> The moment of active projection into the future (which is also the moment of the loss of the self in the intoxication of the in-

stant) lies for the imagination in a past from which it is separated by the experience of a failure *(Scheitern)*. The interpretation is possible only from a standpoint that lies on the far side of this failure, and that has escaped destruction thanks to an effort of consciousness to make sure of itself once again. But this consciousness can be had only by one who has very extensively partaken of the danger and failure. Act and interpretation are thus connected in a complex and often contradictory manner. For those who must interpret it, history is never a simple and uniform movement like the ascent of a peak or the installation of a definitive social order. Rather, it appears much more in that twilight in which for Wordsworth the crossing of the Alps was bathed, in which the coming-to-consciousness is in arrears vis-à-vis the actual act, and consequently is to be understood not as a conquest but rather as a rectification or even a reproach. The future is present in history only as the remembering of a failed project that has become a menace. For Wordsworth there is no historical eschatology, but rather only a never-ending reflection upon an eschatological moment that has failed through the excess of its interiority. The poetry partakes of the interiority as well as the reflection: it is an act of the spirit which allows it to turn from the one to the other. ('WWH' 58–59; translation modified)

It is this insight, dependent as it is on the 'overcoming' of analogical thought, that links Wordsworth's thought to Hölderlin's, which, according to de Man at least, has conquered such analogism 'almost from the beginning' (59). De Man's text wavers slightly on the nature of this link—either it is a matter of Hölderlin and Wordsworth inhabiting the same poetic world ('as well as') or the truth articulated here is actually a result of our having already 'abandoned' Wordsworth 'without being clear about this ourselves' until Hölderlin threw his light across our path—but he is clearly more interested in the relationship between poetry and history he reads into both Wordsworth and Hölderlin as such: 'The comparison stops being an exercise and becomes truly illuminating' (60).

And once again it is Hölderlin's 'Mnemosyne' that must be read 'if we want to pursue our investigation to its end, even though the difficulty of the text is so great that only a few general remarks are possible here' (59). Yet the end had already been reached, and the difficulty of the text seems to put up no resistance to its repetition: the true illumination gained from 'Mnemosyne' only throws light on what was already exposed.

De Man takes issue with readings of 'Mnemosyne' as an 'eschatological poem in which Hölderlin, inspired by the memory of ancient heroism, decides to actively prepare the fulfillment of history' (60). This is to misunderstand the poem's 'temporal perspective,' which corresponds to that in Book Six of *The Prelude* in that it recognizes the equivalent of revolutionary fervor, the historical action of humanity that precedes the poem, as a moment of literal enthusiasm, 'a state that distinguishes itself through the necessity of history to succeed anew in unmediated action'—once again, the river reads the rule ('Ströme müssen / Den Pfad sich suchen' [Streams must / Seek themselves the path])—and which has a positive face 'in which a feeling for the future once again becomes possible' and a negative one in its suspension in 'a time span of uncertainty and the greatest danger' (60–61). This confusion is 'similar' to the one in which Wordsworth's imagination 'springs forth,' and thematizes 'an excess issuing from a fullness which causes us to transgress our own limits' (61). As in Wordsworth, this excess—Titanism—should not be read in any 'direct opposition' to poetry: rather, the relation is one of 'prematurity [*Vorzeitigkeit*]' (62), with poetry acting as the medium in which 'to achieve the transition from the Titans to the interiority of interpretation' and in which 'the traces of both these elements'—the heroic and the ideal—can be preserved (63).

Thus, although poetry participates in the 'Titanic origin,' it 'never allows this power to rush blindly to meet the unknown future of death. It turns back upon itself and becomes part of a temporal dimension that strives to remain bound to the earth, and that replaces the violent temporality of action [*reissende Zeit*] with the sheltering temporality [*schützende Zeit*] of interpretation' (63). Such is the 'protecting [*schonend*] act of the Logos' named at the end of 'Mnemosyne' ('Unwillig nehmlich / Sind Himmlische, wenn einer nicht die Seele schonend sich / Zusammengenommen'), but, as with Wordsworth, this sheltering return 'is possible only after the Titanic heroism has run its course' (64). Hölderlin's 'aber er muß doch' refers to the double necessity for the hero to die in his necessary historical action and for the poet to turn back upon himself as he 'conjures (up) [*Beschwören*] the death of the hero in the form of a memory so mournful that it almost draws him on to a similar dying' (64; translation modified).[20] The heroes' death is necessary, but the poet must avert a similar death in the error of his mourning. This error, then, is the interiorized repetition of the heroic apocalypse, not its memory, for memory, which is always a 'memory of death' (in Hölderlin 'the death of the heroes whose actions engendered history') is what 'resist[s] the temptation to escape from temporality into eschatological or apocalyptic schemes,' precisely by remembering them as past apocalypse ('HEW' 146).

The light that remains after (and of) the apocalypse in the 'temporal doubling of the act and its interpretation' that distinguishes both Wordsworth and Hölderlin further 'discloses a general structure of poetic temporality':

> It lends duration to a past that otherwise would immediately sink into the nonbeing of a future that withdraws itself from consciousness. It is thus an act through which a memory threatened with its own loss succeeds in sustaining itself. . . . The poet decisively separates himself from the hero through his care for preserving memory, even the memory of the heroic act that throws itself into the future and destroys itself in this project. The poet and the historian converge in this essential point to the extent that they both speak of an action that precedes them but that exists for consciousness only because of their intervention. ('WWH' 64–65)

This commemorative enterprise seems to retain only minimal traces of Rousseau's confidence in the 'possibility of practical efficacity' ('IR' 41) of his thought in its thrust toward the generalized ideal of a perfect world. If the poetic spirit in 'The Image of Rousseau' had to forget its own lucidity in order to preserve the future of humanity at a lawful distance from apocalyptic consummation, it now has to remember this future as itself an apocalyptic projection in the past: there is no mention of another, nonapocalyptic future. The logos of Mnemosyne only averts the logos of last things by remembering it as the dissolution of the logos in the past; it is primarily reactive and the 'magnanimity' that marks the poet's self-understanding ('WWH' 63) appears singularly composed in comparison to Rousseau's revolutionary self-extension to 'the entire human community' ('IR' 41).

The dialectic would require a progression from Wordsworth's and Hölderlin's memorial warning against the heroic act's self-destructive projection into the future toward Rousseau's future-oriented promise to restore 'the thought and the destiny of the West' to its 'authentic path' in a full awareness of the limits imposed by 'its own laws' (45). In this logic, the warning would describe past aberrations and thereby put up resistance to their repetition, whereas the promise would interiorize this resistance in the mode of a law for the future: the promise would be the genuinely synthetic *Vollendung* of the antithetical warning against the all too thetic lawless promise of the original transgression. Yet what remains is the warning founded by the poets in response to their participation in the exhilarating but destructive promise. The light that remains is not the properly deflected lawful portion of the lucid insight into the future but the hesitant searchlight cast over the ashes of an all too recent and familiar past that has already had its future and lost (itself in) it.

Past Obsession

It is necessary, then, to take sides, and to act accordingly. But Montaigne proposes to this effect a hygiene of action; it prescribes the preservation of inner 'repose' and serenity, not only in the interest of the individual, but in order to better ensure the justice and the efficacity of the action taken.
— Jean Starobinski, *Montaigne en mouvement*

Consequently, we must correct the perspective and recheck the balance sheet—on which, by the way, his [Sartre's] cursed lucidity, in lighting up the labyrinths of rebellion and revolution, has recorded in spite of himself all we need to absolve him.
— Maurice Merleau-Ponty, 'Introduction' to *Signs*

But we are not, alas!, in an epoch of irony.
— Albert Camus, 'Autocritique'

In this light, it is hard not to recall once more de Man's 1953 account of Montaigne's cautionary memory, 'entertained and justified and content to make a patient inventory of the dangerous structures men have produced in hopes of achieving some sort of rule' ('MT' 10). As we conjure up this recollection, whose imperious law is the hermeneutically and historically satisfying return of the repressed repression of memories of extensive participation in danger and failure, we must also register the violently intelligible analogical scenarios it has the power to produce.

Montaigne's 'moral phenomenology' is governed by the 'fundamental humility of the spirit, which cannot claim to legislate but only to describe,' and in which, '[s]ince Husserl, we have learned to find . . . the best source of resistance to the aberrations of our time' (8). As an instance of this moment of resistance in the descriptive spirit, de Man quotes Montaigne's criticism of the anti-Calvinist *Sainte Ligue:* if at the surface of the moment Protestantism figures as a 'fanatical movement' and Catholicism as the 'tested and tolerant doctrine' that Montaigne pledges his profoundly formal allegiance to, the League's activities nonetheless—but necessarily—elicit from him a 'thundering' criticism, 'that will apply to so many of Catholicism's subsequent excesses' (9–10). The passage, taken from the essay 'On Custom and on not readily changing a received law,' is as follows:

> 'But if the inventors [the Protestants] have done more harm, the imitators [the Catholics] are more vicious in that they wholeheartedly follow examples whose horror and evil they have felt and punished. And if there is some degree of honor even in evildoing, they must concede to the others the glory of invention, and the courage of the first effort.'[21] (10)

The lesson de Man draws from this passage is an unstable combination of topical critique and political principle—it is one of the passages in his writing that continues to haunt my attempts to grasp his thought and compels me to translate it in the terrible stenography of psychosynthesis:

> Let these words be remembered when one pretends to invoke today [*de nos jours*] a conservatism like Montaigne's to justify some such injustice [*justifier telle injustice*]. What orthodoxy, at the present time [*à l'heure présente*], could invoke the breadth and the comprehension of post-medieval Christianity? The miserable myths that surround us are no sooner born than they degenerate into sclerotic bureaucracies. They must appeal to the most factitious loyalties—those of nationalism and of race—to gain any vitality at all [*pour se donner un peu de souffle*]. Imagine Montaigne in such surroundings; no doubt he would be on the side of the rebels [*révoltés*]. (10; translation modified)

What on earth is he talking about? Which injustice, what justification, whose conservatism? Whose are the miserable myths and factitious loyalties to nation and race targeted here? What are the 'aberrations of our time' we must resist? And in the name of which rebels? It is imperative to struggle for some answers to these questions, even while we must recognize the sinister policing of necessary meaning they announce.²²

The time of publication is 1953, a moment in 'a very rich and complex period' of which 'only the remotest echoes filter through' to de Man's writing. I quote from de Man's 1965 comments on Camus's 1942–1951 *Notebooks* ('AC' 147): perhaps the echo (if it is an echo) we should hear in his 1953 invitation to 'imagine what rebellions [*révoltes*] Montaigne is capable of' is what filters through from the bitter conflict generated by the publication of *L'Homme révolté (Man in Revolt / The Rebel)* in 1951. In the absence of whatever notes on current reading de Man may have made, it is difficult to reconstruct this hypothesis into hard genetic insight (itself always risking a questionable oblivion to the very logic of the genetic imperative), yet there is enough in the constellation here to allow us to draw out some figures for de Man's referents and to read them through to 'Mnemosyne' 's warning in an attempt to acknowledge the historical intent of de Man's articulations of Romanticism.²³

The straitjacket harnessing *L'homme révolté* is the tension that obtains between revolt and revolution, innovation and terror. Revolt is the act of 'a man who says no' *and* 'who says yes.'²⁴ It is a double act that defines a limit, a measure, and it is in the loyalty to this limit—whose substantial nature as human solidarity Camus is at pains to specify—that the quality of the revolt as revolt is to be measured:

> In order to be, man must rebel [*se révolter*], but his revolt must respect the limit it discovers in itself and in which men, by join-

ing together, commence being. Rebellious thought can therefore not do without memory: it is a perpetual tension. In following it in its works and its acts, we shall therefore have to say, each time, whether it remains faithful to its primary nobility or whether, on the contrary, through weariness [*lassitude*] or madness, it has forgotten it, in an intoxication of tyranny or of servitude.[25]

Such is the program Camus then indefatigably but tiresomely brings to bear on a sweeping survey of Western ideologies, in whose development he diagnoses a 'desperate effort to found . . . the empire of man'—the disastrous consequences of this effort (in particular, the excesses of nihilism as fascism and Stalinism) being indexes of 'the extent to which the revolt has forgotten its origins, has grown tired of the difficult tension between yes and no and has fully abandoned itself to the negation of all that is or to total submission.'[26] For Camus's political imagination, one of the truly decisive moments in which this oblivion acquires shape is Hegel's *Phenomenology of Spirit*—which he qualifies as 'a metaphysical *Emile*'[27]—and the law of this oblivion is Hegel's 'definitive destruction of all vertical transcendence,'[28] a feat that clears the way for the 'excessive consequences [*conséquences démesurées*]' of 'cynicism, the divinisation of history and matter, individual terror or the crime of the State':[29] Promethean revolt has been perverted into the terrible revolutions of the latter-day Caesars.[30] 'Revolution, obeying nihilism, has in effect turned against its rebellious origins.'[31]

Such is the 'hypothesis' that, for Camus, 'explains, in part, the direction and, almost entirely, the excess of our time [*la démesure de notre temps*]'[32]—in 1950, the 'fate of the world' depends on the conflict between 'the forces of revolt and those of the Caesarean revolution':

> The triumphant revolution must prove through its polices, its trials and its excommunications that there is no human nature.

The humiliated revolt, through its contradictions, its suffering, its renewed defeats and its tireless pride, must give this nature its content of pain and hope.³³

The task Camus defines at the end of his itinerary is the recognition of the light of a new 'renascence' to be prepared 'beyond nihilism,'³⁴ and its law is the rebellious elaboration in the face of history of a 'rule' that is neither 'formal' nor wholly subordinate to historical substance—a rule that recalls (though Camus does not spell out the echo) the historical form of Hölderlin's *vaterländische Umkehr:* 'Instead of killing and dying in order to produce the being we are not, we must live and make live so as to create what we are.'³⁵

The response elicited by *L'homme révolté* was an overwhelming combination of dubious praise and painful acrimony.³⁶ Most notably, it brought about, at last, the radical break between Sartre and Camus that had already begun to leave its marks soon after the Liberation. The terms of the polemic—whose tone was set in Francis Jeanson's acerbic analysis of Camus's soul in the May 1952 issue of *Les temps modernes*—can be summarily rehearsed. For Jeanson, Camus's thought is thrall to a profound metaphysical 'refusal of history,'³⁷ which substitutes a rarefied 'pure dialogue of ideas' (the conflict between authentic revolt and excessive revolution, or, in Camus's own terms, between an 'uprising against the condition [*soulèvement contre la condition*]' and 'an excessive expedition against the sky [*une expédition démesurée contre le ciel*]')³⁸ for a genuine appreciation of the oppositional dynamics of 'concrete situations.'³⁹ The figure with which Jeanson names this 'evasion towards some definitive retreat where [Camus] can fully devote himself to the rebellious delights of an existence without history'⁴⁰ is Hegel's Beautiful Soul, quoted as follows: 'Consciousness lives in fear of soiling the splendour of its interiority through action and being-there, and in order to preserve the purity of its heart it flees the contact of effectivity [*effectivité; Wirklichkeit*] and persists in its stubborn impotence.... Its operation is nostalgic aspiration [*aspiration nostalgique; Sehnen*].'[41]

The most evident form this nostalgia takes in Camus's thought is form itself: Jeanson's primary ironical attack on *L'homme révolté* is that—despite Camus's explicit rejection of the cultivation of form—the book is too formally accomplished: 'This author who "measures" his revolt so serenely' styles his protest in a tireless sequence of formulas that is 'too beautiful, too sovereign, too sure of itself, too much in harmony with itself'—in short, (too) 'transcendental.'[42] It is this formal perfection that allows Camus (now in the words of Sartre's rejoinder) to act the role of 'public prosecutor' for the 'Republic of Beautiful Souls'[43] and 'to establish the synthesis between aesthetic pleasure, desire, happiness and heroism, between fulfilled [*comblée*] contemplation and duty, between Gidean plenitude and Baudelairean dissatisfaction.'[44] In his summation of Camus's evolution, Sartre drives the point home: 'Your morality has first changed itself into moralism, today it is no more than literature, tomorrow it will perhaps be immorality.'[45]

Jeanson and Sartre further determine the genesis of this 'refusal of history' in a critical reflection on Camus's wartime commitment to the Resistance, as he had registered it himself in his 1943–44 'Letters to a German Friend,' in terms of a sacrificial duty.[46] For Sartre, these terms are to be translated as follows: in peacetime, Camus 'waged a timeless war against the injustice of our destiny,' and as the Germans became the preeminent historical incarnation of this injustice, Camus felt forced to 'enter history': 'The circumstances of this combat have anchored you in the idea that sometimes one must pay one's tribute to History, so as to have the right, afterwards, to return to the true duties'[47]—these true duties being the repeated formal acts of revolt against the absurdity of history as such. Thus, Camus's understanding of his involvement in the Resistance could only ever confirm the 'wisdom' his '"strained serenity"'[48] had always already assumed:

So don't deny it: you have not refused History because you have suffered from it and have discovered its face in horror. You have refused it prior to any other experience because our culture has refused it and because you had placed human values in the struggle of man 'against the sky.' You have chosen and created yourself the way you are in meditating on the misfortunes and the anxieties that were your personal fate, and the solution you have brought to them is a bitter wisdom that exerts itself to deny time.[49]

In his reply to Jeanson's first attack, Camus had already explicitly taken issue with this diagnosis of *L'homme révolté* as the product of a congenitally ahistorical Beautiful Soul strengthened in its eternal commitment to celestial combat after having suffered a tour of duty in a historical conflict apparently performing but ultimately perverting the ideality of lawful revolt. Answering Jeanson's suggestion that his thought effectively forecloses a genuine confrontation with concrete contemporary historical suffering (such as the suppression of industrial action and French colonial enterprises against insurgents in Madagascar, Vietnam, and Tunisia),[50] Camus turns the tables by arguing that Jeanson—and, by implication, Sartre and his allies at *Les temps modernes*—remains wilfully blind to the concrete historical suffering that *is* identified in *L'homme révolté* as the latest manifestation of the unleashed revolutionary logic the book sets out to oppose: 'the fact of the concentration camps [*le fait concentrationnaire*]'[51] in the USSR, which, following the Kravchenko affair and David Rousset's 1949 call for investigation,[52] had come to join the earlier Stalinist infamy of the Moscow Trials as a central target in indictments of communism. To Camus's mind, Jeanson is caught in a contradiction, defending Marxism 'as an implicit dogma,' while being unable to accept it as an 'overt politics.'[53] It would have been 'normal, and almost courageous' if Jeanson had recognized the problem of the historical implementation of 'authoritarian socialism' and 'justified the existence of those camps':[54] but as it is, always on Camus's analysis, Jeanson's silence (at this time shared by Sartre) indicates an embarrassment at the core of communist-existentialist thought that betrays its complicity with nihilism in its inability to give another 'form' or 'name' to liberty than that of the necessary despotism of divinized history.[55]

If this conflict is the echo of Montaigne's revolt in de Man's aside on the 'aberrations of our time,' we can—*for instance*—hear it as follows: the 'miserable myths' de Man villifies in 1953 are those of communist thought, degenerated into the practice of 'sclerotic bureaucracies' (the banal evil presiding over the Gulag administration, the Moscow Trials, and, most recently, the November 1952 Slansky trial), appealing to nationalist sentiment (exemplified within the Soviet Union in the forced settlement of non-Russian nationalities,[56] and on a global level in the logic of the Cold War as the perversion of international socialism) and racist loyalties (say—and the blank possibility of this saying is the problem—*zhdanovshchina* anti-Semitism, which attracted international attention in early 1953 with the persecution of the 'White Shirts').[57] 'What orthodoxy, at the present time, can invoke the breadth and comprehension of post-medieval Christianity?' ('MT' 10). In the face of the hardened orthodoxy of totalitarian socialism, which has become 'massive and opaque, wounding anyone who comes up against it,' which has 'no concern but to perpetuate itself as an institution,' and whose 'ritual becomes a police regulation' (9), revolt is the only appropriate response. Invoking Montaigne to 'extenuate' the 'injustice' perpetrated in the name of the revolution is to abuse his suspicion of universal ethical values for the purpose of a cynical acceptance of suffering in the name of the system.[58] If this echo makes sense, the problem is it makes too much of it, and not nearly enough.

When Camus objected to Jeanson's 'fabrication' of an 'imaginary biography' as an etiological frame of reference for the antihistorical sentiment putatively governing *L'homme révolté*,[59] Jeanson retorted that the problem was precisely that in trying to reconstruct Camus's 'intellectual itinerary' on the basis of his writings alone, he repeatedly witnessed Camus's ideas miraculously turning into 'flesh.'[60] Camus has every reason to doubt the good faith of Jeanson's *ab homine* reading with its subsequent justification in terms of ineluctable incarnation, and his objection that Jeanson tendentiously distorts his thought on history is largely convincing. Yet, this does not make the psychobiographical pattern any the less compelling. For us, its dubious attraction is doubled by the fact that this psychobiography is highly enabling for an equally psychobiographical explanation of de Man's enigmatic recourse to the paradoxical rhetoric of topical insinuation in the course of his reading of Montaigne. For it is tempting to imagine a sheltering mechanism of wishful identification allowing de Man to participate in the wisdom of someone whose understanding of historical aberration originated in an experience of revolt against the divinization of history as necessity which de Man himself, 'young and inexperienced,' had first espoused and subsequently witnessed the failure of. The imperative revolt against Stalinist terror would imply a retrospective revolt against the supreme nihilism of fascist historicism (as Camus sees it, 'Hitler was history in its pure state');[61] as revolt, it would further ensure a measure of attractive passion to balance the chastened understanding of past aberration; and this understanding itself, derived from an experience beyond reproach,[62] would be all the more effective insofar as it would allow for an interpretation of this aberration in terms of a compelling mystifying logic so impersonal that its very recognition already amounts to a formal excuse for not having recognized or resisted it. It is easy to imagine such a scenario of 'defensive resistance,'[63] but it will not do to take it as read. Not because it is an excessive inflation of arbitrary hints and suspicions on the basis of a puzzling passage of a few lines only, but because, as a response to the referential imperative of that passage, this scenario is immediately undercut by what it excludes. For there are other referents.

De Man's evidence for Montaigne's moral revolt is his 'thundering' accusation of the *Sainte Ligue* for their 'vicious' imitation of the 'fanatical' Protestants. But Montaigne also grants the fanatics a measure of 'honor' in their 'evil-doing' (be it only by way of hypothesis): theirs is 'the glory of invention, and the courage of the first effort' ('MT' 10).[64] De Man urges us to remember these words, as proof of Montaigne's resistance to an opaque and injust orthodoxy, but if that were their sole purpose he could have chosen far less complicated instances (such as, say, the denunciation of an incomprehensible judiciary system immediately preceding the passage in question).[65] As it is, the suggestion of a vicious imitation disguised as opposition that characterizes the League's reaction establishes a pattern that, when read with some suspicion, becomes disturbingly familiar. The stark form of the analogy would be this: League:Reformation::Purge:Collaboration.[66] The effect of the analogy is disturbing not because it would mark a condemnation of the *Epuration*—the failure of the postwar purge to uphold its integrity had been denounced by an increasing number of entirely nonsuspect intellectuals ever since its inception[67]—but because it would also entail, through the force of this particular quotation, a *pro domo* recognition of honor, glory, and courage in the 'original' fanatics by someone who had, precisely, welcomed the courage of the first effort at innovation in the 'present revolution' (*HVL*, May 1942, 307). The 'sclerotic bureaucracies' ('MT' 10) could now be read as the various postwar organizations (both of the Right and of the Left) self-righteously watching over the preservation of the values of the reborn French Nation, and although this certainly does not imply a celebration of the substantial principles of the first efforts of German aggression itself, it is hard not to hesitate at the formal apologetic admission of honor, however hypothetical, that is involved here, coming as it does from one who registered the effort at its first climax as a necessary development.

And of course there are still other scenarios that would answer the call for reference: the newly born 'miserable myth' could be that of the true Europe styling itself as the sole safeguard against Soviet aggression and/or American imperialism; the 'sclerotic bureaucracies' could be the anti-Communist paranoid administration in the grip of McCarthy, at the height of its powers around the time de Man was writing; the 'factitious loyalties' to nation and race could be specified with reference to French colonial activity in the name of Empire. Et cetera. Which is, evidently, the problem: the proliferation of positions that can readily be taken—and must be taken—in the name of Montaigne's revolt is a direct consequence of the uncompromising formality of its detachment,[68] and this formal detachment is itself the empty and gratuitously gratifying conclusion of the psychobiographic account of this ideology of revolt I have been trying to trace.

In the face of the formal 'injustice' de Man leaves unidentified, Montaigne would revolt. But 'without taking himself seriously' ('MT' 10). The only ground on which the injustice can be condemned is its 'stupidity,' and all that remains after this revolt is 'a patient inventory of the dangerous structures men have produced in hopes of achieving some sort of rule,' recollected 'gently, with a respectful irony and an utter honesty—always asserting their ultimate absurdity, but delighting as a connoisseur in the spectacle of their beauty.' Irrespective of which particular answer we bring to the referential demand stamped on this 'injustice' by the marker 'de nos jours'—and some such answer cannot but be given, irrespective of whether we infuse the phrase with the added pathos of de Man's personal history or 'merely' read it in the wake of the historical catastrophes marking the half-century before it was written—this recollection is terrible. The consciousness displayed here in its performance of superior, 'formal and aesthetic' 'phenomenology' is a monstrosity; it is neither the 'unhappy so-called Beautiful Soul' chastised by Hegel for its ineffectual 'yearning [*Sehnen*],'[69] nor the sublation of this 'objectless self-consciousness'[70] in the active fulfillment of the Absolute Spirit. It does not suffer from 'the fear of soiling the sovereignty of its inwardness through action and existence,'[71] for it does not even take this inwardness seriously, and the very thought of achieving a genuine synthesis with concrete reality is beautiful but absurd, if not stupid. This consciousness 'located beyond failure . . . has a name: it is *form*, a gratuitous but rigorous structure that is made and unmade in our hands but is never completed' (10; translation modified). And this form is writing:

> We can never be sufficiently amazed by the extraordinary nature of this enterprise. A man sits down at his desk and writes, without the desire to communicate with anyone at all, without the need to express some violent sentiment that torments him, without the desire to explain himself to himself or to justify himself morally in his own eyes, without any attempt at fabulation. (10; translation modified)

This act is truly formal, in that it is wholly devoid of intention. It exhausts itself in itself and its 'tense is exclusively the present,' infinitely open 'to every wind that blows.' Even the inventory is ultimately erased:

> The past collapses straight-away into oblivion, because it works loose from the subjectivity of the immediate; have we sufficiently understood the extraordinary fact that Montaigne never refers to his previous declarations? Quite literally, he has forgotten them. The future, it goes without saying, remains open; no conclusion is definitive, and contradiction is the mind's law. (11)

The only thing that is certain is this piece of paper, the writing on which establishes 'a formal separation between the action accomplished in reality and its observation by means of discourse' (translation modified). An observation that is totally pointless: the 'summary image' of this consciousness 'is that of a man who observes himself in the gratuitous and fundamentally futile act of writing,' and it is wholly in keeping with this sovereign absence of intention that the form itself also dissolves. For finally, this consciousness cannot even see itself 'as a form, however transitory': its absolute, restlessly chastened transcendence is that of an objectless, tranquil, and ironic gaze.

In *Serenity in Crisis* I tried to demonstrate how this monstrous detachment is recomplicated in a return to crisis in de Man's essays of the second half of the 1950s, and in the preceding chapters I have pursued this thought up to the point where the complication once more appeared on the verge of being resolved in a relapse into the logic of the inventory. But if Hölderlin's heroes and Wordsworth's revolutionaries now seem to prefigure twentieth-century forms of totalitarian politics—their common denominator being the excess of revolt into revolution—what must interest us here more than the charicaturesque repetition we thus appear to diagnose is the historical implication of the pattern in a relentless and increasingly confident critique of sensory (analogical) reason in the name of authentic (nonapocalyptic) temporality and its emphatic coloring as a warning mourning over a shared past rather than as an ironic contemplation of the beauty of human absurdity. Past analogy, past apocalypse: past apology, obsession. Unlike Montaigne, the figure of the poet read into 'Mnemosyne' cannot satisfy itself in the alacritous *(allégresse)* ('MT' 11; translation modified) assumption of triple failure (epistemological, ethical, and aesthetic); unlike Montaigne's, the critique that it is this figure's responsibility to articulate takes itself extremely seriously.[72] If my history of de Man's thought does repeat itself, the repetition at this point takes shape as a rethinking of monstrously happy ironic distance in the mode of a tragic mourning with a muted but perceptible purpose. The crisis of this purposeful mourning we can now turn to is an incontrovertible moment in de Man's historical determination.

Recall | 113

CHAPTER FOUR

The Crisis of Contemporary Romanticism

What is important is the wholly human drama—and how eternal it is, seeing that we find it in *Hamlet*—of the uncertainty of a man who changes his mind. – Paul de Man, 'André Gide' (1939)

Next to Faust, Heller suggests Hamlet as the romantic prototype; Hamlet is 'the man who has bequeathed to modern literature and thought the obsessive preoccupation with "authenticity."' This concern, he goes on to say, leads to paralysis 'because there is for Hamlet nothing that could possibly be in accord with his inner being.... The action chosen would always, whatever he did, crudely diverge from the subtle and illegible text written within.' To blame Hamlet for what happens at Elsinore is like blaming the German poets of the nineteenth century for the subsequent murder of their civilization. The 'authenticity' that sets Hamlet apart is caused not only by a fastidious desire to make the world accord with his ineffable feeling of selfhood, but by his knowledge of a distressing fact that others seek to conceal. The morbid manner in which he handles this knowledge may well be far from commendable; in the same manner, many romantic and postromantic writers let their original insight become obscured by evasive or obsessive behavior. Still, the value of the insight remains: whether we want it or not, we

cannot hide from the demands of its 'authenticity.' The romantic text we confront is indeed subtle, but it will appear illegible only to those interpreters who prefer not to see what it says.
– Paul de Man, 'The Literature of Nihilism' (1966)

Our backward glance at Montaigne was dictated by the memorial trope of a mournful sheltering logos singled out by de Man as the truth of Wordsworth's and Hölderlin's poetic enterprise—a trope that itself inverted and all but erased the prospective lucidity celebrated in 'The Image of Rousseau.' It is therefore appropriate—as it would be—that in his next substantial appearance in de Man's writing, Rousseau should offer a distorted reflection of both Montaigne's transcendence— '"observing [him]self [in the act of writing—PdM]"' ('RTS' 42)— and Mnemosyne's 'mourning' (26). In order to place this ambivalent mournful transcendence, we must relate it to what de Man calls 'the original intent,' which is also to say we must turn to his formalization of the figure of crisis that had been an intuitive source of attraction for his thought from the start. For origin and crisis are notions inseparably correlative:

> We can speak of crisis when a 'separation' takes place, by self-reflection, between what, in literature, is in conformity with the original intent and what has irrevocably fallen away from this source. Our question in relation to contemporary criticism then becomes: Is criticism indeed engaged in scrutinizing itself to the point of reflecting on its own origin? Is it asking whether it is necessary for the act of criticism to take place? ('CC' 8)

The question, in other words, is whether criticism, like the demigods, acts 'in conformity with the source' ('IR' 32)—or, alternatively, whether it has either forgotten this source or lost itself in excess beyond recollection. The question is also: To what end criticism in the present day?

The Crisis of Contemporary Romanticism | 115

Establish the Unbroken Link

And that which was the general ground for the decline of all peoples, namely, that their originality, their own living nature succumbed to the positive forms, to the luxury which their fathers had produced (examples, vividly presented), that seems to be our fate as well, only on a larger scale, in that an almost limitless prior world, which we become aware of [*innewerden*] either through instruction or through experience, works and weighs upon us (Exposition) – Hölderlin, 'The Viewpoint from Which We Must Look at Antiquity'

Why should we read Rousseau, Hölderlin, Wordsworth? Not merely because we may also happen to be critics who happen to have a philological-historical interest in a 'definition of the concept of Romanticism' and wish to clearly articulate this definition for the sake of institutional credibility (though this is no doubt part of the intent),[1] but because we—and this we is total—*need* this understanding for our own sake: 'The subject is so fundamental that it in fact reaches to the roots of our historical condition' ('IR' 20). If this is the case, reading Romanticism is at once a primary concern for literary studies and, insofar as criticism acts in conformity with this concern, a solid justification for critical practice as such. If the 'main points around which methodological and ideological arguments circle can almost always be directly traced back to the romantic heritage' ('WWH' 48), then a critically conscious reading of Romantic texts is the royal road to a good conscience—the obvious appeal of this assumption being that it weds the integrity of concentration on the literary matter at hand to a genuine commitment to a historical and political—that is, ideological—understanding of ' "modern" thinking' (48).

As a regulative ideal, this original intent is as formidable as it is formal: it takes shape as an ideal form that governs both Romanticism's interpretation of its own formidable origin as act and our interpretation of Romanticism as our own active origin. If the interpretation of Romanticism is difficult, this is because Romanticism is itself the difficulty of interpretation:

> As a near and particularly active moment in the history of consciousness, romanticism necessarily appears to us in a Titanic light, from which no demythologization can wholly release it [*aus dem keine Entmythologisierung sie ganz zu lösen vermag*]. Whence issues our divided attitude toward a phenomenon that always unduly attracts us or repels us, depending on whether we accent the aspect of renewal or of danger. But Wordsworth's and Hölderlin's reflection on the relationship between act and interpretation allows us to state that we should not [*dürfen nicht*] shirk the interpretive task left us by our romantic precursors if, for our part, we would acquire a historical significance. We should not [*nicht dürfen*] allow the poetic magnanimity [*dichterischen Edelmut*] to which our own consciousness owes tribute, to sink into forgetfulness. ('WWH' 65; translation modified)

The 'truth of romanticism,' which is the goal of our 'task of interpretation' (49), is itself Romanticism's 'interpretive task' (65) in the face of its 'experience of the temporal relation between the act and its interpretation' (50). As we know, this experience is only available to those that have 'very extensively partaken [*sehr weitgehend teilgenommen*] of the danger and failure' (58)—which is to say that we will only be able to read it if we, too, have taken part in Romanticism, if Romanticism is a thing of our past. Which is why we must claim an *a priori* understanding of what it is our task to interpret *as* something we have experienced, even if only up to a point (though the point will measure the degree of difference). De Man writes this in so many words—or, more accurately, in too many words, adding vacillation to foreknowledge:

> First of all, we must [*müssen*] be conscious of the fact that with this task of interpretation we find ourselves in a particular position, one that is fundamentally [*grundsätzlich*] different from the one we occupy, for instance, in relation to the Middle Ages or to Ancient Greece. In the case of romanticism it is a matter of the interpretation of a phenomenon that we should [*dürfen*] only consider from the temporal perspective of a duration that we have ourselves lived [*erlebt*]. The proximity of the event on the historical plane is so great that we are not yet able [*nicht vermögen*] to view it in the form of a clarified and purified memory [*abgeklärten und gereinigten Erinnerung*], such as Greece presents to us. We carry it within ourselves as the experience of an *act* in which, up to a certain point [*bis zu einem gewissen Grade*], we ourselves have participated [*teilgenommen*]. Perhaps [*Vielleicht*] this obtains for every attempt at understanding the past [*Vergangenheit*], but it nonetheless remains the case that with romanticism we are not separated from the past by that layer of forgetfulness and that temporal opacity that could awaken in us the illusion of detachment [*Loslösung*]. To interpret romanticism means quite literally [*wörtlich*] to interpret the past as such, *our* past precisely to the extent that we are beings who are defined in relation to a totality of experiences that slip into the past, and who want [*wollen*] to be interpreted as such. The content of this experience is perhaps less important than the fact [*Tatsache*] that we have lived it in its passing away [*daß wir sie in ihrem Vergehen erlebt haben*], and that it thereby has contributed in an unmediated way (that is, in the form of an act) to the constitution of our own time-consciousness [*Zeitbewußtsein*]. Now it is precisely this experience of the temporal relation between the act and its interpretation that is one of the main themes of romantic poetry.[2] (49–50; translation emended)

The passage is remarkable for its combination of imperative authority *(müssen, dürfen)*, hesitation *(vielleicht, bis zu einem gewissen Grade)*, certainty *(grundsätzlich, Tatsache)*, desire *(wollen)*, and impotence *(nicht vermögen)*. To read this combination we must relate it to its source, that is, to the tension in the first person plural the passage proceeds from: 'First of all, we must. . .' The interpretation of Antiquity *is* fundamentally different from that of Romanticism because we *should* only consider Romanticism as our own lived experience. Yet, perhaps this is the case for every interpretation of the past. Though the fact remains that we have lived Romanticism in its passing away, whereas Greek Antiquity is present to us a 'clarified and purified memory' from which, at the same time, we are separated by a 'layer of forgetfulness' that could awaken the 'illusion of detachment [*Loslösung*].'

Romanticism, we know, cannot be 'released [*lösen*]' in this way: no 'demythologizing' can translate its Titanic light into the illusion of pure, forgetful memory. It is by this Titanic light that we are defined as historical beings and it is as the product of such definition that we want to be interpreted. The privilege of Romanticism, then, is that it itself enacts this interpretive process in reflecting on its own Titanic origin. Romanticism is itself a *mise en abyme* of our relation to Romanticism: it performs the task we too must perform while its performance is also the material our performance must process. Yet this *mise en abyme* opens a fracture in the system: if the truth of Romanticism is its interpretation of its own Titanic origin, and if our task is the interpretation of our Titanic origin—that is, Romanticism—then the interpretive moment in Romanticism is itself Titanic. In other words, Romanticism's auto-interpretation becomes for us itself the transgression the interpretation reflects on: the interpretation of the act is the act we must interpret. Their interpretation of the act in which they have extensively taken part is their act in which we have taken part up to a point even in its passing away and which we must now interpret.

What will concern us in the next pages is de Man's attempt to locate his own critical enterprise in this complicated setup by marking out his particular participation in the historical 'we' defined in relation to Romanticism. The preliminary assumption of this attempt is that 'the interpretation of romanticism remains for us the most difficult and at the same time the most necessary of tasks,' and our own critical task here will be to understand to what extent de Man's thought lives up to the original intent of this assumption—that is, how it comes to terms with its fracture. The methodological fiction I shall be using as a grid in which to place the principal terms of this setup is an exploded version of de Man's own projection of Romanticism as necessarily appearing in a Titanic light. The advantage of this pseudoallegorical strategy is that it allows for a perspective on de Man's writing that disarticulates the heuristic reification of this work in terms of a sequential oscillation between critical and metacritical concerns in which Romanticism figures at best as a contingent corpus, not as a privileged past.[3] Put more positively, this perspective allows us to come closer to de Man's persistent attempt to make sense of this oscillation by understanding it from the vantage point of a truly synthetic insight historically determined in relation to Romanticism. However, as this attempt is itself already disarticulated in the texts under consideration here, my reading here will amount to an attempt to rehearse in a synthetic mode an ideational pattern whose synthetic intent is always fragmented and never accomplished—but only in this way can I avoid the unproductive preemptive understanding of final fragmentation and abortive completion as itself the comforting figure of de Man's failure that is too often taken to be the conclusive name of unreadability.[4]

Naive

If the time should ever come when what is now called science, thus familiarised to men, shall be ready to put on, as it were, a form of flesh and blood, the Poet will lend his divine spirit to aid the transfiguration, and will welcome the Being thus produced, as a dear and genuine inmate of the household of man.
— Wordsworth, Preface to *Lyrical Ballads* (1802)

The most obvious way not to live up to 'the most difficult and most necessary of tasks' is to collapse the internal doubling of Romanticism by celebrating it as a moment of prophetic power—that is, by seeing it as Romanticism itself sees its own Titanic origin, but without the appreciation of the transgressive moment that characterizes this Romantic vision. Such a 'reading of romanticism turns to the period to find values by which it can live, examples of past strength by means of which it can sustain its own particular dejection and uncertainty' ('RTS' 27). Romantic thought becomes a repository of 'reassuring myths about the certainty of a better future' ('RH' 212), a dwelling-place for a reactionary nostalgia that seeks to compensate its own impotence by deriving from Romanticism 'the hope that a truer insight into the nature of existence *(Dasein)* will be of direct benefit to the empirical world' ('RTS' 26), either in the sense of a prophetic vision with truly performative eschatological power or in the sense of a primitivist harmony gained by an equally prophetic (or retrophetic) return to pantheistic naturalism.

The inner division of this 'bland admiration' of Romanticism as either the locus of the historical effectiveness of revolutionary prophecy or the most recent recovery of Edenic innocence responds to the temptations of, respectively, apocalypse and analogy in Hölderlin and Wordsworth, temptations that de Man simultaneously acknowledges and qualifies as having been decisively overcome in Romantic thought at its highest moments. Insofar as these temptations can now be recognized as partaking of the Titanic dynamic that no demythologization of Romanticism can dissolve, we can propose a first more coherent reading of de Man's ambivalent modulation of authentic thought as Romantic renunciation.

If 'the main affirmation of the period is precisely the need to renounce the hope that a truer insight into the nature of existence *(Dasein)* will be of direct benefit to the empirical world' ('RTS' 26), we must simultaneously hear both the echo of this hope in Mallarmé's 'fantastically high claims . . . for literary creation' ('PHDM' 4) as a depository of the faith that 'action will follow from itself, when this insight has been gained' (102) and the source of this echo in the 'practical efficacity' and the 'profound . . . impact on history' ascribed to Rousseau's 'radically revolutionary spirit' ('IR' 41). Similarly, when we find this same efficacity questioned in the statement, 'The romantics . . . had fewer illusions about their impact on the practical world' than we have now ('PT' 51), we must remember the previous statement that 'they found it far less difficult than we do now to reconcile the demands of history with those of the self' ('JPS' 122). And perhaps most graphically, we must acknowledge that if, on the one hand, de Man can claim that the French Revolution 'takes its origin in [Rousseau's] solitary thinking' ('IR' 42), the same hand can write only about a year later that 'it is just as absurd to praise Rousseau for the French Revolution as to blame Nietzsche for Hitler' ('LN' 164).[5] Regarding the notion of a harmony with nature through the power of analogy, the pattern is less clear-cut (at least from this perspective), but here too we can observe a remarkable shift from Rousseau's stabilizing ability 'to apprehend things in such a way that they may appear as secondary in relation to a more fundamental entity that supports them and subtends them' ('IR' 39) to Wordsworth's 'endlessly precarious state of suspension: above an earth, the stability of which [our mind] cannot participate in, and beneath a heaven that has rejected it' ('WWH' 54).⁶

The logic of these shifts can be summarized as moving from an affirmation of the positive possibility of the Titanic moment, which is Romanticism's original intent, to a bracketing of this possibility in response to the uncritical celebration it has received. The fact that, as I have tried to demonstrate, this bracketing of the analogical/apocalyptic impetus in Wordsworth and Hölderlin requires a considerable amount of countertextual pressure could then—at least according to the logic of this narrative—be charitably construed as part of a deliberate strategy to free Romanticism from a naively nostalgic reception of its power and to restore the original intent of our interpretation as the articulation of a link with Romanticism's participatory interpretation of its Titanic moment. In other words: de Man's determinate negation of this impetus could be read as a necessary station on the road to a true understanding of Romantic insight.

This pattern receives a measure of support in de Man's comments on the second obvious way not to read Romanticism, the way taken by those who are 'unduly repel[led]' by its 'aspect of danger.' Here, too, Romanticism is reduced to its Titanic origin, but with an exclusive emphasis on the destructive dynamics of this origin that is not contained in a recognition of Romanticism's reflective elaboration of this source in 'the interiority of interpretation' ('WWH' 63). Rather, in this reductive reading, interiority itself is qualified as the primary aberration, and Romanticism becomes 'the moment of maximum delusion' in 'the life of societies and civilizations' that are 'growing increasingly destructive, violent, and irrational as they come closer and closer to the moment when their motives will be revealed' ('CCR' 16). This true motive, in a phrase de Man borrows from Erich Heller's *The Artist's Journey into the Interior*, would be '"the retreat of the Spirit into human subjectivity,"' interpreted as 'a deliberate alienation of the consciousness from the outside world' ('LN' 165). Romanticism becomes a 'secularized' appropriation of transcendence aimed at an apocalyptic moment when, now according to René Girard's indictment of the *Mensonge romantique*, '"men will be gods for each other"' ('CCR' 16), in the grand finale of 'the Promethean claim to confer upon the human will absolute attributes reserved to divine categories of Being' (6). The Romantic 'reassertion of the self' is read as 'a proud, Promethean (or even Faustian) statement of the power of the mind over nature' ('LN' 167), a 'sin of intellectual pride' pushing a 'power-hungry Spirit' that 'can only come to rest when it has carried out the death sentence it has pronounced on the world of the senses' (168). On this account, the catastrophes of the twentieth century betray a direct lineage to, specifically, German Romantic thought: it is this tradition that has 'provided the intellectual basis for Nazism' and has been 'discredited' by 'recent events (not only Nazism) . . . to such an extent that it should now be abandoned' (162).

The argument here derived from, among others, Heller and Girard clearly resembles Camus's analysis of the divinization of humankind and history that perverts revolt into revolution and destroys (human) nature. For Camus, as de Man indeed writes, 'History is a diabolical invention of German philosophers, a modern curse,' and he goes on to quote a passage from the *Notebooks* that qualifies the 'whole effort of German thought' as an attempt 'to substitute for the notion of human nature that of human situation and hence to substitute history for God and modern tragedy for ancient equilibrium' ('AC' 150). 'But like the Greeks,' Camus adds, 'I believe in nature.' In de Man's framework, this reference to Greek Antiquity is symptomatic in the sense that it amounts to a displaced rehearsal of the familiar misunderstanding of Romantic neo-Hellenism in terms of 'nostalgic envy' ('LN' 169). To the extent that Camus fails to appreciate that the 'nakedness,' the 'dénuement' ('AC' 151) of Greek art is a sign of the contingency of the human condition rather than a tribute to harmonious physical freedom, he repeats the ahistorical appropriation of Greece as a 'lost Garden of Eden' ('LN' 169) that is a temptation for Romanticism but never its truth (see also 'RH' 212). Camus 'does not seem to realize that [the] equilibrium [of Greek art] is the final outcome and not the starting point of a development that is anything but "natural"' ('AC' 151), and in this blindness he misses an understanding of Romanticism's lucid encounter with this 'barrenness,' trading it instead for a version of the illusory 'purified memory' ('WWH' 50) of a history that is in no way our past, and thereby foreclosing both 'historical insight' and 'ethical profundity.' Fatally 'dated' by this misunderstanding, Camus's thought 'falls apart, on the one hand, in a seductive but irresponsible dream of physical well-being and, on the other, in a protective moralism that fails to understand the nature of evil' ('AC' 151).

As was the case for the uncritical celebration of the Romantic promise, these modern warnings against the aberrations of Romanticism are revealed as degraded forms of Romantic self-understanding, which is also to say that they do, be it uncritically, entertain a degree of contact with the source. The destruction of the senses in the name of tyrannical interiority denounced by Heller has its forgotten moment of truth in the original intent of the transcendence of the sensorium announced in the solipsistic imagination of 'Intentional Structure' and truly consummated in Rousseau's *Aufhebung* of perception through his affirmation of the ontological priority of earth-as-consciousness. Similarly, Camus's 'defensive and protective' stance as 'the goalkeeper of a society that was in the process of suffering a particularly painful historical defeat' ('AC' 152) is a belated and deluded imitation of Yeats's warning song 'against the danger of unwarranted hopeful solutions' ('WBY' 238), the song with which 'he accomplished all that the highest forms of language can for the moment accomplish' by reestablishing a measure of contact with 'the protecting act of the logos' ('WWH' 63) memorized in 'Mnemosyne.'

The pattern that emerges from the stark genealogical simplifications I have here construed from the conflicting traces of de Man's text is one in which partial understandings of Romanticism's Titanic original intent are distorted to the point of massive misunderstanding. The conclusion de Man draws from this pattern is that 'there seems to be no better way to interpret the movement than by understanding the misunderstandings it created among its interpreters' ('RTS' 26), and his most systematic attempt to activate this conclusion occurs by way of his understanding of 'the crisis of contemporary criticism' as a more critical but exactly parallel misreading of our Titanic origin.

Critical

At stake here is the future of structuralism as an intellectual movement but also as a methodological blueprint for scientific research that, like Rousseau's state of nature, 'no longer exists, has perhaps never existed and will probably never come into being' but which we nevertheless cannot do without. – Paul de Man, 'Roland Barthes and the Limits of Structuralism'

'The Crisis of Contemporary Criticism' is the titular subject of a lecture delivered by de Man in December 1966; parts of it were subsequently inserted in 'Romanticism and Demystification,' the first of the six Gauss lectures on 'Romanticism and Contemporary Criticism' de Man presented in the Spring of 1967; and it was finally republished in a revised version called 'Criticism and Crisis' (a stark return to the original a-Romantic title) as the first of the *Essays in the Rhetoric of Contemporary Criticism* collected in *Blindness and Insight* in 1971.[7] The various emphases in these titles and contexts indicate de Man's awareness of a certain discomfort with his 'double-barrelled topic,' a discomfort he compares to 'the rather tiresome grimace well known to anyone who has ever played in an orchestra, where one has to keep track simultaneously of the score and the conductor' ('THW' 74). If the score is the Romantic text and the conductor is its modern critical commentator, de Man is the player of period instruments proposing to bring out the original intent by underscoring the conductor's failure to accurately record the still sad *Wechsel der Töne* in authentic Romantic thought. The underlying assumption of this performance, which saves it from being an exercise in puritanical pedantry (something for which de Man, incidentally, shows no talent), is that the conductor's inability to recognize the source is intimately related to his talent to hear its echo displaced in his own voice. Our task here will be to double the grimace of de Man's trope in order to capture the distinctive dissonance of his Romanticism.

The composite figure that plays the role of conductor in 'The Crisis of Contemporary Criticism' is the 'recent developments in Continental criticism' ('CC' 3), conveniently collected by de Man under the label 'the structuralist aberration,'[8] and the primary goal of the essay is to demonstrate that this brand of criticism is witnessing a crisis—that is, a separation between its 'original intent' and 'what has irrevocably fallen away from this source' (8). For this demonstration, a preliminary definition of this original intent is required:

> The main intent of French structuralism, whether it derives its language from sociology, psychoanalysis, ethnology, linguistics, or even from certain forms of philosophy, including that of Heidegger, can be quickly summarized: it represents a methodologically motivated attack on the notion that a literary or poetic consciousness is in any way a privileged consciousness, whose use of language can pretend to escape, to some degree, from the duplicity, the confusion, the untruth that we take for granted in the everyday use of language. ('CC' 8–9; o.v., 45)

For this attack to function as genuine criticism, it must necessarily fail, in the sense that it must encounter its crisis: for 'all true criticism occurs in the mode of crisis' (8). Only when it does not succeed in carrying out its 'overwhelmingly anti-romantic' ('CCR' 5) intent can structuralism be recognized as genuine—that is, in the last analysis, Romantically determined—criticism. But before this restoration of structuralism to its Romantic source can be established, a number of preliminary questions require an answer. First, what precisely is this duplicity, confusion, and untruth we take for granted in the everyday use of language; second, how is this phenomenon contained and elaborated in the structuralist enterprise; and third, what are the stakes involved in the structuralist intent to deny literature the power to escape from this state of affairs—what is the necessity of the structuralist attack?

The first question is not answered as such—de Man merely expands what 'we take for granted' in the mode of the 'we know,' appealing to our presupposed common understanding that 'our entire social language is an intricate system of rhetorical devices designed to escape from the direct expression of desires that are, in the fullest sense of the term, unnameable—not because they are ethically shameful (for this would make the problem a very simple one) but because unmediated expression is a philosophical impossibility' ('CC' 9). It is not quite clear what it can mean to have a system designed to avoid what is impossible anyway, and neither is it immediately clear why 'the individual who chose to ignore this fundamental conviction' would either be 'slated for crucifixion, if he were aware, or, if he were naïve, destined to the total ridicule afforded such heroes as Candide and all other fools that appear, fortunately, more often in fiction than in life' (o.v. 45). As Richard Klein has noted, the uncertainty of de Man's text here 'may betray a more general, persistent uneasiness' involving a complex tension between 'a certain inherent philosophical necessity' and 'the ethical realm'[9]—the exposition of this tension in its relation to our commonsensical ridicule of Romanticism and Romantic fiction and suffering may well be what the text is strictly about.[10]

Having voiced his 'common knowledge,' de Man moves on to 'the particular structuralist contribution' to its analysis, which consists of 'an astute rephrasing of the problem that develops when a consciousness gets involved in interpreting another consciousness' ('CC' 9; o.v. 45–46). The way structuralism proposes to come to terms with this 'built-in discrepancy within the intersubjective relationship' (11) is illustrated by means of two examples, Lévi-Strauss's structural anthropology and post-Saussurian linguistics.

Lévi-Strauss's enterprise is portrayed as an attempt to safeguard anthropological reason, by way of a preliminary exercise in 'self-demystification,' from the earlier positivistic anthropologists' blindness to the fact that their allegedly detached and objective observations in fact remain heavily 'determined by the inhibitions and shortcomings of their own social situation' (9). Such an exercise, however, cannot be undertaken in isolation: the observing self can only be properly interpreted (demystified) when this interpretation involves the interpretation of that self's observation and interpretation of others. Nor are the observing subject and the subject observed constants: the observation itself changes both, and the consequent 'oscillating progress seems to be endless' (10), even to the point that the very distinction between them becomes radically blurred. The structuralists' answer to the threat to reason spelled in this *'vertige'* is to propose a 'radical relativism' that, on the one hand, rejects any 'standpoints that can a priori be considered privileged' and any 'postulate of ontological hierarchy that can serve as an organizing principle from which particular structures derive' (such standpoints and such a postulate being irreconcilable with the rigorously demystifying scientific intent of the method), but that on the other hand, and at the same time, retains the notion of what Lévi-Strauss calls 'un foyer virtuel': a virtual 'privileged point of view to which the method itself denies any status of authenticity,' a 'privileged' standpoint that is only ever an instrument, not a truth postulated as truth.[11]

Such is what Derrida a few months earlier (at the Johns Hopkins colloquium on *The Languages of Criticism and the Sciences of Man* de Man also attended) [12] had called Lévi-Strauss's 'double intention': 'to conserve as an instrument that of which he criticizes the truth value.'[13] De Man comments:

> Lévi-Strauss' method aims at preventing this virtual focus from being made into a *real* source of light. The analogy with optics is perhaps misleading, for in literature everything hinges on the existential status of the focal point. It is one thing to say that the focal point is privileged but virtual, another to subscribe to Lévi-Strauss' further statement that 'the determination of the real center of a work is impossible,' that, therefore, 'myths have

no authors,' and that, in the terms of Jacques Deridda [*sic*], the absence of the center is equivalent to the disappearance of the self as a constitutive subject.[14] (o.v., 47)

Refraining from explaining just what this difference between 'one thing' and 'another' consists of, de Man then immediately makes the transition to his second example, structural linguistics. In 'everyday language,' we are reminded, much the same discrepancy as that encountered by Lévi-Strauss in anthropological discourse obtains 'in the impossibility of making the actual expression coincide with what it signifies' (11). Hence, the 'interpretation of everyday language is a Sisyphean task, a task without end or progress, for the other is always free to make what he wants differ from what he says he wants.' In order to confront this difficulty, structuralist linguistics, in its turn, has to postulate a kind of 'foyer virtuel': 'As Lévi-Strauss, in order to protect the rationality of his science, had to come to the conclusion of a myth without an author, so the linguists have to conceive of a meta-language without a speaker in order to remain rational' (11–12).

Having postulated this much, de Man can make an attempt at answering the third question preliminary to an identification of the crisis of structuralist/contemporary criticism: Why is it necessary to attack the notion of a privileged literary consciousness? The answer was already hinted at: the scientific viability of the structuralist enterprise depends on the accuracy of its claim that a structure of human comportment can only be properly interpreted if one discards the notion of an ontologically superior standpoint, a point of view that would be closer to the real truth of the matter than any other. Such a stance would radically compromise the notion of the virtual or hypothetical focal point, and with it the doctrine of demystified radical relativism, by introducing a focalizing subject transcending the mystification structuralism conceives of as an essential feature of the subject as such. This would be the stance of 'the self as a constitutive subject' (the disappearance of which was the 'other' thing structuralism subscribes to); 'constitutive' in the sense that it engenders truth in an effective transcendence of the impossibility of interpretation that the virtual subject is only a hypothetical response to—a response, in fact, that derives its scientific legitimacy wholly from its hypothetical nature. The relevance of literature as a field of human comportment to be taken into consideration by way of testing this response is itself obvious: literature has its existence in a particularly conspicuous relation to language, and if the structuralist notion of virtual interpretation—which entails language as its methodological and/or conceptual core—is valid, it should be able to maintain itself in the face of literary language.

> If the radical position suggested by Lévi-Strauss is to stand, if the question of structure can only be asked from a point of view that is not that of a privileged subject, then it becomes imperative to show that literature constitutes no exception, that its language is in no sense privileged in terms of unity and truth over everyday forms of language. The task of structuralist literary critics then becomes quite clear: in order to eliminate the constitutive subject, they have to show that the discrepancy between sign and meaning *(signifiant* and *signifié)* prevails in literature in the same manner as in everyday language. (12)

The task, in other words, is an exercise in demystification showing up that the 'so-called "idealism" of literature is . . . an idolatry, a fascination with a false image that mimics the presumed attributes of authenticity when it is in fact just the hollow mask with which a frustrated, defeated consciousness tries to cover up its own negativity' (12). The privileged target of this exercise, which also reveals the 'historical scheme within which [this demystification] operat[es],' is what structuralism conceives of as 'a specifically romantic delusion': the 'romantic myth embodied in the recurrent topos of the "Beautiful Soul"' (13), functioning as the *'figura* of a privileged kind of language' projected by 'the theoreticians of romanticism' in their attempt to give a face to their belief in the 'unity of appearance (sign) and idea (meaning),' of *Schein* and *Idee*:

> Its outward appearance receives its beauty from an inner glow (or *feu sacré*) to which it is so finely attuned that, far from hiding it from sight, it gives it just the right balance of opacity and transparency, thus allowing the holy fire to shine without burning. The romantic imagination embodies this figure in the shape of a person, feminine, masculine or hermaphrodite, and seems to suggest that it exists as an actual empirical subject: one thinks, for instance, of Rousseau's Julie, Hölderlin's Diotima, or of the beautiful soul that appears in Hegel's *Phenomenology of the Spirit* and in Goethe's *Wilhelm Meister* (13).

It is the apparent suggestion of empirical reality that turns this figure into the irresistible sitting duck it has proved to be for the chefs of demystification ('from Voltaire down to the present'). Once removed from 'the fictional world in which it exists' (be it in Rousseau, Hölderlin, Goethe, or Hegel), the Beautiful Soul becomes 'even more ridiculous than Candide,' and it can subsequently be unmasked as only ever a myth springing 'from fantasies by means of which the writer sublimates his own shortcomings.' This discovery can then be brought to bear on the development of literature in the wake of Romanticism, a development that comes to be read as 'a gradual demystification' leading from Romantic lies to realist truth. In this 'historical scheme,' 'Romanticism represents, so to speak, the point of maximum delusion in our recent past, whereas the nineteenth and twentieth centuries represent a gradual emerging from this aberration, culminating in the breakthrough of the last decades that inaugurates a new form of insight and lucidity, a cure from the agony of the romantic disease' (13). Thus, Romanticism figures essentially as the origin of a pattern of 'apocalyptic self-discovery' ('CCR' 16): it is an epoch of extreme error that inaugurates its own demystification in 'a totally enlightened present' as 'literature finally comes into its own, and becomes authentic, when it discovers that the exalted status it claimed for its language was a myth' ('CC' 14). Criticism, insofar as it is the revelation of this authentic demystificatory intent, participates in the articulation of 'a new, postromantic dispensation' ('CCR' 17)—it responds to 'our desire for lucidity' and offers a remedy for 'our impatience with a difficult present.' But it also radically misses the point, even while it does dig among the roots:

> This scheme is powerful and cogent, powerful enough, in fact, to go to the root of the matter and consequently to cause a crisis. To reject it convincingly would require elaborate argument. My remarks are meant to indicate some of my reasons, however, for considering the conception of literature (or literary criticism) as demystification the most dangerous myth of all, while granting that it forces us, in Mallarmé's terms, to scrutinize the act of reading 'jusqu'en l'origine.' ('CC' 14, O.V. 50–51)

With this puzzling cautionary promise, the ground has been cleared for de Man's initial question: we have been told what it is the structuralists seek to attack, why this attack is at all necessary, and how it is eventually carried out. Now, in order to show that this criticism comes up against its own crisis, de Man has to demonstrate that the attack is ultimately unsuccessful: that the demystificatory intent of contemporary criticism misfires in the face of Romanticism.

At this juncture the text very consciously makes a detour around another cape, thereby raising the argument to a level of conspicuous generality: 'We must ask ourselves if there is not a recurrent epistemological structure that characterizes all statements made in the mood and the rhetoric of crisis' (14). The question is broached by way of an example, Edmund Husserl's 1935 lectures on 'Die Krisis des europäischen Menschentums und die Philosophie' ('The Crisis of European Humanity and Philosophy').[15]

In this text, de Man detects a significant conflict between two governing concerns—that is, on the one hand, the analysis of a certain crisis whose remedy must be sought in the constitution of a true *'ratio'* as 'the truly universal and truly radical self-explicitation of the Spirit in the form of a universal responsible science [*Selbstverständigung des Geistes in Form universaler verantwortlicher Wissenschaft*]'[16] (this latter being Husserl's own project for a transcendental phenomenology), and on the other hand, the exclusive grounding of this analysis and this remedy in European civilization. De Man's argument is simple: if, as Husserl contends, the only way to attain the true universality of philosophical knowledge is by discarding the 'externalization [*Veräußerlichung*]' of the *ratio*, by combatting its 'implication [*Versponnenheit*] in "naturalism" and "objectivism,"'[17] by turning away from 'empirical knowledge' (16) and toward the 'self-interpretation' (15) of the 'Spirit as Spirit [*Geist als Geist*],'[18] then 'Husserl's listeners and his present-day readers may well be tempted to turn this philosophical criticism on Husserl's own text, especially on the numerous sections in which philosophy is said to be the historical privilege of European man':

> The privileged viewpoint of the post-Hellenic, European consciousness is never for a moment put into question; the crucial determining examination on which depends Husserl's right to call himself, by his own terms, a philosopher, is in fact never undertaken. As a European, it seems that Husserl escapes from the necessary self-criticism that is prior to all philosophical truth about the self.[19] (16)

It is this inconsistency, then, that 'reveals with striking clarity the structure of all crisis-determined statements.' The important truth established by Husserl—'that philosophical knowledge can only come into being when it is turned back upon itself'—is immediately undercut by the text's refusal to proceed in accordance with this truth: 'The rhetoric of crisis states its own truth in the mode of error,'[20] and this 'recurrent epistemological structure' can now, by convenient analogy, be read back as the 'pattern of self-mystification' riddling the demystificatory intent of structuralist criticism:

> [Husserl] was, in fact, stating the privileged status of philosophy as an authentic language, but withdrawing at once from the demands of this authenticity as it applies to himself. Similarly, the structuralist critics are in fact asserting the privileged status of literature, but withdrawing from the implications by cutting themselves off from the source from which they receive their insight. (16–17)

More specifically, structuralism's determining error is that the authenticity it ascribes to literature (its recognition that the exalted status it claimed for its language was a myth) is not the *'telos'* of a gradual process of demystification but rather the *'archè'* from which authentic literature always already sets out (o.v., 54). Literature never was the idolatrous privileged consciousness as invented by structuralism as *raison d'être* for its attack:[21] literature never was mystified by the unity of sign and meaning, of *Schein* and *Idee*, targeted by the structuralist demystifiers: 'It is the only form of language free from the fallacy of unmediated expression' (17).[22] And it asserts this freedom insofar as it 'always designate[s] [itself] as existing in the mode of fiction.'

In the process of further laboring this point, the plot of de Man's text thickens beyond repair, even as it begins to articulate its original intent: an understanding of the essence of literature, that is, Romantic thought.

What is the essence of literature?

> The self-reflecting mirror-effect by means of which a work of fiction asserts, by its very existence, its separation from empirical reality, its divergence, as a sign, from a meaning that depends for its existence on the constitutive activity of this sign, characterizes the work of literature in its essence. It is always against the explicit assertion of the writer that readers degrade the fiction by confusing it with a reality from which it has forever taken leave. ('CC' 17)

The structuralist demystification is one such degradation of the fiction: it confuses the fictional entity with an empirical entity in order to show that this fictional entity does not match the empirical one.[23] What the demystification thus misses is that the fiction (was) never meant to be a match. Demystificatory critics who see the Beautiful Soul as a sitting duck are taken in by a red herring of their own imagining, diverting attention from the true 'priority of fiction over reality, of imagination over perception.' This priority, de Man adds, with reference to Rousseau, is by no means 'the compensatory expression of a shortcoming, of a deficient sense of reality'; it is not the sublimation of a frustrated desire but a recognition of the necessary impossibility for desire to be satisfied. If desire is thought in terms of actual fulfillment, it is totally alien to the affirmation of this priority, which is essentially a full recognition of nothingness—'le néant des choses humaines'[24] and 'le néant des chimères,' the nothingness of fiction itself: 'The consciousness does not result from the absence of something, but consists of the presence of a nothingness. Poetic language names this void with ever-renewed understanding and . . . never tires of naming it again and again. This persistent naming is what we call literature' (18).

Literature does not represent subjects but 'invents fictional subjects to create the illusion of the reality of others,'[25] and never is it deluded about this its own enterprise: 'The fiction is not myth, for it knows and names itself as fiction.' Consequently, there can be no demystification of literature that would then uncover literature's hidden authenticity in the recognition of the noncoincidence of sign and meaning: literature is always already authentic; 'It is demystified from the start.' This, then, is the crisis of the structuralist enterprise as a central representative of modern anti-Romanticism: it arrives at a truth about the authenticity of literature, but it states this truth erroneously as the outcome of an apocalyptic demystification of the origin of literary consciousness in Romanticism. As a result, it is unable to turn this truth back upon itself—it blinds itself to the truth that literary consciousness is, always has been, and always will be radically privileged by virtue of its being nothing other than the total truth of which structuralist criticism only manages to catch a fleeting impression through the dark glass of demystification. Once recognized in full, this total truth effectively demolishes the fiction of the virtual focus introduced as an alternative for the prematurely aborted constitutive subject—once resurrected, this subject demystifies the scientific, theoretical fiction of virtual focalization as not being nearly fictional enough, as being, in fact, a myth constitutionally inferior to the absolutely fictional and therefore metamythic subject constitutive of literature:

> When modern critics think they are demystifying literature, they are in fact being demystified by it; but since this necessarily occurs in the form of a crisis, they are blind to what takes place within themselves. At the moment that they claim to do away with literature, literature is everywhere; what they call anthropology, linguistics, psychoanalysis is nothing but literature reappearing, like the Hydra's head, in the very spot where it had supposedly been suppressed. The human mind will go through amazing feats of distortion to avoid facing 'the nothingness of human matters.' In order not to see that the failure lies in the nature of things, the structuralists chose to locate it in the individual 'romantic' subject, and thus retreated behind a historical scheme which, apocalyptic as it may sound, is basically reassuring and bland. (18)

The 'individual "romantic" subject'—and in particular Rousseau, 'the author the structuralists consider the most deluded of all'—is in no way a deluded consciousness whose obsession is to be remedied by a historical progression toward the radical relativism of a virtual focus: as a literary—that is, in the final analysis, Romantic—consciousness, it figures instead the maximum realization of the ontological truth of the self as a constitutive and real, as opposed to virtual, nothingness. In order to discard the notion of the subject, which it mistakenly cast as essentially and inextricably implicated in distorting determinations, structuralism invented the notion of the virtual focus, 'a mere hypothesis posited by the scientists to give consistency to the behavior of entities'; insofar as this virtual focus is styled as a nothingness, it comes upon an important truth, but it blinds itself to this truth when it assumes that this virtual nothing can dislodge the subject as a delusion whose disappearance can put a stop to the *vertige* of interpretation. When it discards the subject, structuralism fatally forgets the fiction of its own fiction: it neutralizes this fiction by returning to reason as an order ultimately independent from constitutive invention and therefore superior to the merely instrumental fictionality of the virtual focus. It blinds itself to the real nothingness of the subject that has always already terminated the *vertige* by stating its truth (cf. 'LB' o.v., 49), and in so doing it deprives itself of the knowledge of this nothingness persistently named in literature, as the realm in which the ontological truth of the self comes into its own.

> The virtual focus is a quasi-objective structure posited to give rational integrity to a process that exists independently from the self. The subject merely fills in, with the dotted line of geometrical construction, what natural reason had not bothered to make explicit; it has a passive and unproblematic role. The 'virtual focus' is, strictly speaking, a nothing, but its nothingness concerns us very little, since a mere act of reason suffices to give it a mode of being that leaves the rational order unchallenged. The same is not true of the imaginary source of fiction. Here the human self has experienced the void within his own being, and the invented fiction, far from filling the void, asserts itself as pure nothingness, *our* nothingness stated and restated by a subject that is the agent of its own instability.[26] ('CC' 19; o.v. 56)

In establishing this difference between the adherence to the 'rational order' and the assertion of 'pure nothingness,' de Man's argument moves toward a momentous historical inference which, muted here, leaves its severe imprint elsewhere in his writing. It is because it has failed to recognize the truth of 'our nothingness' that structuralism—as well as any other thought that espouses demystification as its original intent—can still conceive of its own activity as historically effective, an illusion Romanticism at its highest moments has renounced: 'Our own great demystifiers, Freud, Marx and Nietzsche, are much more naïve than their romantic predecessors, especially in their belief that the demystification can become a praxis beneficial to the personality or to the society' ('PT' 51). Romanticism has 'left the problems of the empirical self behind,' and if we tend to picture the arch-Romantic Rousseau as a 'comically proverbial' case of 'fatal confusion between two selves: the one specific, particular, historical, and chaotic, the other capable of the lofty lucidity of total self-understanding' ('RTS' 27), then this is a mistaken projection of a 'modern' or 'postromantic' schizophrenic predicament onto the utterly composed Beautiful Soul of authentic Romanticism ('PT' 51)—a Soul that, unlike Husserl's European transcendental phenomenologist, is a genuinely undeluded, privileged (non-)entity. If Rousseau, in his confessional moments, 'relapses' into some such predicament, this only means that his true Romantic nerve failed him. In his 'major literary achievements,' the 'dialectic between an empirical and an ideal subject' and the 'persistent conflict between fiction and reality' we tend to read into his writing are already fully transcended and 'entirely subsumed in the fiction' (50).[27] He knows that this fiction can be used 'to serve the personal, social and moral interests' of others (and of his own, relapsed self); at times, he 'cautions against' such abuse; but 'he has few illusions that he can prevent this degradation, and turns away from it toward things that matter more to him'—such as 'le néant des choses humaines.'

Barren

Prophetic denunciations of human stupidity are never out of date; they were never more apposite than in Spinoza's Europe, wasted as no civilization had ever been wasted by perverse and 'inadequate' ideas. . . . The intellect and vision are passive in Descartes as in Aristotle. The active principle is the will. Above all 'the actions of the soul are *desires,* since we find in experience that they proceed directly from our soul and appear to depend upon it alone.' And so the European tragedy was launched, not indeed by Descartes, but by these direct actions of the soul, desires released from the intellect and bereft of vision, and the process as it gathered momentum seemed to discover the power which Hobbes likened to the fall of heavy bodies, a huge impotence resembling power only from the bigness of its catastrophe. The subject-object relation might serve almost as a name of the increasing system of estrangement and enmity, religious, political, economic devised in the service of 'our desires.' It is the fruitful source of epistemological confusion down to our own time.
 – T. S. Gregory, Introduction to *Spinoza's Ethics*

To be interested in 'le néant des choses humaines' is to take a stance of 'disinterestedness' ('RTS' 39) toward anything related to 'the self that lives in the world of material and pragmatic substances' (37).[28] It is to take the stance of 'the authentic self engaged in the interpretation of its own being-there and capable of comprehending the truth of its fallen destiny' ('LB' 44; O.V., 72), impervious to the seductive interpretation of this knowledge 'as a *means* permitting to influence the destiny it reveals'—an interpretation that would amount to abandoning 'the ontological inquiry for ontic concerns that can only betray it' (48; o.v. 76). Such a betrayal is understandable—'it is difficult to rigorously maintain oneself in the total disinterestedness of ontological thought' (49; o.v., 77); it is tempting to forsake 'the barren and impoverished world of ontological truth and to nourish oneself with the riches of lived experience' (49; o.v., 78)—yet only by resisting this temptation and by embracing this difficulty can criticism lay claim to being 'one of the most advanced and most audacious forms of contemporary thought' (50; o.v., 78). Only in this way can we establish a proper contact with our source in the truly transcendental self of the Romantic Titans.[29]

This Titanic self is the object of our desire. It is the reflection of Romanticism's own authentic object of desire, and to this extent our desire is a reflection of Romantic desire. Yet, because it is a reflection, it must also necessarily mark a difference, and the quality of our desire therefore depends on our ability to accurately register this difference. The naive as well as the critical reading of the Titans fails to honor this difference: they partake of a general regression from Romantic rigor and take shape as more or less subtle 'strategies . . . devised to avoid confronting the self-insight achieved by their predecessors' ('AIB' 103). The only way to counter this regression is an obstinate insistence on the rigorous indifference to matters empirical proper to an absolute intent on the ontological, in which all that is solid melts into the void of authentic, negative truth. A privileged figure in which this insistence can be read is the translation of the Beautiful Soul as it figures in Romantic thought to our own (de Man's) post-Romantic modernity.[30]

De Man does not thematize this translation in a consistent analytical frame: it is often difficult to distinguish between, on the one hand, his imitation of Romantic insight from the inside of Romanticism and, on the other, his representation of our task to rehearse this repetition from the point of view of post-Romantic modernity—a confusion that allows for an understanding of the pattern of his thought as the afterlife (or a strong rereading) of Hegel's progressive unfolding of the Spirit in the *Phenomenology*.

It will come as no surprise that the transpositions readable in this pattern have history and sensation for their operative terms.

✻

Romantic desire can still (or, more accurately, already) conceive of itself in a special relation to sensory beauty: it is 'oriented toward its authenticity, which it lost in the fallen world of empirical experience' and which 'it wants to possess in order to be complete' ('RTS' 45), but it is also able to find an intimation of this universal authenticity in a 'particular incarnation' of 'the symbolical figure of the "beautiful soul" . . . in an actual person' (45). The only error would be to believe that such a particular person 'could be sufficient to fill a void that does not exist on an interpersonal but on an ontological level.' It is to the precise extent that the truly undeluded Romantic consciousness knows this error that it has earned the right to celebrate the 'sensuous aspects of beauty' characteristic of the incarnated Beautiful Soul: for this consciousness 'there is no reason to renounce the desire that such a figure can inspire,' for it knows that the figure 'only exists as a prefiguration of an imaginary entity' (45–46). By virtue of this knowledge, Romantic desire at once 'transcends the notion of a nostalgia or a desire since it discovers desire as a fundamental pattern of being that discards any possibility of satisfaction' ('CC' 17). Because it transcends itself as a notion intent on actual satisfaction, Romantic desire need not renounce its inspiring figure of actualized beauty.

For us, to the contrary, such a provisional celebration of the sensory is forbidden. Our constant temptation is to restore the Beautiful Soul to the empirical world from which, in its authentic form, 'it has forever taken leave' (17). Because Romanticism understands this 'forever' as an 'always already,' it transcends both the naive nostalgia that would celebrate the fictional figure as a positive full actualization of authenticity in the past, and the critical suspicion that would ridicule it for its ineptness as an empirical entity. For us, who erroneously perceive this leave-taking as a temporary absence prefiguring a renewed presence in our own empirical condition or as a false escape from the demands of that condition, the truth of the Beautiful Soul, which must redress these mistaken conceptions, is that 'she is nothing' ('RTS' 47), *un rien,* and as such represents the invention of nothingness that is the face of our authenticity 'from an empirical point of view.'

To the extent that we positively espouse this inauthentic empirical point of view, we can only perceive this nothing as mystification or actualization and are consequently ourselves mystified, either because we naively embrace the mystification or because we propose to critically demystify it. The only truth for us is therefore *askesis,* an audacious divorce from the empirical perspective, an absolute intent on barrenness ('LB' 49; O.V., 78). The source we can then reestablish contact with is our modern, post-Romantic equivalent of the Beautiful Soul, the Barren Titan. Such is de Man's (in)version of the 'vaterländische Umkehr.' *Es ereignet sich aber das Nichts:* what occurs is nothingness. If this (in)version lacks the synthetic articulation of the original turn in terms of destiny, it is because, unlike our Romantic predecessors, 'our weakness' is not 'the lack of destiny, the dusmoron,' but its excess: our *Haupttendenz,* instead of being a reactive desire for what we do not have, has been all too decisively realized as what we are.[31]

The Titanic is barren because it cannot figure for us as the *Beautiful* Soul, as we are unable to think beauty other than on the level of empirical experience: wishfully, as an object of harmonious fulfillment, or critically, as the regulative surrogate of evasive aestheticism. At the same time, the Titanic is barren because it cannot figure for us as the Beautiful *Soul,* as we are unable to think this soul other than in hopelessly simplified terms of historical effectiveness—either emphasizing the absence of such effectiveness, when the Beautiful Soul appears either as a ridiculous figure of impotence or as a blissfully extrahistorical *eschaton;* or emphasizing its presence, when it appears as either the embodiment of Terrorist purity or the prophetic prefiguration of an all too empirical ideal. The Titanic is barren because this is the only mode in which it can lawfully appear to our post-Romantic modernity, which is essentially fallen away from the 'truly historical consciousness' ('FG' 97) of the Romantic 'historians of the self' (96). In this fallen condition, Romanticism appears to us as a warning or as a promise. Both the warning and the promise concern the ability 'to reconcile the demands of history with those of the self' ('JPS' 122), but in our 'misguided antiromanticism,'[32] as much as in our wishful nostalgia for Romantic energy, we fail to register the true import of the in itself entirely legitimate concern with such reconciliation. Romanticism was able to mark a more subtle and effective understanding of the difficulty of this demand, and this is the measure of our difference:

> This ability seems to have been lost in the course of the nineteenth century. The romantic historical consciousness declined on the one hand, into [a] kind of parody of idealism . . . and, on the other hand, into the materialism (dialectical or otherwise) that made many historically oriented minds forget their own idealist origins. (122)

Both the latter-day idealist, who, 'beneath the surface of [his] virtues,' hides 'the nihilistic terror of a man who has deliberately removed himself from reality' (119), and the hard-line materialist, who thrives on the eclipse of his idealist origins, leave us open to what for de Man is the central aberration of our time: they have 'surrendered the autonomy of the conscious mind to the unquestioned hegemony of the physical world' ('WM' 143–44). It is because we are implicated in this positively embraced or blindly resented submission—such is our excessive destiny—that we are unable to properly understand the laws of this consciousness in its historical elaboration and lose the lucidity of our predecessors in misguided eschatological projections or—more importantly—scientific 'reification' ('FG' 95, 97). Our destiny, to put it differently, is realized in our separation from the following truth:

> Historical 'changes' are not like changes in nature, and the vocabulary of change and movement as it applies to historical pro-

cess is a mere metaphor, not devoid of meaning, but without an objective correlative that can unambiguously be pointed to in empirical reality, as when we speak of a change in the weather or a change in a biological organism. ('CC' 6)

Putting it crudely—in empirical terms that can be isolated as recurrent components of isotopical constellations in the changing system of de Man's writing—that is, putting it in actual terms: history is not the laboratory's business.

De Man's original question, one of the governing concerns of his wartime journalism, is still waiting to be read. In the 'study of human beings and society' the 'phenomenon to be analyzed' cannot be 'isolated': there is no 'inert matter,' there are no 'measurable forces,' there is no way to 'accurately determine' the 'variable elements' (*HVL*, September 1942, 331). In 1942, the problem posed by human and social imperviousness to laboratorial practice is resolved in the empty prefiguration of a sociology infused with literary intuition.[33] In 1966, such an alliance of literature and sociology in the service of both practical and theoretical reason is precisely what is to be opposed: 'The recent tendency to renew literary studies by placing them in a context that includes some of the social sciences is a fallacy' ('CC' o.v., 56). For what is lost in such a contextualization is precisely the point that literature needs no such reinforcement: in the understanding of history, literature is not the intuitive auxiliary of sociology, and neither does it need to plead to sociology for a recognition of its relevance. To the contrary, literature—Romantic literature—is for us the only authentic way to save history from the reifying gaze of objective, natural reason, whose dependence on a subject/object dichotomy marks the betrayal of Romanticism's universal historical consciousness. For the proper meaning of the 'mere metaphor' 'historical "change"' is 'change in the history of consciousness,' the history written by the 'historians of the self,' even as it masquerades in the guise of what, to us, has become mere literature:

Events or changes in the history of consciousness, in the historical process of the act of understanding, are not like events in nature, and no objective correlative can ever be found to prove that such events have actually taken place, as when we speak of a change in the weather or a change in a biological organism. The change does not occur as something that happens factually at a definite time and place, but in the increased self-understanding that takes place in the historical observer as he interprets the event. ('FG' 95–96)

For us, the event to be interpreted is Romanticism, and in order to effect historical change our interpretation must overcome the 'regressive' period 'in terms of self-insight' that separates us from this event (98). That is: we must deliberately refuse to let our historical understanding be predicated in any way—be it negative or positive—on the regressive demands of the empirical. This means that we must oppose the 'misrepresent[ation of] the "artist's journey into the interior"' as essentially a 'nihilistic' and 'power-hungry' 'deliberate alienation of the consciousness from the outside world' ('LN' 165), for such a deliberate alienation misses the mark of authentic self-reflection to the precise extent that it is the defensive mechanism of an idealism that parodies its true origin. It also means that we must oppose the appeal to a logic of necessity that castigates this interiority as essentially a retreat for quietist impotence—as in Jeanson's and Sartre's 1952 attack on Camus (irrespective of the question of whether Camus is an impotent quietist or no)—or as essentially the dwelling-place for complacent metaphysical dreamers—as in de Man's 1942 attack on Romain Rolland's *Voyage intérieur* (irrespective of the question of whether Rolland is a complacent dreamer or no).

We have arrived at a point where we must begin to explicitate more clearly a retrospective understanding of de Man's wartime thought in terms of his own diagnosis of misconceived anti-Romanticism. Establishing this (un)broken link is necessarily a trivial and banal exercise, but an attempt to retrospectively read this misconception can only be dispensed with at the risk of, precisely, trivializing de Man's entire enterprise as a special case of the pathos of negativity, or a bad case of the 'bad faith' involved in 'buying a good conscience by substituting for genuine abnegation the stance and the rhetoric of sacrifice,' the bad faith from which he emphatically wishes to exempt Camus ('AC' 148). For de Man, what is 'to be questioned' in Camus 'is not his good faith but the quality of his insight,' which 'depends, finally, on the intrinsic quality of his inner experience.' We can hardly avoid the temptation to turn this question to de Man's own text, even though such a reflection risks betraying his insight.

*

Here is de Man in one of his most dogmatically anti-Romantic moments:

> In reality, Romain Rolland's evasion in ethereal realms sprouts from a curious incapacity to see things as they are. It was the reaction of an excessive sentimentality, incapable of finding an object to which it could attach itself, finding no other refuge than the adoration of a deformed and adapted image of the heroes of the past. There is something unhealthy in this exaltation that does not dare to acknowledge its responsibilities and escapes in a fog of empty phrases [*paroles creuses*]. (LS, April 1942, 224)

(Rousseau, Fifth *Rêverie:* 'There is nothing solid [on earth] to which the heart could attach itself'[34]—Hölderlin, 'Mnemosyne': 'Am Feigenbaum ist mein Achilles mir gestorben'[35]—Wordsworth: 'blest in thoughts that are its own perfection and reward'[36]—de Man, *passim:* 'the nothingness of human matters.')

The attraction of such evasive sentimentality—an attraction the enlightened journalist confesses to have been seduced by himself at one time—is a function of human history, as much in the ontogenetic as in the phylogenetic sense:

> In a certain era, the public could fervently welcome this kind of thought. This was at a moment when—as during adoles-

cence—one stands apart from the realities. Stabilized in an easy life, without anxiety about tomorrow, endowed with the assurance that the practical problems were resolved or on the way to resolution, a society can let itself slip toward this nebulous metaphysics, toward this verbal humanitarianism that flatters its need for sacrifice without requiring the commitment of its action. At present we are no longer in this state. Our existence has been burdened with an increasing number of precise concerns and we clearly sense that if we do not learn very soon to direct our ship we risk capsizing. Science and thought must serve our security and guide our route toward a greater stability. There is no room anymore for a reverie that, under the pretext of elevating and ennobling us, sets us apart from reality and makes us lose our way in sterile meditation. And one should not fear that this immersion in the real [*bain de réel*] will forever drown the most precious values of the spirit, by debasing them for basely utilitarian missions. It is when thought closely adapts itself to the exigencies of life and exerts itself to clarify the immediate that it is most fertile. And it is when faith wants to simply help men to surmount their difficulties with courage that it is most alive. (224–25)

On an adolescent, caught in the 'painful crisis in the course of which he tries to bring into accord an intelligence smitten with grandeur with a surrounding world that in no way reflects his desires . . . as he is as yet incapable of seeing its resources,' Rolland's sentiments must needs leave a deep mark (224). But when 'the laws of the real have imposed themselves upon him with their servitudes and their riches, [this] teaching soon becomes an evasion [*faux-fuyant*] and a harmful reverie.' Now, in 1942, Rolland 'belongs for us to a past gone by [*un passé révolu*] and his words no longer reach us.' The total divorce of his thought from the 'tangible realities of existence' and his naive 'vigorous imposition of a belief in the life of the spirit, whose beneficent power purifies and glorifies all things' are the features that now force us to see that 'we no longer have a lot in common' with 'the intimate evolution of his soul.' We may still acknowledge the rare moments of 'clairvoyance and candor' when Rolland's 'humanitarianism turns itself to its real object' as he 'unveils the treasures hidden in the soul of the poor and the untalented'; we can still look on his work as one of the 'most striking of an era gone by [*une époque révolue*] but which we nonetheless like to remember now and again, even if only to search for the few qualities it preserved among its many faults' (*BD*, June 1942, 353).[37] But granted this exception, this 'false revolutionary who has so badly translated the mysteries of genius' is of no further concern to us: 'We must resolve to smash this idol of our youth, who was also the idol of the century at a moment when this century did not yet have, with its maturity, its tragic preoccupations and heavy responsibilities' (*LS*, April 1942, 225).

In his terrible maturity, de Man articulates the decisive error of this broken idol in terms that allow us to tighten our deceptively simple but irrepressible genealogical construal of his thought:

> For [Rolland's] entire work seems to be a false interpretation of a saying of Spinoza's that, he tells us, had a profound influence on his formation: 'By the series of causes and real beings, I do not mean the series of particular and changing things, but solely the series of fixed and eternal things,' Spinoza wrote. Availing himself of this phrase as a springboard, Rolland hastens to conclude from it a disdain for all that is tangible and an adoration for all that to him seems to incarnate 'the fixed and eternal things.' Yet Spinoza had taken care to declare beforehand 'that it is absolutely necessary to derive all our ideas from physical things, that is to say real beings, proceeding, following the series of causes, from one real being to another real being, without passing to abstract and universal things, either to conclude anything real from them, or to conclude them from any real being: for the one and the other interrupt the true march of the understanding.' Which clearly means that all values, and above all the fixed and eternal values, emanate from the things of this earth and not from the phantoms of the spirit. This is one of the most fertile and most useful of Spinoza's ideas. Yet, by falsifying it, Romain

> Rolland began to march against his master [*a l'encontre de son maître*].³⁸ (224)

As a result of this mistake, Rolland transforms science as well as art into 'ethical values,'³⁹ failing to see that science 'is not good or bad, but false or exact' and that art 'inspires admiration for the talent and the imagination of the creators but is not valid as a moral orientation, that is to say, has no relation to the actions and duties of men.' Art, as the realization of aesthetics, has nothing to do with morality—'If one were to submit art to moral imperatives, one would end up with catastrophes'—and science is primarily the epistemological arbiter of truth and falsehood—with the important further implication that insofar as science properly observes 'the true march of understanding' it can accurately legitimate the true 'fixed and eternal values' that emanate from 'the things of this earth.' Art, for its part, can only manage to become 'a true message' when, 'by a rare miracle, true virtue and pure talent are reunited in a single being.' Such as this one, for instance:

> Look at Péguy. On the one hand, there is the man with his two feet riveted to the ground and who must loudly speak the truths that this ground has taught him. On the other hand, there is the poet of the singing phrase and of the ringing formulas. The two are united in an admirable synthesis, cumulating the merits of the moralist and of the artist. But the moralist Péguy is not valuable thanks to the poet but at the same time as the poet. Someone is not better because he is more talented. (224)

Science may not be an ethical value, but it is the scientific stance—literally fixed onto the things of this earth—that enables the moralist to learn the eternal values of true virtue. In this, art is no more than a singing and a ringing supplement: the alleged synthesis is only ever dispensable cumulation. While the 'fundamental signification' of art (the realization of talent and imagination independent of any expression of 'lines of conduct' and 'lessons in elevation') is readily taken into the bargain, it is clear that the one thing needful is the turn to reality in the footsteps of Spinoza properly understood, in search of a true understanding of the 'series of causes' leading 'from one real being to another real being,' without moving to 'abstract and universal things,' yet still ending up with an insight in the 'fixed and eternal values' necessary for our 'security' and 'stability.'

But the supplement to this stability, as supplements do, interrupts the true march of understanding: a few months later, it makes an inconclusive bid for recognition as an unacknowledged but constitutive contributor to truth by way of sociological intuition (*LS*, October 1942, 276);[40] ten years later, it begins to march against Spinoza.

In an unpublished 1953 graduate essay on 'Taine and Baudelaire,' de Man sets out to account for the 'strange and touching points of weakness' in the 'monument of system and order' we tend to associate with Taine's thought, and to argue that these points are of a nature to reveal what, appearances notwithstanding, this 'solid theoretician' and the 'haunted poet' Baudelaire 'have in common' ('TB' 1–2).[41] At the end of the exercise, it transpires that this common feature is the failure of their opposite enterprises in 'the same central defeat': that is, the failure to effect a reconciliation of the 'causal stability' of 'objective nature'—the realm of science—with 'the existence of Form as a living phenomenon'—the realm of art (21).

For Taine, the central problem is his discovery of 'the deep and tragic split between order, revealed through nature, and free chaos in human consciousness' (12). His 'fundamental passion' is his 'imperative urge for order' (2), his 'profound desire to transpose the majestic order of the exterior world [onto] the chaos of the human soul' under the aegis of a mechanistic conception of universal reality (3). To the extent that this attempt runs into the primary obstacle of 'the limitation of our knowledge of the exterior world,' it suffers 'frustration,' but it can still find refuge in 'the great metaphysical intuitions of which mechanism is one among many other offsprings.' Taine's 'master' in this connection is Spinoza: living in an era marked by 'the proud hope that the order of nature, through science, was [made] accessible to the human mind,' de Man argues, Taine must have been deeply attracted to Spinoza's 'seventh proposition': 'Ordo et connexio idearum idem est, ac ordo et connexio rerum.' [The order and connection of ideas is the same as the order and connection of things.][42] For the lesson of this law, as read by de Man in the name of Taine (whom it is tempting to imagine here as a bourgeois prefiguration of Antonio Negri),[43] is that 'in conquering the system of nature, the mind (being identical to it) would thus conquer itself, which meant that ideal problems such as ethics, politics and aesthetics were susceptible of solution' (3). For this promise to hold, however, it is necessary that this identity between mind and nature be wholly contained in the premise of an 'efficient cause,' which stands in a necessary and determinate relation to its effect: Spinoza's monism requires a concept of causation sufficiently powerful to unequivocally explain any event 'by the correct enumeration of its causes' (4). And this original assumption is precisely what is effectively disproved by the existence of the work of art as '*form*,' as a formal 'total unit in itself' whose 'coherence' is 'organic' rather than 'analytical.' As such, the work of art cannot be analyzed in terms of 'a series of imperative equations' between its component parts:

> Instead, it is a statement of equalities, differences, contrasts, oppositions and contradictions, linked together by an arbitrary act of free will. These proportions *are*, and that is the end of it; they cannot be brought back to a generative system that transcends them. They have no other finality than their ontological intent to constitute themselves into what we call form. (5)

The true merit of Taine's enterprise is that he recognized this rift in his thought even while he tried to suppress it: if he had restricted himself to 'natural science' alone, even if—though 'at the cost of some error'—he had 'transposed his *Weltbild* into the field of psychology and sociology,' he could have succeeded in upholding the illusory promise of his Spinozan monism (11);[44] but insofar as he genuinely acknowledged the 'aesthetic consciousness . . . which was an active part of his own nature,' he performed the defeat of the metaphysics he adhered to:

> He knows, more or less consciously, how essential it is to safeguard the hope that objective and subjective reality can be fused by means of an act of knowledge; he realizes that, if such were not the case, we would find ourselves completely adrift, without any guarantee of meaningful existence, and that the construction of an ethical system would then meet with almost insurmountable difficulties. He states, therefore, that his analysis must stop short of the recognition of failure, beyond which there can be only despair, and that he must hold on to his monistic postulate like a shipwrecked traveler to a life raft. (11)

The equally desperate reverse side of this despair is represented by Baudelaire—who, be it said in passing, and to speed matters up, stands in roughly the same relation to Taine as does Mallarmé to Baudelaire in 'The Double Aspect of Symbolism.' The 'haunted poet' starts out from the 'opposite pole' ('TB' 21): for him, the first commitment is to form as 'a rebellious imitation of nature' through 'the re-creation of an equally coherent universe made this time of purely human power, by means of purely human faculties' (13). He aspires to a 'perfect formal stability,' which presupposes the 'eliminat[ion of] nature' (24)—a presupposition that, in turn, meets its defeat in a recognition of the inimitable 'causal stability' of an 'objective nature' (21) that it is not in the power of form to eliminate (18). In the final analysis, Baudelaire's 'formal intent' is 'structurally self-destructive' and founders on the painful knowledge that it 'can never achieve the status of objective existence' (23).

The pattern that emerges from this double failure—this 'same central defeat' (21)—is predicated on a dichotomy between the 'causal stability' whose revelation is the province of the natural sciences and 'the existence of Form as a living phenomenon,' of which a constitutive 'awareness' is central to the work of art. An obvious objection to this 'diagnosis' (10) would be that it is blind to the historical determination of the scientific paradigm it espouses: the notion of an exhaustive comprehension of the physical world in terms of 'deductive causality' (11) alone is, for scientific theory and practice from the early twentieth century onward, a thing of the past, and this observation could invite the suggestion that the missed encounter between form and cause (both within and between the respective enterprises of Baudelaire and Taine) must be understood as an accident of history that it would be wrong to diagnose as an essential conflict. In 'Taine and Baudelaire,' de Man hints at a possibility to better understand the relation between form and cause along Hegelian rather than Spinozan lines (a task Taine envisaged but never quite managed to face) (6), but the figure through whom he implicitly proposes to meet the potential objection that his diagnosis only holds in the discursive context of mechanistic—essentially Newtonian—science is Gaston Bachelard, who, arguably significantly for de Man, 'was a professor of chemistry before becoming a philosopher of science and then a theoretician of literature' ('BB' 5).

Having 'lived the breakdown of Newtonian physics' (6) in the recognition that its constitutive logic—deductive causality—was merely 'a certain type of rational operation, which had perhaps erroneously been considered the only one of which the mind was capable,' Bachelard set himself the task to establish a framework in which 'the necessary pluralism of scientific truth' (7) revealed in this recognition could be accommodated. In this adapted paradigm, the key concepts of science are translated as 'conglomerate[s] of . . . different truths' interacting in the cognitive intent on 'objective reality' and riddling this cognition to the core. The consequent 'increased complexity is best expressed by stating that causality is no longer deductive but formal, thus putting emphasis on the existence of certain relationships (both within one concept and from concept to concept) but excluding the determined point to point correspondence between cause and effect implied in the term "deductive"' (8). In order to prevent this post-Newtonian epistemology from foundering in radical indetermination, Bachelard (prefiguring the enterprise de Man would later ascribe to Lévi-Strauss) further had 'to prove that formal causality is rational too, and that, provided the concept of rationality is made flexible enough to include plurality of thought, it can keep making claims of truth that are precisely the claims of rationality.' For de Man, the central question for this exercise in rational 'formalization' of cognitive activity concerns those activities of the mind 'that have no cognitive intent':

> Our concern with the objective realities of the outside world is not always motivated by the desire to *know* this world, in a reflective sense. Specifically, whatever pertains to the general realm of what Bachelard includes under the term 'imagination' seems to disregard the rigors of knowledge with a puzzling *désinvolture*. There seems to exist a pre-rational apprehension of the world which states itself, in works of art for instance, and keeps interfering with the objective vision that rationality . . . sets out to achieve.[45] (9)

Like Taine, Bachelard is unable 'to evade the issue, by dismissing the imaginative attitude as simple aberration': like Taine, he is troubled by 'a poetic sensitivity' interfering with an 'almost mystical desire for clarity and rational harmony,' and he is unable to simply 'discard a part of himself that he feels to be of equal power and importance' (9; cf. 'TB' 11). But like Taine, he does not succeed in coming to terms with the art he refuses to discard. The specific character of this failure can be summarized as a deliberate blindness to the formal structure of products of the imagination. Where Taine desperately unsuccessfully tried to wed his recognition of the formal totality of art to the concept of efficient causality he envied in Newtonian physics and Spinozan metaphysics, Bachelard denies the work of art any formal intent whatsoever and claims such intent as the exclusive and distinctive province of cognitive rationality. Art, for its part, is the privileged domain for the 'resistance to knowledge' ('BB,' 10): its activity consists of a total submission to 'the temptation of imaginative, natural and spontaneous perception,' and it deserves recognition precisely for the purity of its difference from genuinely rational 'formal thought,' which is itself essentially 'exercized against the natural perception of the world' (11). Bachelard's intent, then, is 'to show that imaginative knowledge is nonformal or preformal and thus to provide a screen through which it could be sifted out of scientific knowledge' (12). The 'fundamental thesis' shaping this intent is that 'the poetic imagination is always and necessarily rooted in matter itself; in matter, not as it is seen by physics (a formal system of causal coherences), but as it is immediately perceived by direct sensation.'

Not surprisingly, de Man takes objection to the 'metaphysical presuppositions' underpinning this aesthetics: although it is true that 'the aesthetic intent' of the poetic image 'is undeniably aimed toward matter' (17), it is equally—and more importantly—true that, from 'the point of view of matter,' 'the image is altogether a dematerialization.' Bachelard's 'material monism' ultimately amounts to a misguided inversion of the metaphysical substructure of Taine's failure: the poetic image is seen as being effectively caused by way of an unmediated, naive perception of matter, a 'purely intra-material intuition' devoid of 'intentional structure' (21); whereas rational thought is granted 'total intellectual purity' (10) on the basis of an elimination of 'naive conceptions' that can only be recognized as such when they are identified as instances of the 'unscientific perception' (11) whose purest (non)form is poetic imagery. The point being that the failure to register the nonnaive and truly formal structure of poetic language as it opposes any reduction to material monism deprives Bachelard's method from the yardstick with which to measure the pluralist rationality of formal science.

It is because he wished to protect his rationalistic system which . . . is itself a formalist one, that Bachelard had to devalorize the concept of aesthetic form. Hence his neglect of linguistic and intentional structures. . . . For if one grants the full formal quality of the poetic, the argument that founds rationality on the formal nature of mental activity collapses. It would then apply just as well to obviously non-rational activities, such as poetic creation. (21–22)

Taine's clutching to the mechanistic 'monistic postulate' of 'deductive causality' was a 'pathetically inadequate' attempt 'to erect a barrier against the rising tide of subjectivism' ('TB' 11) thwarted by his sensibility to aesthetic form; Bachelard's work 'is a rather desperate attempt to save rationality from the problem of subjectivism' ('BB' 21) by means of a 'material monism' unable to come to terms with aesthetic form. The crisis of both nineteenth- and twentieth-century forms of scientific rationality is a corollary of the failure to 'eliminat[e] the obstacle that aesthetic activity, by its mere existence' (22) forms for both 'the Spinozan axiom of monism' ('TB' 13) and the post-Newtonian attempt to rigorously formalize 'the necessary pluralism of scientific truth' ('BB' 7).

Hastily, if in 1942 the boat had not yet capsized and Spinozan monism could still function as a reliable rudder, in 1953 the vessel is decisively broken and the best Taine can do is to pretend, even against his own better insight, not to have noticed that art has already shattered the life raft as well. More specifically: If in 1942 de Man is still confident about the prospect of policing the boundaries between epistemology and aesthetics in the service of objective judgment, in 1954 he decides that the exactly similar project he now ascribes to Bachelard—'an attempt to circumscribe the realms within which both faculties [objective vision and poetic sensitivity] operate, and thus to avoid their disharmonious interference' ('BB' 9–10)—can only remain consistent at the cost of a damaging exclusion of the truth of artistic form.

But there was always another discipline to be taken into account. We must recall here that in October 1942, de Man hints at a productive disturbance of the clear demarcation between science and literature:

> For reasoning reason is not the only means to attain a truth. There also exists a poetic comprehension that immediately grasps the lessons of the world, in the very contact with concrete things, objects, and beings. This mode of knowledge has been denied a scientific value since it would lack the indispensable qualities of generality and objectivity. It is nonetheless true that certain sciences constantly make use of it, even without admitting it.[46] (*LS*, 276)

The 'science' in which this disturbance by intuition is to be accommodated is sociology (Jünger's *Marmorklippen* being a privileged experiment), and sociology, now represented by Kenneth Burke, is also the second, subordinate subject of de Man's essay on Bachelard.

De Man starts out by backhandedly praising Burke's 1935 *Permanence and Change* for its implication in 'the sociological fallacy of the thirties,' which, 'however naive it may seem in retrospect, was backed by the best of intentions': to address 'the feeling of impending collapse of capitalism, the inequity of overproduction contrasted with utter poverty, fascism as a desperate rear guard action of the bourgeoisie in the class struggle, unemployment, etc.' ('BB' 23). If these problems now, in 1954, 'seem dated,' this is not because 'they have been solved, but because we have lost illusions about the possibility of solving them by the mere manipulation of political and economic institutions.' The saving trait of Burke's efforts to articulate such manipulation is the suggestion that 'social consciousness could take on the form of a criticism of deductive causality,' whereby 'sociological reasoning,' in its opposition to the 'atomistic philosophy of production' in 'the hated technological and capitalist society' (an opposition whose immediate analogy is that between Bachelard's scientific rationality and the 'linear system underlying Newtonian metaphysics'), would become a '"formal"' exercise of reason (23–24).

> Since they [sociologists like Burke] had to justify the necessity for a total and revolutionary change, the discontinuity of social evolution had to be proven; one had to reveal a plurality of social truths, which leads to a formal vision of history, very similar to the formal concept of reason . . . in Bachelard. That the term 'dialectical' should suddenly have become a key word from political meeting halls to laboratories, indicates the depth of the change involved in replacing the concept of deduction by that of form. (24)

One further effect of this introduction of 'the discontinuity of paradox into deductive and continuous schemes' was that it seemed to allow for a recognition of 'semirevolutionary intentions' in literature as a 'formal activity' congenital to sociological thought: by virtue of this shared sense of form, Burke's 'extravagantly naive claims' about the '"poetic"' nature of communism or 'the poet as *the* political rebel of the age' received 'a certain cogency that is not unsympathetic' (24). But when turned to literature in its own right, this sympathetic extravagant naiveté deteriorates in an 'endless conversion of aesthetic symbols into social facts,' which is not only 'not too fruitful' for sociology but, more importantly, simply damaging for literature.

Where Bachelard could still be praised for his distorted understanding of the poetic image's intent on matter, Burke is taken to task for his failure to realize that this intent 'is always aimed toward a relation between consciousness (which can be social) and matter,' so that it can only be understood as 'a formalization of the social,' never as 'a socialization of the formal' (26).[47] Instead of investigating the 'inner motivation' (25) of literature as an attempt to give form to the dialectic of matter and consciousness, Burke explains literature away into 'almost vulgar banality' (29) by relating its structures to 'their surface analogies in social conduct' (25). He thereby not only slights literature as an activity whose constitutive concern is metaphysical rather than sociological, but also fatally misses the possible social power that de Man still holds up as a *telos* of literature's formal 'inward concentration' (28):

> When [the poetic imagination] returns to social statements, as in the case of prophetic poets like Blake, Hölderlin or George, it speaks from the depths of an overall metaphysical intuition that was gained by inward contemplation, far removed from the values of the social as such.[48] (27)

With this empty statement, de Man's formal logic once again reaches its self-imposed transcendental point of reference: contemporary 'critical theory' of literature is flawed by its inability to filter out the 'extraliterary concerns' stemming from the 'nonpoetic disciplines' whose potentially deceptive proximity to 'poetic consciousness' as a formal activity they are unable to accurately articulate.(30) What remains to be established is a 'correct and complete phenomenology of the poetic image, entirely within the structure of the poetic intent' (31). The development of this project in pursuit of a substantial historical determination is one name for a sustained paraphrase of de Man's original intent.

To recapitulate and to simplify: de Man's wartime espousal of a scientific realism whose superiority depends on its constitutive pretense to derive value from the proper observation of fact (a realism whose synthetic alliance with literature and sociology is given unpursued expression only in the second half of 1942) is replaced in the 1950s by an anatomy of modern thought as a theater of intense conflict in which the actors are consciously or unconsciously thwarted by a central impotence in the face of literary form. For Taine, this impotence takes shape as the inability to extend the realist perspective to the 'free chaos in human consciousness' manifested in aesthetic form ('TB' 12) (which implies a tragic impotence in the face of problems ethical, political, and aesthetic);

for Baudelaire (or Mallarmé), it is the failure to radically eliminate the realist perspective by surpassing the enviable coherence, permanence, and stability of the objective world, and with it of natural science ('TB' 18–19), on the strength of the formal totality of consciousness alone; for Bachelard, it is the untenable intent to preserve rational formalization from contamination by the formal nature of the poetic imagination's intent on matter; for Burke, it is the misguided project to harness poetic form to 'a superficial sociology' ('BB' 29).

These versions of impotence are gradually rarefied by de Man as corollaries of the assumption of the ontological superiority of the natural object, an assumption he himself shared even as he diagnosed its paralyzing implication in the governing model of a subject/object dichotomy that no modern monism has the power to transcend and no modern thought—including, necessarily, his own—has the language to address: 'We have no language to handle a problem that questions precisely the logic by which we have lived for so long,' and 'this difficulty prevents us from dealing with the entire realm of problems that result from this awareness of separation, and this includes most matters of contemporary history, literature, and, to a large extent, ethics and theology' ('IG' 15). Again: Because we have no language with which to adequately frame our inability to 'fuse' 'objective and subjective reality . . . by means of an act of knowledge,' our attempts to 'construct an ethical system . . . meet with almost insurmountable difficulties' ('TB' 11). The intent that governs the totality of the form we aspire to 'can never be perceived' (23) and our language is fatally implicated in the dictates of perception: our task, the 'crucial' problem of both 'criticism' and 'modern philosophy,' is 'the invention of a language capable of dealing with intents, to replace a language only fit to deal with objects, and the concomitant invention of a logic capable of ordering what cannot be described' (23). That is: a language that radically supersedes the language of 'physics, where an event is entirely contained in and explained by the correct enumeration of its causes'; a logic that can successfully think what cannot be described and can thereby function, as formalized rationality and formalized sociology cannot, as a truly radical alternative to the powerful dream of Spinoza's concept of causation, which, 'by the isolation of variables, reduces complexity to a skeleton of fundamental *données*, which are capable by themselves of engendering reality as a whole,' and which, 'inversely,' is able to 'effectively act . . . upon [reality] through the medium of these *données*, and through them alone' (4).

Faced with our '*unhappy* consciousness' of the absence of this logos, our modern temptation is 'to repress the original anxiety' ('IG' 15). In this, the object of our desire is the 'serenity' we hope to acquire by 'giv[ing] up our awareness of ourselves' and by 'fall[ing] back on something that would not be conscious, namely, nothingness,' or—but it is the same (no)thing—by 'sacrificing,' as does Bachelard in his 'poetics of "unmediated vision,"' 'the demands of consciousness to the realities of the object' ('IS' 7–8). This is our modern predicament, and the answer de Man with increasing confidence brings to it in the course of the 1960s occurs by way of the translation of modernity as, specifically, the post-Romantic condition. The events that cannot be 'described' and 'ordered' ('TB' 23) by our language since they 'are not like changes in nature' ('CC' 6) are the events of history, and Romanticism is the locus of a 'truly historical consciousness' ('FG' 97) fit to articulate what we cannot speak: its poets 'assume that [the predicament of poetry] can be changed by present and future decisions, including their own *poetic* decisions' ('PHDI' ii), and to them this is never a 'merely' poetic undertaking: 'The ordering of human experience within successive time is a conscious theme of their work'—their power resides in their ability to thematize, to describe and to order what our language is unable to deal with. The key to this power is their ability to recognize 'the error which hid the true predicament from sight' ('AIB' 102), and this error is precisely our mistaken submission to the subject/object dichotomy as the original truth of our unhappy consciousness. Romanticism states the error of our crisis in the mode of truth:

The error is that of a self that tries to forget its own temporal fate by patterning itself on the eternal aspects of nature; hence a conception of the self as the pole of a subject/object relationship becomes the illusion that has to be renounced. The somber light, the harsh serenity that prevails in authentic romantic literature, expresses the difficulty of this renunciation. And the persistent intellectual refinement with which the successors of romanticism have pursued the dialectic of subject and object to its most extreme form indicates the increased strength with which this renunciation is being resisted. The major poets that came after romanticism are mostly impressive as negative figures, by the subtlety of the strategies they devised to avoid confronting the self-insight achieved by their predecessors.[49] (102–3)

This 'harsh serenity' that recognizes 'le néant des choses humaines' lies beyond the false serenity aspired to in our reactive nihilist desire to fall back on 'something that would not be conscious, namely, nothingness' ('IG' 15). It is also crucially distinct from the sentiment of the 'so-called beautiful soul'[50] that revels in the self-congratulatory sense of its mistaken purity and superiority, and it has nothing in common with the defensive self-aggrandizement of 'an excessive sentimentality, incapable of finding an object to which it could attach itself' and stuck in a 'fog of empty phrases' at a perverse remove from the 'bain de réel' (*LS,* April 1942, 224–25). Rather, it proceeds from the 'authentic reflection' that has renounced 'not only the hope of overcoming pain, but even the hope of justifying itself by means of that pain, of making it serve self-glorification' ('RDS' 177). Its figure is the true Beautiful Soul, whose 'somber happiness' (177; translation modified) bespeaks 'the serenity of ideal knowledge' ('IR' 44): it is a 'fictional character who knows all there is to know of human happiness and who is about to face death with Socratic equanimity' ('CC' 17). Its operation is not the 'compensatory expression of a . . . deficient sense of reality' (17), its language is not 'the hollow mask with which a frustrated, defeated consciousness tries to cover up its own negativity' (12), its practice is radically different from post-Romantic poets' attempts 'to elude the problem by means of a substituted language that covers up the original desire as under a mask' ('DA' 155), and consequently its greatness surpasses that of those among its descendants who, 'at rare moments,' reestablish a measure of contact with their source by 'drop[ping] the mask' in order to 'name again [the] "rich, dark nothing"' (156). Beyond the sublational imperative, whose logic necessarily diagnoses it as a 'form of defective selfhood,'[51] this Beautiful Soul preempts the predicament Hegel projects onto it when he burdens it with the 'yearning [Sehnen] that in the becoming of itself as an object without essence [wesenlosen Gegenstande] only loses itself and falling over and above this loss back onto itself only finds itself as what is lost.'[52] Living on after Hegel, the truth of the Beautiful Soul is the recognition of '"an unexplainable void"' within, which no realization of the Spirit can fill ('CC' 18) and which can only be honored in 'the nothingness of fiction.'[53]

The *Phenomenology of Spirit* may find its prefiguration in the *Bildungsroman*, but with this difference: that, as Jean Hyppolite points out, at the end of history this 'history of consciousness' is 'not a novel but a work of science.'[54] In the eyes of the Absolute Spirit, at least as read by Alexandre Kojève, the Beautiful Soul may figure as the last refuge of unfulfilled 'post-revolutionary Romantic man' into a 'purely literary existence,'[55] in which 'he describes himself, reveals himself complacently to all,' and 'flees the World, not himself,—the *only* Selbst he knows and is interested in.'[56] The Absolute Spirit, who has left this unproductive auto-affection behind, understands that 'the acme of romantic expression would be the novel of a novel, the book of a book,' the *Gattungsgeschichte* of a *Gattung;* it recognizes the 'analogy' between this expression and its own history, the *Phenomenology,* 'which explains how this Phenomenology itself is possible'; but it insists that, unlike the self-description of the Beautiful Soul, the *Phenomenology* has 'a *real* content: Man as the agent of History.'[57]

The Crisis of Contemporary Romanticism | 165

There is just one catch to this history: the realization of this content—for Kojève's Hegel this is Napoleon as the figure of '(universal) Action' and 'Bewußtsein'—needs to be revealed as '(absolute) Knowledge' by the figure of 'Selbstbewußtsein,' Hegel. And for this revelation itself to be real, it needs to be recognized by the real: here is Hegel's (Kojève's) terrible condition (1937):

> This could be managed (and even then!) if Napoleon 'recognized' Hegel, like Hegel has 'recognized' Napoleon. Did Hegel expect (1806) being called to Paris by Napoleon, in order to become the Philosopher (the Sage) of the universal and homogeneous State there, having to explain (justify)—and perhaps direct—Napoleon's activity?
>
> Since Plato, this thing has always tempted the great philosophers. But the text of the Phenomenology that relates to it . . . is (deliberately?) obscure.
>
> However this may be,—History/the Story has come to an end [*Quoi qu'il en soit,—l'Histoire est terminée*].[58]

As Rousseau writes, with characteristic arrogance, 'It would not be difficult for me to prolong this Note, but that would be to wrong the intelligence of the only Readers I care about.'[59] However this may be, history has not come to an end and instead insists on the end of the 'unproblematically forward-directed' nature of dialectical time 'in the Hegelian sense' ('PT' 72). The missed crossing of Hegel and Napoleon leaves us with the task not to demystify 'the beautiful soul that appears in Hegel's *Phenomenology of the Spirit*' ('CC' 13) and to recognize that this 'nothing' ('RTS' 47), for all its apparent 'pessimism and negativeness,' may well bespeak 'a greater awareness of the historical forces that brought about such catastrophes as Nazism' ('LN' 164), even while it harbors 'few illusions that [it] can prevent this degradation' ('PT' 50)—illusions such as those that were cherished, tragically, by Husserl, claiming 'European supremacy' while 'speaking in what was in fact a state of urgent personal and political crisis' ('CC' 16), illusions for which, maddeningly, he can be excused:

Since we are speaking of a man of superior good will, it suffices to point to the pathos of such a claim at a moment when Europe was about to destroy itself as center in the name of its unwarranted claim to be the center. Who, speaking in Vienna in 1935, three years before the *Anschluss,* could not be excused, in Husserl's situation, for indulging in wishful thinking? (16; o.v., 52–53)

The 'historical forces that brought about such catastrophes as Nazism' ('LN' 164) are impervious to such thinking—not because this thinking is wishful, not because its intent at *Entmythisierung* misfires, but because these historical forces thrive on the eclipse of the source critical thinking, especially when it is wishful, is in the process of reestablishing contact with:

> If Hitler triumphed in Germany it was in spite of the intellectual tradition of the country, rather than because of it. There was *trahison des clercs* to the precise extent that literary thought and political action had lost contact with each other. The problem is not that a philosophical tradition could be so wrong but that it could have counted for so little when it was most needed. The responsibility rests not with the tradition but with the manner in which it was used or neglected, and this is primarily a sociological problem. (163)

The history of this sociological problem is that of a treatment of 'literature and politics as being entirely isolated within their own fixed spheres,' in a 'baffling' 'discrepancy between intellectual values and actual behavior' that radically betrays the essentially Romantic tradition, which in no way 'advocated a separation between mind and action,' without therefore considering them as 'so closely interrelated that passage can be made from one to the other, as from cause to effect, without trace of mediation'(163). Only when we fail to accurately grasp 'the complexity of the relationship between thought and action'—and 'one would think that, after some of the experiences of this century,' this relationship 'would be better understood'—can we condemn the special impotence of authentic thought as the mark of nihilism:

> It is not in the power of philosophy or literature to prevent the degradation of the human spirit, nor is it its main function to warn against this degradation; Nietzsche could rightly be criticized for having warned too much and perhaps for not having thought enough. A literature of nihilism is not necessarily nihilistic, and one should be careful about praising or blaming writers for events that took place after they had ceased to exist: it is just as absurd to praise Rousseau for the French Revolution as to blame Nietzsche for Hitler. This does not mean that philosophers and poets have no moral or political responsibility even when their work is apolitical. But it means this responsibility should be evaluated within the full philosophical or literary context of their work, not their lives, still less the effect that their work may have had on other people. ('LN' 164)

For the work of Romanticism, this context is saturated as the lucidity of nothingness: a lucidity that precisely did succeed in claiming its own transcendent coherence by concentrating exclusively on the workings of superior consciousness alone, beyond the subject/object dialectic post-Romantic thought is still/once more enthralled to; a lucidity that therefore paradoxically (and, to us, incomprehensibly) was able to contain, in the richest sense of the word, 'the separation between thought and action' (163)—for instance in its 'natural' ability to read Napoleon as 'the practical side of Rousseau's ideality' ('IR' 296 n.47)—and could consequently muster the 'audacity to affirm' the 'possibility' of the 'perfect world' (23), in a true performance of the mistaken promise that neomonism and modern formalism failed to deliver. Through the 'subtler language'[60] of this promise, genuine Romantic insight disclosed 'the moments, the articulations, of consciously understood historical becoming' as a *Vollendung* decisively distinct from 'the "end of history" in a Hegelian sense' (294 n.28) and thereby was 'able to safeguard the future of humanity' (45). In its insistence on 'the complex and primarily negative relationship prevailing between any kind of reflective language (including that of poetry) and the more immediate experience of reality that is a necessary part of history' ('RH' 212), it stated the truth of its 'wisdom' as 'the knowledge of its own historical ineffectiveness,' a wisdom that has its own crucial effectiveness in its radical difference from 'schemes that conceive of history as either apocalyptic failure or salvation.'

There is just one catch to this history: the humanity of Romanticism's future misreads this mediating promise as the failure to bring history to a post-Hegelian and hyper-Heideggerian end in the realist nihilism of an 'unmediated proximity to being' ('PT' 73); it mistakes 'the stagnation of [its] own mind for the stagnation of history' ('WM' 137) and settles at best for a complacent compromise in the face of a future apocalypse.⁶¹ At best: for there are worse mistakes than that of the stagnation of compromise—such as (as if this could ever be a convenient example) the 'dangerously arbitrary' assumption of a 'messianic attitude' ('MP' 158) attendant on the nationalist recuperation of Hölderlin ('RH' 211). The all too familiar point of reference for this recuperation can be read in the 'far from reassuring' 'political overtones of [Heidegger's] commentaries [on Hölderlin] (especially when juxtaposed with the Rectoral Address of 1933)' ('PT' 55; cf. 'RH' 211), but for an understanding of de Man's post-Romantic determinations, the more salient source here may well be the semiarticulated figure of Stefan George. One more return:

In a 1954 graduate essay on 'Yeats and the German Romantic Tradition,' de Man points out that interpretations of Yeats 'within the continuity of the English tradition' fatally miss an 'extremely important dimension': 'the fact that Yeats is and considers himself to be a nationalistic poet, concerned with the cultural and political emancipation of his country' ('YRT' 3). 'The obvious comparative analogy' that could be useful in order to come to terms with this dimension, de Man suggests, 'is with those European literatures of approximately the same period that were also concerned with national problems' (4). France is immediately ruled out ('since few literatures take their national existence more for granted than the French' [4], and 'aggressive literary nationalism' only appears on the scene with Barrès and the *Action française* [5]), and so are 'minor nationalist literatures' (6) like that of nineteenth-century Flanders, since (unlike Yeats), its proponents primarily took to writing 'in a minor language' (5).[62]

The 'most fruitful' comparison would therefore appear to be 'the overall German romantic tradition, as it evolves from its beginnings around 1800 up to Rilke and Stefan George' (6):

> During this period, German poetry and German thought tended to overstate and overreach themselves constantly, following up each line of thought to its most extreme consequences. This has not exactly generated a balanced and secure culture, but it provides us with a remarkable series of test cases for the study of European intellectual phenomena. In Germany, one can study them in their purest and most magnified forms; like new species bred in a hothouse, they reveal their best and their worst sides to the fullest. Any one interested in the overall motivations that stand behind modern hopes and anxieties—of which modern poetry is one—will find Germany to be an inexhaustible mine of information.[63] (6–7)

The terms of these 'overall motivations' are those of 'Romanticism' and its 'philosophical counterpart' in 'idealist philosophy,' and they involved 'a conflict between the real and the ideal, between the objective being of the natural world and the subjective freedom of human consciousness' as it is 'experience[d]' in the 'two principal areas' of 'history' and '(human and divine) love.' This Romanticism:

> far from having reveled in the polarity of being . . . has been a heroic attempt of the human mind (in the sense of the German word 'Geist') to posit itself, in its own right, as an essential element of being, next to and sometimes instead of the objective

world. Whether this attempt failed or succeeded is beside the point; human destiny is not written in terms of contests and competitions. What matters is that, in the course of this effort, our awareness of our own being has increased, and that this increased consciousness is henceforth a part of our reality that no feigned ignorance can eliminate. From the point of view of literature, it is of great importance that romantic poetry (using the term in a broad sense that includes symbolism up to the present) has been the principal vehicle of this effort. (7–8)

But the failure or success of this effort can hardly be 'beside the point' if there is to be a full understanding of the 'best' as well as the 'worst sides' of the (German) Romantic tradition. As it turns out, some 'measure[ment]' of the 'relative greatness' of those who have participated in this effort is always implied (25), and it does not come as a surprise that Hölderlin should be the most crucial figure to have emerged from the hothouse, 'with a strange lucidity that still lies well beyond our understanding, in which nature and the gods are reborn, and man has again opened up to a contact with reality that is not painful beyond endurance'—a strange lucidity that 'cost [him] his mind.'[64]

In the wake of this 'strange lucidity,' the hothouse, equally unsurprisingly, also produces an 'aggressive and assertive' monstrosity that spells 'the total subjectivation of reality, the enclosure, within the inner self, of the entire outside world,' the swerve of a 'defensive movement' in the face of 'the duality between self and other, between subject and object' that has turned into 'an unbearable and paralyzing torture' (22). The figure of this 'fanaticism' (23) is George, who 'tries, to the point of blindness, not to see his irrevocable defeat' (24):

> His mask become so hardened, so desperately and continually forced upon himself, that he manages to look like a statue. By repetitively and repeatedly stating the total victory of the subjective self he tries to believe in its reality and lives, hard and cold, within the ever-narrowing circle he claims to be the entire

> world. When reality intrudes upon him he simply claims not to recognize it, which compels him to persist in a curious mixture of deceit and heroism. (24)

De Man stops short from articulating precisely what the 'extreme consequences' of George's sterile self-petrification are, and in the absence of such development, we can only jump to George's marginal reappearance in de Man's work in the mid-1960s as, yet again, a figure of 'aberration' ('LN' 164) in the face of the nation. Together with Nietzsche, Yeats, and Gide, George ranks among 'the most unsettling figures of the recent literary past' ('AG' 131), figures that contemporary criticism has all too eagerly 'reduced to a reassuring common denominator' involving various mixtures of 'nihilism' and 'aestheticism.'[65] One ground for this reduction is that George, like Wagner (though 'in a less one-sided way'), is one of those who 'adopt[ed] nationalistic attitudes' as a result of a 'confusion of values' through which 'the nation, a perfectly legitimate concept in itself, acts as a substitute for something more fundamental and more encompassing.' To resist the reassuring reduction of this confusion as a mere index of the nihilist aestheticism of a recent past would require a densely articulated argument, but here, too, de Man fails to specify the particular aberrative substitution he diagnoses in George. Perhaps, however, we can approximate its logic by turning to his roughly contemporaneous (and not much less formal) comments on the 'messianic' conception of poetry associated with George and his circle.[66] Surveying the state of German poetics, de Man ascribes a laudable impact to 'George's disciples'—in the sense that they reestablished a 'closer contact with live poetry'—but adds that their 'militant[] aware[ness] of the need for poetic autonomy' failed to develop into a viable poetics, and this primarily 'because their insistence on the messianic element tends to overshadow the formal element of poetry altogether' ('MP' 157–58).

> In their master, George himself, the tangible expression of the transcendental value of poetry was to be found in the perfec-

tion of the form; it was by the act of extreme formal discipline, a kind of ascesis of the form, that the poet earned the right to statements of prophetic weight. If this formal discipline is taken away, the entire messianic attitude becomes dangerously arbitrary. (158)

Which is what happens—to hastily complete the thought—when the ascetic commitment to form that George inherits from Hölderlin, and that in Hölderlin leads to a superior wisdom, is abandoned for a fatally premature commitment to the nation as the substantial substitutive figure of accomplished aesthetic form: the fiction of the political[67] as a well-wrought lie.[68] The failure of 'George''s formal imitation of Hölderlin takes its historical shape as a fatal impatience with ascesis swerving into a blind presumption to prophetic power. The renunciation of such power—or such weight—in the nothingness of fiction marked the moment of its success in the genuinely historical and legitimately ideological (cf. 'IR' 296 n.47) consciousness of Romanticism, where the quality of faith in poetry precisely precluded the mindless realization of this faith in the confusion of nation and form that is one of the ulterior historical names of (German) ideology. The oblivion of this renunciation in post-Romantic illusions of unmediated historical impact is the determining factor in our modern failure to authentically mediate such impact.

As de Man wrote in 1960, we are no longer able to understand the 'Vaterländischer Umkehr' ('PHDY' 174) as primarily 'a revolutionary decision in the use of poetic language' as it 'cease[s] to strive for natural things that are forever inaccessible to us' (175): 'Since 1800, the word "national" has more and more meant the opposite of what Hölderlin intended it to signify, and it has been the most alien word used by modern man.' He continues that in a few poems by Yeats, the 'remote possibility of a poetry which dares to say what it really is, which dares to be truly "national" is perhaps being "born" . . . though it be in the guise of a "terrible beauty."' Perhaps. Perhaps the nonoccurrence of this birth is what happened in George's 'dramatization of the problem of the image, carried to its most extreme consequences' ('PHDI' iv), but the fragments of this failed finale are not there to be read.⁶⁹

✳

If we are to survive in the environment we have made for ourselves, may we have to be monstrous enough to greet our predicament?
— Nicholas Mosley, *Hopeful Monsters*

✳

Here is the inventory: Because this failure is still too much with us, because, 'all eyes,' we are 'fingering slave[s]' 'wrapped closely in [our] sensual fleece,'⁷⁰ we must name our predicament in the mode of barren truth—in an 'asceticism of the mind' ('LB' 49) that takes shape as an 'ascesis of the form' ('MP' 158) whose extension to 'statements of prophetic weight' must be rigorously suspended. Because the 'human mind will go through amazing feats of distortion to avoid facing "the nothingness of human matters"' ('CC' 18) that is 'our condition as it really is' ('LN' 169); because, like Husserl, and despite his proscription of *Veräusserlichung*, we keep 'committing precisely the mistake that Rousseau did not make when he carefully avoided giving his [fundamental] concept[s] . . . any empirical status whatever' ('CC' 16); because, like Mallarmé as he was praised by de Man in the 1950s and demystified by de Man in the 1960s, we still aspire to the 'universality' of consciousness by way of a 'dialectic with the object' predicated on a 'central intuition that situates being in sensible substance' ('MB' 71; o.v., 554), and are consequently unable to recognize 'the illusory character of [this] dialectic' and to reject it as a case of 'philosophical blindness,' an invention of 'false becoming' regulated by 'the reassuring myth of progressive temporality' with which we try to 'hide from our sight a movement we refuse to face,' thereby 'obey[ing] passively to the attraction of being' (73; o.v., 556);⁷¹ because, like Lévi-Strauss, we still adhere to Spinoza's manner in that we conceive of our task as a mere 'fill[ing] in, with the dotted line of geometrical construction, what natural reason had not bothered to make explicit' ('CC' 19) and are unable to abandon the 'illusion of physical continuity borrowed from the geometrical world of space' ('HEW' 145) for the true morphology of nothingness; because, like Bachelard, 'we limit ourselves to the pastoral resonance' of Rousseau's earth and read his 'reverie of repose' as 'only an idyllic interlude' ('IR' 37; cf. 'IS' 14); because, like Sartre, whose thought in this respect is remarkable for its 'similarity to Bachelard's theory of material imagination,' we neutralize our insight in 'the radical distinction between perception and imagination' by returning to the model of an 'interpenetration between matter and consciousness' ('MP' 155), a model that 'led Sartre to substitute his own obsessions for those of Baudelaire' ('AIB' 105) in much the same way as de Man did in 'The Double Aspect of Symbolism'; because, in short, we are not in a position to adequately question the 'hegemony of the physical world' ('WM' 146), the Romantic promise must be suspended as 'a warning against the danger of this delusion' only ('PT' 73).[72]

The position assumed in this suspension is that where 'the human self has experienced the void within itself and the invented fiction, far from filling the void, asserts itself as pure nothingness, *our* nothingness, stated and restated by a subject that is the agent of its own instability' ('CC' 19). If it is 'perfectly legitimate' to suppress this awareness in 'an attempt to protect the scientific status' of the study of humankind, such suppression also necessarily 'deprives this science of any claim to grow into a philosophical anthropology—while such an anthropology would be inconceivable without the consideration of literature' ('CC' o.v., 56)—'as a primary source of knowledge' ('CC' 9). And insofar as literature is a source, it must cause a crisis—as it did, for instance, at the symposia de Man attended in 1966, where 'nothing was said that had the remotest connection to literature' and where literature therefore returned with a vengeance:

Yet all these meetings mentioned literary criticism as their central concern and the particular polemical tension that characterized the tone was due to the silent presence of the unmentioned topic, literature, haunting the minds of the speakers as a ghost to be exorcized. No comparable tension would have existed if these meetings had merely been devoted to sociology, psychoanalysis or ethnology. The slightly apocalyptic irrationality, the mood of crisis that prevailed in all of them, was due entirely to the innocent and innocuous presence of literature, present in the mediated form of the reflection of literature that we call literary criticism. ('CC' o.v., 45)

But insofar as literature is itself the place where nothing is said in the mode of presence, where nothing is persistently named 'with ever-renewed understanding' ('CC' 18), something has fallen away from the original intent. In de Man's Titanic perspective, this crisis takes shape in the form of understanding.

The Beautiful Soul as it originates for Romanticism is for us a strictly incomprehensible (if not a savage) anomaly, since we are cut off from its original source in the Titanic intent. Our task, therefore, is to translate the Beautiful Soul as itself a Titanic entity: 'We are to understand the original from the perspective of the translation' ('WB' 83). But to the extent that this understanding takes shape as a monumentalization, it must necessarily miss the point that 'the original was always already disarticulated' (84)—a point de Man would begin to read explicitly in his later work but which now leaves its mark as a fissure in his monument to the Titanic Romantic. The resistance of this fissure can be summarily formalized: If the Titanic origin of Romanticism is the transgressive apocalyptic heroism of revolt under way to revolution and the equally transgressive analogical oblivion of consciousness's precarious exile from the natural order, and if true Romanticism, figured in the authentic Beautiful Soul, is an interpretive recollection of these transgressions in and beyond crisis, then Romanticism as our Titanic origin is the transgressive culmination of this recollection in a total obliteration of Romanticism's original Titanic intent on nature and history.

As de Man's thought encounters this fracture in the system he imposes on our historical understanding, it meets its programmatic (or retrogrammatic) crisis: if the original intent of 'the most difficult and the most necessary of tasks' ('WWH' 50) was the articulation of a historical understanding of our relation to our Romantic origin as the only way for us to 'achieve a historical significance' (65), what we are left with is the barren and overdetermined repetition of a renunciation of history in the name of nothingness, '*our* nothingness,' the nothingness of fiction. This nothingness is what must prevent the fiction from becoming the fiction of the political that has cut off our post-Romantic history from its source by cutting it into tragic catastrophe. For 'history,' actual history 'is not fiction' ('LH' 163), which is also why, as an 'empirical mode of manifestation' ('THW' 84), it interferes with the inalienable nothingness of the ideal fiction that is our necessary reaction-formation to the constitutively premature aesthetic fiction of the political.

Even as our barren counter-*Bildung* derives its *raison d'être* from a historically determined resistance to the fallacious stabilization of history in terms of scientific reason, it cannot avoid being beset with the history that is not its intelligible fiction and critically interferes with its harsh serenity, much as 'authentic criticism' interferes with the composure of literary studies,[73] much as 'wars... interfere with the serenity that is indispensable to an orderly pursuit of [the] discipline [of historians]' ('CC' 8), i.e. fiction. And because history is thus what interferes with understanding in that it involves the disarticulation of its *Vollendung* through reading—actual reading, a practice that cannot come to rest in a vicarious retrospective celebration of somber magnanimity and authentic wisdom—de Man's failure to recognize this critical fissure as the scratch from which he must always start again ('PRR' viii) takes shape as the formalization of its post-Romantic translation in the transcendence of total hermeneutics. The Barren Titan, our figure for what little light remains from the holy fire infusing the Beautiful Soul's lucid understanding of the nothingness of human matters, has a home in the achievement of full understanding. The final metamorphosis, which is always already undergone, is the surpassing understanding of the total circle.

PART THREE

Trope

CHAPTER FIVE

A Time of Total Form

Above all, writing does not lead to the truth of being. One could say that it leads to the error of being—to being as a place of errance, to the uninhabitable.
— Emmanuel Levinas, 'Le regard du poète'

In his preface to *Narcisse*, Rousseau sets out to answer those who would detect an inconsistency between, on the one hand, his marked depreciation of arts and sciences as being conducive to moral corruption and on the other, his literary practice. The stark form of his refutation of this objection is as follows: given the fact that moral virtue has already been corrupted, and considering that such corruption is by nature irreversible, there is no point in abolishing the cause of corruption. On the contrary, arts and sciences, having destroyed virtue anyway, may play a vital stabilizing role in the post-moral condition: 'the same causes that have corrupted the peoples sometimes serve to prevent even greater corruption,' and the necessary function of arts and sciences in observance of this law is to prevent the 'vices' they themselves have 'hatched' from turning into 'crimes.'[1]

They destroy virtue but leave its public simulacrum which is always a beautiful thing. In the place of virtue they introduce politeness and *bienséances,* and for the fear of appearing bad

[*méchant*] they substitute the fear of appearing ridiculous. . . .
   It is no longer a matter of leading people to do good but only to distract them from doing evil; they have to be kept occupied with inanities [*niaiseries*] in order to turn them away from evil action; they have to be amused instead of being lectured. . . . Since there are no morals anymore, one must only think of discipline; and it is sufficiently known that Music and Spectacles are one of its most important objects [*Lorsqu'il n'y a plus de mœurs, il ne faut songer qu'à la police; et l'on sait assez que la Musique et les Spectacles en sont un des plus importans objets*].²

The function of entertainment in the present time, then, is to inculcate 'a certain gentleness of manners [*mœurs*],' as a surrogate for the 'purity' that has been irredeemably lost. In this, the postmoral apparatus of the literary 'simulacrum' establishes 'a certain appearance of order which prevents horrible confusion' and invites 'a certain admiration of beautiful things which keeps the good things from falling into total oblivion': literature is 'vice putting on the mask of virtue, not, like hypocrisy, in order to deceive and to betray, but in order to remove, under this kind and sacred effigy, the horror it has of itself when it sees itself uncovered [*à découvert*].'³

Having offered this theoretical 'justification' of literature as a principal instrument for the Beautiful Vice Squad, Rousseau adds that the one question that still concerns him is whether he himself has succeeded in practising literature in conformity with this intent. On the answer to this question depends his inclusion among the few 'privileged souls,' the few 'sublime geniuses who are able to penetrate the veils in which truth envelops itself' while 'resisting the stupidity of vanity, base jealousy, and the other passions engendered by the taste for literature':⁴ 'It is only in observing myself that I can judge if I can count myself among the small number, and whether my soul is capable of supporting the burden of literary exercises.'⁵ As, not entirely surprisingly, turns out to be the case:

   I needed a test to complete the knowledge of myself, and I have carried it out without wavering. After having investigated the state of my soul during literary successes, it remained for me to examine it in adversity. I know now what to think of it and can defy the public. My Play has had the fate it deserved and which I had foreseen; but, except for the trouble it has caused me, I have come out of the performance [*représentation*] a good deal more satisfied with myself, and with more just cause, than if it had been a success.[6]

Satisfied with this self-knowledge, Rousseau advises his detractors to think twice before accusing him of inconsequential conduct again, and promises to burn all he has ever written should they find anything at all they could justly reproach him with. Innocent till proven otherwise, he will continue to write books, verse, and music, even as he will repeat the low opinion he has of letters and those who cultivate them. The last word will be spoken beyond the grave:

> It is true that one day it could be said: So sworn an enemy of the sciences and the arts nonetheless produced and published Pieces for the Theatre; and this discourse will be, I admit, a very bitter satire, not of me but of my century.[7]

On this epitaph for the spirit of the age, the curtain goes up.

The Ontological Priority of the Circle

For if the narrow circle of the lamp was once equal to the vast circumference of an appetite which only the universe can satisfy, the immensity of this universe is now reduced to the periphery of a memory that can no longer dilate itself.
— Georges Poulet, *Les métamorphoses du cercle*

Almost a century and a half after this performance, Mallarmé repeated Rousseau's strategical question: 'à savoir s'il y a lieu d'écrire'—'whether it is necessary for the act of writing to take place' ('CC' 7). Half a century later still, de Man rehearses the question as an index of the 'profound skepticism' ('DA' 150) riddling 'symbolist literature' in 'the postromantic tradition' (149) even as it makes 'the extraordinary claim that poetry is man's only way of salvation out of an inner division that threatens his very being' (150). A decade later, de Man retranslates the question once more into the constitutive performance of crisis, rephrasing Rousseau's answer in the form of writing consciousness:

> As part of a culture, of a corrupt civilization, art is used only for reasons of deceit or, at the very best, to soften the harshness of the utter estrangement that self-love has created between all men. No writer can write with a good conscience in this situation, and Rousseau is hard put to give any reason why he should write at all. . . . The only reason for writing is to put oneself to the test in the solitude of one's own consciousness: 'It is only in observing myself [in the act of writing—PdM] that I can judge if I can count myself among the small group. . . . I needed this test to bring the knowledge of my own self to completion.' Clearly, there is a great deal of apparent conceit in

this very assertion, but next to a genuine insight into the disinterested character of the work of art—for Rousseau clearly recognizes that the authenticity of an aesthetic consciousness is defined by the ability of the self *not* to use the product of its aesthetic activity for its own gratification. ('RTS' 42)

With a five-word graft, Rousseau's triumphant vindication of the historical-strategical necessity of his literary production as a socially beneficial simulacrum of virtue is transfigured into a concern for the self engaged in the critical act of writing. The intent of this act is self-transcendence toward nothingness, and its fulfilment is the Romantic *Vollendung* of crisis in the form of language: 'The transcendence of the self occurred for them [Rousseau, Wordsworth, Hölderlin], much more consistently than for us, in their exclusive concern with *poetic* language, the medium in which the transcendence fulfilled and preserved itself' ('PT' 51). Our departure from this consistent commitment is the result of our tendency to 'reify form into an object, a thing that can be described independently of its intentional structure,' which has made us forget 'the difficult problem of form as a consciousness, as a constitutive project that exists temporally . . . that is not empirical . . . that is directed toward being instead of being directed toward particular entities' (52). This oblivion is our crisis, its soteriological *Vollendung* is the performance of 'authentic interpretation' ('MB' 65), an act 'primarily and exclusively' concerned with 'the truth of [the] language . . . in which the aesthetic self is constituted' ('PT' 53), independent of 'the observation of things' and of 'the analysis of individual subjects' ('MB' 65), intent only on 'the ontological priority of the work' (64) as a 'totality . . . rigorously included within the hermeneutic circularity that . . . connects its beginning with its end and constitutes its form' ('PT' 71).

The interpretive task must therefore locate its source in the source of the work, which 'is not to be sought outside, whether in [the poet's] empirical experience or, as in Heidegger, in an experience of being that would precede the language of the text':

The source of the poem is exactly [its beginning], its *telos* is [its ending], its form the temporal process that brings both together in an act of interpretive reading which is an extension of the interpretive act that takes place in the poem itself. At no time do we have to leave the realm of language that constitutes the poem in order to understand it (71).[8]

As Blanchot (one of de Man's acknowledged elective sources at the time) declares, this act of interpretive reading is an exercise in adding nothing:

> Reading does nothing, adds nothing; it lets be what is; it is freedom, not the freedom that gives or grasps being, but the freedom that welcomes, consents, says yes, cannot but say yes, and, in the space opened up by this yes, allows the overwhelming decision of the work to affirm itself, the affirmation that it is—and nothing more.[9]

To which de Man adds that to add nothing 'marks a positive intervention': 'this "nothing" that reading should not add is the very definition of authentic language' ('MB' 64; O.V., 549)—the only language that can properly articulate form and intent by virtue of its genuine 'ontological orientation' ('PT' 72). The origin of its 'principle of totalization' is 'the discontinuous structure of being itself' (72), the '*unfailing* law that governs the natural, personal and historical existence of man' ('THW' 94), named 'dissolution' in the form of 'the authentic temporal consciousness of the self' at the far side of the 'misleading myth' of 'progressive temporality' ('MB' 73). Such is de Man's reading of Rousseau's recollected 'sentiment de l'existence': a state in which time is truly nothing for the soul, *un rien*.

What remains when nothing has been added is the work in its true temporal structure: the circle. *Un coup de dés jamais n'abolira le hasard* (not even if the dice were cast in eternal circumstances)— such is for de Man the profound statement on the negativity of

Being and the indetermination of thought in the 'mature' (that is, critically post-Romantic) Mallarmé as he has 'finally moved beyond the dialectic of object and subject by penetrating into the field of the authentic action of being' ('MB' 74; o.v., 557). The insight gained through this penetration is that authentic consciousness cannot interfere with the 'historical temporality' ordained in the inexorable 'jamais': the indetermination inflicted by the ineluctable contingency of existence cannot be transcended in actual history. The true activity of consciousness therefore consists in the creation of immense *'appositions'* to historical temporality in the mode of fiction—'comme si...' These appositions—in the English version of this essay de Man specifies them as 'grammatical'—are intended not to determine the concrete historical destiny of consciousness but to determine the impossibility of doing just that, by 'mediating the experience of destruction through the intercession of a language that names it with precision' (75; o.v., 558), that is: 'not as an actual experience . . . but as the generalized statement of the truth of this experience' ('THW' 94). And the outcome of this exercise in fictional veridiction is necessarily the nothing it set out to address: 'le "rien" de l'abolition accomplie et inconnaissable' ('MB' 75; o.v., 558).

And yet: 'This knowledge of the circular structure of fictional language,' this knowledge of nothing, can lay claim to a positive 'temporal destiny' (75). For the circular structure effected in fiction is what 'philosophy' has long recognized as 'the circularity of consciousness that characterizes every entity capable of putting its own being in question' (75; o.v. 558), and although such questioning spells the end of reassuring illusions, its experience as 'time itself acting in its authentic being' opens up 'a certain form of becoming.' The moment Blanchot's authentic interpretive language uncovers the becoming of the circle, he joins 'a philosophical trend which tries to rethink the notion of becoming by starting from a hermeneutic structure of consciousness, by reflecting on the historicity of understanding' (76; o.v., 558–59).

The 'principal impulse' for this thought 'in our century' is Heidegger, but even as he recognizes this source, Blanchot refuses to follow the ulterior course of Heidegger's thought.[10] Closer to *Sein und Zeit* than to *Erläuterungen zu Hölderlins Dichtung*, Blanchot 'does not believe that the literary act [*démarche*] could ever coincide with that of being, not even that, in its most profound intention, it tends towards this identification' (76; o.v., 559). Instead, the circularity of literary becoming is 'an undertaking [*démarche*] that maintains and measures our distance in relation to being,' and its ever-renewed constitution 'serves as a verification for the authenticity of our undertaking [*démarche*]. The "becoming of the circle" is this hesitant search [*tâtonnement*] towards circularity which gives form to poetic language.'[11] The circle is not itself Being, but rather traces 'the authentic relation of consciousness to being': it is the form of the poetic self engaged in the total self-'purification' in which it discards 'all the pseudo-structures derived from everyday reality, intersubjectivity, reification, and an excessive subjective valorization of nature and sensation' (78; o.v., 560). In this light, criticism reveals 'how poetical language always traces the curve of this movement' of 'dissolution [*chute*] and forgetting,' and thereby figures as 'a kind of demythification on the ontological level, by which we learn to conceive being as it is, in all its evanescent negativity' (76; o.v., 559).

But in order to avoid a total loss of the self in a coincidence with Being—in order to escape the attraction of Heidegger—the form of the authentic self must never assume a final shape. The only question is whether hermeneutic understanding can succeed in thus falling away from the power of its 'principal impulse,' for the principle through which this understanding is constituted, the principle of circularity known to philosophy as 'the circularity of consciousness that characterizes every entity capable of putting its own being into question' (75; o.v., 558), is itself nothing other than the principle of the priority of *Dasein*[12] always already under way to its construal as achieved superiority.[13] The question, in other words, and again, is whether hermeneutic understanding can avoid speaking the last word of crisis by assuming the valorization of its circular structure as the coincidence of authenticity and the truth of Being in the unfailing fulfillment of intentional form under the touch of totally determined time.[14]

Intimation of Totality

One can as little wish away the innovative and subversive impact of these essays by attributing it to oedipal struggles as to academic provincialism.
— Paul de Man, Introduction to *Studies in Romanticism*

The critical traveler bringing America intelligence of the 'cannibalistic patricidal' 'dogfight' raging among Parisian intellectuals also informed these latter of the instructive errors of their American counterparts ('CC' o.v., 40). We know what is wrong with structuralism: it stares itself blind to the truth of literature by hiding its form under the sciences of man. Yet the 'structuralist experiment' at least has 'the winning characteristics of grandiose error' (o.v. 56–57)—on the other side of the Atlantic, where 'formalist and narrowly historical methods of literary study' still prevail, the dominant mood is one of 'boredom,' be it tinged with a certain 'restlessness' in response to the awareness 'that something essential is being avoided' (o.v., 57).

The problem with 'American formalism' as presented by de Man in 'New criticism et nouvelle critique' (later revised as 'Form and Intent in the American New Criticism')[15] is that it dutifully stares itself blind on form but fails to understand what it might be about. That is: American formalism conceives of literary form as if it were an entity whose 'full meaning' equals 'the totality of [its] sensory appearances' ('FI' 23), thereby 'postulat[ing], in fact, that the language of literature is of the same order, ontologically speaking, as a natural object' (24). What is thus inevitably suppressed is 'the intentional factor.' More precisely: American formalism's explicit rejection of the 'intentional fallacy' derives from a 'radical misunderstanding of intentionality' (25; o.v. 31) as a mere matter of transferring psychical contents from the mind of the poet to that of the reader. It is the intention of formalism to protect the verbal icon from the interference of psychological or historical notions of causality so as to 'safeguard the autonomy and the unity of poetic consciousness,' but because it mistakenly conceives of intentionality as a notion involving causal determinism, it erroneously hypostatizes the poem as an object. The truth of the matter being that, for de Man, 'far from menacing the autonomy and the unity of the poetic entity, it is in fact intentionality that establishes this unity' (25; o.v. 32).

Yet American formalism has its heart in the right place—that is, in literary form, and for this it deserves full recognition. Its 'ontological presuppositions' may be 'questionable' ('FI' o.v., 31),[16] but the technical expertise and the sense of formal context it deploys 'allow for considerable refinement in catching the details and nuances of literary expression' (27): the insistent refusal to 'isolate the constitutive parts from the whole' enriches this criticism with 'an exceptional sense of structural unity' (o.v., 33). Such praising and blaming evidently courts contradiction, and de Man spells it out:

> On the one hand we blame American criticism for considering literary texts as if they were natural objects but, on the other hand, we praise it for possessing a sense of formal unity that belongs precisely to a living and natural organism. Is not this sense of the unity of form being supported by the large metaphor of the analogy between language and a living organism, a metaphor that lies at the basis of so many aspects of thought and poetry since romanticism? . . . The introduction of the principle of intentionality that runs counter to this organic analogism would therefore risk destroying the sense of form which the New Critics have every reason to jealously conserve. (27–28; o.v. 33)

Except, of course, if the true sense of formal unity is essentially different from any 'continuity affiliated to the one that establishes the coherence of the natural world' (28; o.v. 33).[17] As is the case. But in the course of rehearsing this *a priori,* de Man touches a point that might make another difference altogether.

What New Critical practice brings to light, despite its misguided 'theoretical assumptions,' is 'a plurality of significations that can be radically opposed to each other,' a revelation that 'takes us into a discontinuous world of irony and ambiguity':

> Try as it may to reduce these discontinuities to simple ornamental particularities of baroque or symbolist rhetoric, [New Criticism] ends up, almost in spite of itself, pushing its interpretative act so far that the analogy between the organic world and language finally explodes. This unitarian criticism finally becomes a criticism of ambiguity, an ironic reflection on the absence of the unity it had postulated.[18] (33; o.v., 28)

Having read what de Man had not yet written when he wrote this, it is hard not to welcome this introduction of ironic fragmentation as a first figure of actual reading. Yet, no sooner has the text hinted at irony's disruptive potential than—just like the formalism that stands in need of demystification—it turns to a strategy intended to contain its effects. It is imperative that we carefully follow this strategy, especially since the temptation to abandon it in favor of a celebration of the final arrival of a different reading under the sign of irony is itself wholly determined by the eminently classical gesture of understanding organizing the disciplinary strategy de Man himself turns to.

What, then, is the nature of the 'exceptional sense of structural unity' New Criticism is credited with, even while its reading has been forced to abandon analogy in the face of irony? The answer is (pre-)determined:

> It appears that this unity, which is in fact a semi-circularity, resides not in the poetic entity as an object but derives from the

act of interpreting this entity. The circle we find here and which one could call 'form' does not stem from the poetic entity's supposed belonging to the order of natural things, but from the fact that it constitutes the hermeneutic circle. (29; o.v., 34)

Taking recourse to Heidegger's development of the 'ontological signification' of this circle, de Man then rehearses its formal unity as an intricate interplay between two central principles: foreknowledge and totality.[19] Before we question this dialectic, we must briefly indicate the eccentricity of this return to the source.

'Any interpretation [*Auslegung*] which is to contribute understanding [*Verständniss*], must already have understood what is to be interpreted':[20] such is the principle of foreknowledge or *Vorhabe*.[21] The task of the *Auslegung*, then, as de Man sees it, is to explicitate this foreknowledge, to render it accessible to the discursive reason of intentional understanding, wholly distinct from the natural reason of the physical sciences, which never tries to understand but only ever measures. 'In the act of understanding, we do not add a new network of relations to an existing reality, but we make relations that were already present appear in broad daylight [*au grand jour*], not only in themselves (like the [f]acts [*faits*] of nature) but also *for us*' (29; o.v. 34). As Heidegger puts it, 'In interpretation understanding does not become something different. It becomes itself. . . . Nor is interpretation the acquiring of information about what is understood; it is rather the working-out of possibilities projected in understanding.'[22]

Yet—and this is the eccentricity of de Man's turn—Heidegger is not speaking of literary criticism—or, for that matter, of speaking (or writing) in any form—here. The notion of *Auslegung* as it is developed in *Sein und Zeit* cannot be unproblematically (and arguably even not at all) construed as a linguistic operation, an elaboration of the projected possibilities of understanding in linguistic form, and de Man consequently has to transfer the principle of *Dasein*'s *Ausbildung* of its *Verstehen* in its *Auslegung* to the realm of the interpretation of texts (linguistic *Gebilde*).[23] This transfer is swiftly established in an (unacknowledged) analogy between the *Auslegung* of *Verstehen* and literary criticism: the literary critic's task is to allow the foreknowledge of the literary text (and this 'of' will turn out to be the crux) to shine forth in all possible explicitness, 'à la pleine lumière,' allowing the text to come forward in its own 'initial richness, given from the start' (34; o.v. 30). Ideally, the critical commentary should render itself superfluous, adding nothing to the text, decisively effacing itself in the face of its object. However, de Man adds, 'it goes without saying that this ideal critical text can never exist as such': if it did, the very notion of foreknowledge would be annihilated and 'the temporal nature of the hermeneutic process' would be violated. As is the case in Heidegger's *Erläuterungen*, which claim to be written 'from the perspective of the ideal commentator' and thereby illegitimately catch up with 'the implicit foreknowledge that is always temporally ahead of the explicit knowledge that exerts itself to join it' (30–31; o.v., 34; see also 'PT' 70–71).

The problem with this explicit distancing from Heidegger's hermeneutic self-satisfaction is whether the eternal belatedness of interpretation proclaimed in this distance can at all be reconciled with the notion of the specifically literary unity accessible to 'good' reading (or, more accurately, understanding), which de Man seeks to preserve. The answer to this problem is 'the notion of circularity, or totality':

> There can be no true understanding unless it be total, that is, capable of re-establishing a conscious contact with this foreknowledge it could never equal. The fact that poetic language, contrary to everyday language, is an entirely *formed* language indicates that it tends towards this totality. In interpreting poetic language, and particularly in revealing the 'form' of the language, the critic is therefore dealing with a privileged language: a language engaged in its highest intention, since it aims at the plenitude of self-understanding. It follows from this that the critical interpretation is oriented towards a subject (the author)

which is itself engaged in an act of total interpretation. Literature is the foreknowledge of criticism. Far from modifying or deforming it, criticism can only reveal literature for what it is. ('FI' 31; o.v. 34–35)

But criticism can never claim this revelation as an accomplished structure: the process of revelation is irremediably temporal. Since the 'total form' of the literary work whose essence the interpretation sets out to reveal is itself also only ever 'a process under way to its totalization,' never 'a concrete property of the work that would coincide with a sensory or signifying dimension of its language,' the 'act of understanding' is destined to remain suspended in a temporal predicament eternally foreclosing its own totalization.

This, then, is the unity the New Critics 'intuited' but mistakenly conceived of as analogous to an organic unity: only the true hermeneutic act can account for ironies and ambiguities as tokens of a genuine and authentic totalizing intent that is genuine and authentic precisely because it never attains its own totality. Yet de Man is not satisfied. Even though he has just answered the question he set out from, the problem remains: 'The problem remains therefore to define a mode of totalization that applies to literary language and that makes it possible to grasp what is distinctive about it' (32; o.v. 35). In relation to the preceding definition of the dialectics of literary form, this 'therefore' marks a curious disruption: for if this preceding definition is adequate—and it is presented as such—the required 'mode of totalization' has already been defined, and the 'therefore' projecting the task to arrive at this definition should therefore be canceled.

Yet, de Man is right: the definition definitely jars. To the extent that the dialectics of literary form are absolutely understood as the process of total interpretation, the distinctive insistence of literature is abandoned to a preconceived totalization that precisely misses the resistance of literature as an event that has nothing—and least of all the totality of time as the medium of genuine understanding—to be suspended in. The hermeneutic determination of literature as spatially and temporally suspended in the total circle erases the occurrence of literature as what is there to be read.

Yet what, exactly, is what is there to be read? Perhaps the mode of totalization in which it is erased can help us to repeat this question.

A first and obvious moment for reflection here is the unargued transfer of Heidegger's ontology of circular *Auslegung* to the discipline of literary interpretation, or even to the realm of everyday language interpretation. De Man assumes implicitly that what Heidegger writes about everyday *Dasein*'s *Verstehen* of tables, doors, carriages, bridges, and houses also holds for the interpretation of (literary) language, but fails to argue this swerve.[24] To say that 'all language, be it everyday language or poetic language, is to a certain extent involved in an interpretive act' (31; o.v. 34) is enough of a truism to pass muster, unless one reads it—as does de Man—as a truth on the strength of which the coincidence of Heideggerian *Auslegung* and the interpretation of (literary) language can be established.[25]

In fact, de Man himself suggests a crucial difference between ready-to-hand intentional objects such as chairs and tables and the particular intentional object that is the literary text in this respect (though he does not acknowledge this difference as difference but rather frames it into his argument as if it did not exist) when he contends that literature is itself the *Vorhabe* of criticism. For in Heidegger's analysis, a chair is not the *Vorhabe* of *Dasein*'s *Auslegung* of its understanding of the chair 'as' chair: to all reasonably relevant intents and purposes, a chair is not an interpretive act. A literary text—or any linguistic construct—may itself be the expression (the *Aussage*) of the *Auslegung* of the *Vorhabe Dasein* has of, say, a chair, or, less modestly, of Being (as when de Man suggests that the literary work is 'interpretive in relation to being' ['MB' o.v., 549]), but this also entails that an interpretation of that text or construct should be guided by the *Vorhabe* of an *Aussage* of a *Vorhabe*. What it should properly focus on is the language itself ('as' language), and the moment this is recognized any analogical shortcut must be suspended. For it is by no means evident that to try to explicitate an understanding of a text 'as' text would be commensurate with an explicitation of an understanding of a chair 'as' chair. To put it differently: de Man's dialectic as it is here sketched proposes to read the text (the 'form') as *Vorhabe* rather than as text—reading is presented as an attempt to catch up with the *Vorhabe* of a *Vorhabe* rather than as an elaboration of the *Vorhabe* of something that does not itself perform an interpretive act (this latter elaboration being the model for Heidegger's analysis).

The point is that if we are to come to some understanding of a text 'as' text, we cannot afford to assume that the best way to go about this is by conceiving of this text as primarily the predicative expression of an understanding rendered expressible precisely by the *Vorhabe* of the agent of expression (the author). The halfthought this leads us to is that if literature is the 'foreknowledge' of criticism, this need not signify that the interpretation of literature is of the same order as the Heideggerian *Auslegung*, but instead could be a corollary of the trivial but crucial fact that the interpretation of a linguistic construct is of necessity a primarily linguistic operation. If literature is a prefiguration of criticism, it is not impossible that this is less the result of a postulated foreknowledge than of processes of, precisely, figuration. In which case it would be better to actually try to investigate the operations of figuration than to accept the prefigurative structure they are thought to develop as an ontological necessity and, therefore, a moment of authenticity.

The inevitable further point would then be that the 'necessary presence of a totalizing principle in any critical undertaking [*démarche*]' (32; o.v., 35) should itself also become an object of reflection for, rather than an *a priori* legitimation of, interpretation. This is emphatically not to suggest that a totalizing principle can be simply dispensed with in the performance of interpretive acts;

rather, it means that we should allow for the possibility that such totalization is itself an effect of processes of figuration that remain unthought in any interpretation that starts out from the assumption that totalization is a necessary and intelligible prerequisite for a critical encounter with text—an interpretation, in short, that insufficiently problematizes the relation between its performance and the cognitive legitimation of that performance. That is to say: although a totalizing principle may be indispensable for understanding, the understanding of understanding should engage in a reflection on the possibility that in order to critically pursue (if not fulfill) its intent (the understanding of understanding) it must bracket the necessity for totalization (deferred or not)—and must conceive of it, too, as a product of figurations that should themselves be considered as such, in their constitutive linguisticity.

In this connection, it may be instructive to briefly turn to another text by de Man, roughly dating from the same period, in which a further friction between a certain totalization and the workings of irony is (ef)faced.

In a short reflection on Georg Lukács's *Theorie des Romans* (*The Theory of the Novel*) written for a 1966 conference at Yale, de Man sets out to reveal a certain discrepancy between the author's insight into the disruptive power of irony and his overall presentation of the history of the novel. In de Man's view, it is Lukács's singular merit to have conceived of irony as 'a structural category' whose operations must necessarily divorce the novel from any 'preconceived notions' about its being an 'imitation of reality':

> Irony steadily undermines this claim at imitation and substitutes for it a conscious, interpreted awareness of the distance that separates an actual experience from the understanding of this experience. The ironic language of the novel mediates between experience and desire, and unites ideal and real within the complex paradox of the form. This form can have nothing

in common with the homogeneous, organic form of nature; it is founded on an act of consciousness, not on the imitation of a natural object. ('GL' 56)

In developing this notion, de Man argues, Lukács comes very close 'to reaching a point from which a genuine hermeneutics of the novel could start' (57). Yet, *The Theory of the Novel* sadly fails to live up to this promise and proceeds to introduce a concept of linear temporality that runs counter to the effects of irony and ends up by wholly containing them: 'The organicism which Lukács had eliminated from the novel when he made irony its guiding structural principle, has reentered the picture in the guise of time' (58)—in the guise, in fact, of the 'reified idea of temporality' (59) that also informs the very structure of the *Theory* as the narrative of 'the Novel itself. . . tell[ing] us the history of its own development, very much as, in Hegel's *Phenomenology*, it is the Spirit who narrates its own voyage' (53).[26] Put differently, what Lukács's analysis fails to live up to is its own concession of the 'crucial difference' between the 'unchallengeable authority' of, precisely, Hegel's Spirit and the contingent, irony-ridden consciousness of the novel.

We are not concerned here with the adequacy of this critique insofar as Lukács's thought is concerned[27]—what is important to our present purpose is de Man's persistent unwillingness to confront the disruptive power of the language of irony itself. As is the case in 'New criticism et nouvelle critique,' irony is identified as the mark of the noncoincidence of experience and understanding, and as such, it is played out against the organicist conception of history germane to naively mimetic theories of representation. Yet, at no stage is this disruptive potential considered in its own right (or lack of it). No sooner has its presence been acknowledged than it is recuperated as a principle whose power it is to 'unite . . . ideal and real within the complex paradox of the form' (56). The pattern of this recuperation repeats the harnessing of New Critical irony: everything happens as if the concession of irony's disturbance of organic totality immediately justifies its reintroduction as an agent of nonorganic totality, but the workings of irony supposed to bring this unification of reality and ideality about remain wholly uncharted.

Again, my objection to this recuperative pattern is not powered by an *a priori* rejection of the very idea of totality (that would be too dogmatic a reversal of the image, leaving its constitutive presuppositions intact): the point is merely that as long as a concerted reflection on the actual workings of the language of irony remains in abeyance, any promotion of this language to the level of totality and ontological authenticity is, at the very least, premature (which is not to say that in the actual event of such a reflection, this authenticity would be ripe for the picking). Before praising irony for its putative capacity to figure as 'the positive power of an absence' (56) on the basis of which a genuine hermeneutics of the novel, free from the fallacies of reductionist mimeticism, could start, it is necessary to think through the positing forces that supposedly enable irony to represent the totality of form in the mode of the absence of what mimeticism uncritically assumes to be represented.

At the end of 'New criticism et nouvelle critique,' de Man rehearses his central thesis on the totalizing intentional structure of the literary work by way of a critique of Serge Doubrovsky's misreading of Merleau-Ponty's phenomenology of perception as a matrix for literary creation and interpretation. Doubrovsky deserves credit for opposing 'structuralist objectivism' ('FI' o.v., 35), which effects a 'lethal reification' (o.v., 36) of consciousness much as American formalism is in danger of reducing the entirety of literature to 'a single "cosmic" thing' that is in fact 'a gigantic cadaver' (26; o.v. 32).[28] Yet, the problem with the perceptual model of harmonious integration Doubrovsky wishes to oppose to this reification is that it has no room for what really matters, that is, nothing:

> Far from fulfilling a plenitude [literature] originates in that empty space that separates intention from reality. The imagi-

nation takes its flight only after the void, the inauthenticity of the existential project has been revealed; literature begins where demystification ends, and criticism has no need to linger over this latter. Considerations of the 'real,' empirical or psychological existence of writers, to which Doubrovsky, following the example of Sartre, seems to invite us, are a waste of time for criticism. This regressive stage cannot interest criticism, since it can only reveal a nothingness which the writer, in general, knows as such. 'Such is the nothingness of human matters, Rousseau says, that apart from the being existing by itself, there is nothing of beauty other than what is not.'[29] (34–35; o.v., 36–37)

The linguistic name of this originary nothingness once again fails to make a difference:

> Baudelaire has never stopped designating this loss of the real that marks the beginning of poetry:
>
> > ... palais neufs, échafaudages, blocs,
> > Vieux faubourgs, tout pour moi devient allégorie

This ' "allegorical" dimension' is the mark of literary greatness and the 'true profundity of literature' that Walter Benjamin (Baudelaire's best critic, according to de Man) has rightly understood 'when he defined allegory as "a void that signifies precisely the non-being of what it represents" ' (35; o.v. 37).[30] Allegory is hereby identified as that dimension of literature that distorts the representational continuity posited by organicist mimetics, and in this its function is highly similar to that of irony. It consequently comes as no surprise (though it is a letdown) that immediately after this recognition, allegory, too, is made to participate in 'that negative totalization which American criticism had unwittingly discovered when it committed itself, without realizing what it was doing, to the temporal labyrinth of interpretation.' The originary nothingness from which literature takes its flight is the intentional corollary of totality—or, to explode the figure: the owl and the nightingale merge as mere allegories of the symbol, and the discontinuous

A Time of Total Form | 201

universe of irony is lifted up in the palingenesis of allegorical nothingness in the mode of truth. For here, too, the actual operations of this negative totalizing representation are exempted from (further) reading: allegory, like irony, is the name of the essence of the totality of literary consciousness and form, but the essence of this name is itself located in a realm of understanding whose linguistic modality is absentmindedly effaced in an afterthought that lingers on but is never properly faced. 'Tout pour moi devient allégorie'—the next line of 'Le Cygne' is familiar: 'Et mes chers souvenirs sont plus lourds que des rocs.'[31] What was 'read' in 'The Double Aspect of Symbolism' as a moment of maximum delusion ('DA' 151)[32] is now identified as the real depth of literary insight—but neither here nor there is the labor of reading leading up to these diametrically opposed interpretations followed through in a critical reflection on the possibility of its occurrence. A reflection we only miss because it has already taken a turn in our past—as trope.

CHAPTER SIX

Resurrexi

> After all, Christian ritual too was invented.
> – Paul de Man, 'Montaigne and Transcendence'
>
> One may think of the event as one will, either as an audacious, and at least partly successful, attempt to wrest the pomps of the devil to a spiritual service, or as an inevitable and ironical recoil of a barred human instinct within the hearts of its gaolers themselves. – E. K. Chambers, The Medieval Stage

In one of his last writings, the 1983 foreword to the second, augmented edition of *Blindness and Insight*, de Man identified in his own work a virtual structuring moment both forbidding and enabling a 'dramatize[d] . . . figurative and narrative interpretation'[1] of his thought in terms of chronological periods, both inviting and demystifying the critical fictions of 'academics driven to establish sharp cuts in what does not support partitioning.'[2]

With the deliberate emphasis on rhetorical terminology, ['The Rhetoric of Temporality'] augurs what seemed to me to be a change, not only in terminology and in tone but in substance. This terminology is still uncomfortably intertwined with the thematic vocabulary of consciousness and temporality that was current at the time, but it signals a turn that, at least for me, has proven to be productive.

> I am not given to retrospective self-examination and mercifully forget what I have written with the same alacrity I forget bad movies—although, as with bad movies, certain scenes or phrases return at times to embarrass and haunt me like a guilty conscience. When one imagines to have felt the exhilaration of renewal, one is certainly the last to know whether such a change actually took place or whether one is just restating, in a slightly different mode, earlier and unresolved obsessions.[3] ('FBI 1983' xii)

After de Man, a 'productive turn' can hardly avoid being read as a trope, whereby the production (of meaning) out of the turn is the operationalization of a tendency inscribed in, but ultimately irreconcilable with, the trope.[4] The trope here turns out to be a turn toward tropology, toward the exhilaration of renewal brought about by the hypothetically epochal 'deliberate emphasis on rhetorical terminology.' As such, it has come to figure as a privileged organizing moment in the reading of de Man's work—a reading that, in turn, has enabled many to articulate a similar trope in their own readings or to draw on its potential as a point of departure for their own critical attempts. In this sense, the turn admirably lives up to the promise inscribed in it (contingently, no doubt, but not therefore controvertibly) by the etymological tropologetics engendered by its translation as trope. For what is a trope?

Here is one (and '[t]here is nothing farfetched in such a reference' ['LM' 177]):

> Is not this as if a man should undertake to supply an account of a building, and be so intent upon what he had discovered of the foundation as to conclude his task without looking back at the superstructure? Here, as in other instances throughout [this] volume, the . . . Author's mind is enthralled by Etymology; he takes up the original word as his guide, his conductor, his escort, and too often does not perceive how soon he becomes its prisoner, without liberty to tread in any path but that to which it confines him.[5]

To identify de Man's momentous trope is, no doubt, to be enthralled by the archaeological trope of excavation, digging in the grounds for the old foundations, hoping these foundations will turn out to be broken fragments whose future promise can be guessed. It is also to be enthralled by etymology.[6] For what is a trope?

Troping is not only 'turning' in (and here: toward) Greek, the history of the trope also narrates its installation as an exemplary figure of interpretation, and it is this moment that calls for exploitation here. For what is a trope? It is, for instance, an interpolation of dramatic speech interrupting the progress of liturgical song in a staged interpretation of the scriptural text of the Resurrection: the birth of medieval drama out of the spirit of the letter—the narrative (the point need not even be driven home) of 'the exhilaration of renewal.' More accurately, this trope is an interpretation occurring within the frame of the interpretive ritual represented by the Mass itself: the trope is an interpretation within, or even of, an interpretation; an interpretation to (at least) the second power; a dramatization expanding the dramatization of a preexistent text.[7] As a dramatization of an occurrence recounted in a text dramatized in a ritual service, the trope is an attempt to render the text's purport (the occurrence it narrates) accessible (tangible, visible, audible, speakable), transmuting it into what is recognizable (and recognizably human). The trope anthropomorphizes the possibly unintelligible into the simulacrum of immediate comprehension.

As an interpretive gesture, this historical trope also in its turn engenders a narrative (or, rather, several narratives). It figures as an organizing moment in the narrative of the life and the afterlife of the protagonist of the interpreted text; it participates in the narrative of the reading of that life and that Resurrection (the history of Christianity read as the history of the interpretation of its founding texts); it stands at the origin of the development of medieval drama; and, as an 'object lesson in literary evolution,'[8] it constitutes a privileged point of departure for the reading (and constitution) of the narrative of that development by literary history.

To spell things out, no doubt imprudently: just as the liturgical trope is an interpretive moment generating (or figuring in) a (number of) narrative(s), so the turn or trope isolated in de Man's apophatic retrospective self-interpretation engenders the critical narrative of his career as a coherent development revolving around a moment of momentous renewal. More truly challenging: the trope isolated by de Man is itself a turn toward an articulation of the conditions of (epistemological and performative) possibility of, precisely, the turning of the trope under way to narrative. Only this awareness can partially redress the suspension of reading in the anxious interpretive rush powering the formalization of de Man's trope as a preface (if not a *praefatio*) to the work to come.

When the three Marys visited the grave they were greeted by angels. This is the founding trope:

> Quem quaeritis in sepulchro, [o] Christicolae?
>
> Iesum Nazarenum crucifixum, o caelicolae.
>
> non est hic, surrexit sicut praedixerat.
> ite, nuntiate quia surrexit de sepulchro.
>
> *Resurrexi*

Such is the founding dialogue,[9] structured by 'a gesture of dialectical imperialism that is an inevitable part of any hermeneutic system of question and answer' ('DD' 112). The angels do not ask what the three women are doing, or even who they are—they ask what they, *ex post facto* members of the Christian cult, are looking for. As such, the question postulates in its very performance the existence of the object of the quest it ascribes to the questioned: it casts the women as questing; it understands them as looking for something it simultaneously prefigures and constitutes. The question thus apostrophizes the three visitors in the most classical of tropes: it gives them an identity and a purpose open to understanding.

In this way, it also confers upon them the possibility of extending the intelligible: it invites them to apostrophize the questioners in return, it demands that they participate in the distribution and the exchange of meaning the question itself has instituted. And the Marys duly respond in one voice and in one name: their object is the crucified body of Jesus the Nazarene.[10] Yet this quest is in vain: they shall not find this body, it has risen from the grave as he had said it would. The here of the grave is empty. Yet their quest is not in vain, nor are their preaching and their faith: they shall not be found false witnesses. True meaning is deferred and speaks, in the first person, in the mode of perfection (or *Vollendung*): I have risen, *Resurrexi*.

The analogism projected in this trope can be hastily completed: *Quem quaeritis in sepulchro, o Christicolae?* : *Quid quaeritis in lectione, o criticuli?* We have come in search of empirical plenitude; effective commitment; referential meaning; recognizable life; the wealth of lived experience; objective reason; historical significance; identifiable, tangible, workable truth: we have come in search of the ontic. Yet our search is in vain: we shall not find this reconciliation; it has been suspended, as the text had said it would when it designated itself as existing in the mode of fiction. The here of the text is empty, a void. Yet our quest is not in vain: true meaning reaffirms itself in the total form of the absolutely ontological. It reads: 'Poetic language names this void with ever renewed understanding and . . . never tires of naming it again' ('CC' 18). It speaks: 'Tel est le néant des choses humaines qu'hors l'Etre existant par lui-même, il n'y a rien de beau que ce qui n'est pas.' It maintains, across numerous modifications and deviations of the hermeneutic dialectic riddling it to the core, that literature, no matter how menaced by emptiness and barrenness it must appear to us in our post-Romantic crisis, will always remain 'the depository of hopes of resurrection that no other activity of the spirit seems able to offer' ('IS' 17; O.V., 84), because it 'reveals degrees of authenticity that no other activity is able to reach' ('JPS' 122) and can thereby 'alleviate' the 'tragic isolation of postromantic literature' and thought, which will 'allow us, in turn, to recognize ourselves for what we are in our real precursors' ('AIB' 119).

Such is the hermeneutical imperative of post-Romantic ontologism:[11] go and testify that you will find nothing in reading. But such is also its imperious promise of a colored—be it bleak—future: you shall find nothing and this nothing is the authentic translation of the Beautiful Soul as a Barren Titan writing the truth of Being in the form of a circle intent on total time. What you shall find is the absence of the empirical self, 'the void, the inauthenticity of the existential project' ('FI' 34–35), but this absence marks the presence of the truly authentic ontological self. It signifies 'the authenticity of [y]our undertaking' ('MB' o.v., 559) and thus designates you as true witnesses of the splendid profundity of literature: this presence marked by absence is the true temporality of your mystified quest for meaning. It is, ultimately, the genuine object of this quest—as you knew all along, in the authenticity of your foreknowledge.

This 'restrictive, negative conclusion' ('PT' 69) for our post-Romantic present requires that we forsake 'the wealth of lived experience,' but the act of renunciation itself is immediately recuperated and stabilized into the truth of critical insight. The truth is the spot of time in which the totality projected by the conception of reading as a spiraling movement along the circumference of the hermeneutic circle comes into being as the indisputable 'ideal' center of that circle. The hermeneutics of renunciation develops itself as a rush forward toward the intelligibility of the meaning of nothingness constituted by the text: it embraces the hermeneutical imperative as a founded promise of negative knowledge. The claim to authenticity is exempt from all ulterior concerns, divested of whatever is liable to interfere with the harsh serenity of the absolutely ontological. But this serenity can only be taken for granted when the possibility of reading has been determined as a search for meaning whose deferral is only ever a comprehensible corollary of the nothingness already assumed as the reward for the courage of ontological *askesis*. Reading is merely the road of hermeneutics, and its end is the discovery of the emptiness proper to impassible, resurrected truth.

*

De Man's 1966–67 essays in the rhetoric of contemporary criticism fully participate in this resistance to reading, despite the face-value of his oft-quoted *a posteriori* legitimation of the metacritical approach, which centers on the observation that since critics 'deal more or less openly with the problem of reading . . . it is a little easier to read a critical text *as text*—i.e. with an awareness of the reading processes involved—than to read other literary works in this manner' ('FBI 1970' viii). The fracture in this justification is that if criticism is indeed the activity in which the complexities of reading are being faced, there seems to be no logical reason why critical texts would themselves be privileged places for an articulation of these complexities. And in fact, such articulation is precisely what does not take place in de Man's metacritical commentary on structuralism, formalism, and other aberrations: what does find its empty place instead is a model in which the literary text is read as *Vorhabe* of ontological, supratextual, and extralegible truth.

But perhaps we should read this pattern differently: perhaps the observation of a deeply ingrained nonreading at the core of (meta-)criticism is precisely the crucial point these essays should be allowed to make. That is to say: the reading of critical texts would be a reading of these texts *as texts* insofar as they allow us to register the complexities of reading even as they are evaded. These complexities, de Man argues, 'are so deeply embedded in the language [of literature in general] that it takes extensive interpretation to bring them to light' ('FBI 1970' viii)—and perhaps we should read this thesis not as the projection of an actual critical 'unearthing' of the complexities of reading but rather as an oblique reflection of the possibility that it is the very act of unearthing—

or understanding—that brings to light the genuine complexity of the impossibility for reading to be brought to light as the light of interpretive, hermeneutic, determinately negative cognition.

No text does not clamor for understanding, and to the extent that this hermeneutical imperative is rendered explicit in the reading processes constitutive of criticism, criticism can indeed pretend to be literature come into its own. As a result of this self-appropriation of literature in criticism, criticism can therefore also be read more easily as text, that is, with a foreknowledge of what a text is already understood to be (that is, a foreknowledge), with a preposited understanding of a text *en tant que texte,* or even, to point up the analogism underlying such reading, *comme texte.* Yet, and at the same time, insofar as literature is marked as language that is to be read, the fact that criticism shows a tendency to maximize the hermeneutic imperative at the expense of this task of reading effectively transforms such criticism into the most stubborn oblivion of the literary resistance to literature—to that in its text that has neither a proper place to come into as it comes into its own, nor a proper space to leave empty as it takes its true flight. But, and still at the same time, a conception of literature as language there to be read—be it in its unreadability—can, in turn, not be celebrated as criticism's final awareness of what it means to read a text 'as' text—say, as the province of reading (unreadability) rather than of hermeneutics, or of history, or of empirical or existential or ideological issues. For to pretend to read a text as text is still to remain implicated in the structure of hermeneutic knowledge dependent on a *Vorhabe*—the *Vorhabe,* in fact, of the text as a self-enclosed system of pure sign, unadulterated by the everyday exteriority of reference—be it the reference to the nothingness of human matters—which interferes with the preemptive mathematical model of absolutely readable unreadability, itself the hypostasis of the angels' question into the formal imperative of a pure *Noli me tangere: Tolle, lege.*[12] And because this interference does emphatically upset de Man's later thought, his 'rhetorical' turn, which begins to work on the stutter between hermeneutics and reading that is one figure for this interference, must figure here as a trope.

✳

Yet has the trope actually occurred? Is there 'a change not only in terminology and in tone but in substance,' or is de Man 'just restating, in a slightly different mode, earlier and unresolved obsessions' ('FBI 1983' xii)? Relapsing, perhaps, into former error under way to the work to come? Just like Saint-Preux when he revisits, in the company of Julie, 'the northern bank of the lake from which he had, in earlier days, written the letter that sealed their destiny' ('ROT' 200)—revisiting, that is, the intermediary station between his exile in the Valais, where he wrote the letter whose imagery 'determine[d]' Rousseau's 'fate' and 'mark[ed] it as being an essentially poetic destiny' ('IS' 15), and his return to Vevey on the opposite bank of Lake Leman—just like Saint-Preux, then, as he nearly fatally 'relapse[s] into former error' ('ROT' 201) when he rehearses the imagery of his mountain retreat in Meillerie. For if this imagery is now recognized—as previously it was not—in its 'sensuous intensity' (201), its sublation in a landscape that is 'not emblematic of error, but of the virtue associated with Julie' encounters resistance—our resistance—when that virtuous landscape turns out to be, precisely, the 'allegorical' representation of the '"beautiful soul"' (201). And if allegory thus appears to retain the authentic nothingness of the Beautiful Soul, is there not also an 'ultimate irony' in 'the survival of irony itself,' which 'rises again serenely . . . as the climax [of de Man's mature work] on the final page of *Allegories of Reading?*'[13]

> Irony is no longer a trope but the undoing of the deconstructive allegory of all tropological cognitions, the systematic undoing, in other words, of understanding. As such, far from closing off the tropological system, irony enforces the repetition of its aberration.[14] ('RC' 301)

Is this the true Titanic light burning through the veil of naive serenity as the symbol is disarticulated by irony and allegory ('ROT' 208, 214), a serene resurrection that, like the 'historical and aesthetic system of recuperation' monumentalized at the end of 'Shelley Disfigured,' 'repeats itself regardless of the exposure of its fallacy' ('SD' 122)? A prefiguration of the self-supporting ironical transcendence in which '[t]ropes are taken apart with such casual elegance that the exegeses can traverse the entire field of tropological reversals and displacements with a virtuosity that borders on parody' ('SR,' 498)?[15] Or can there be another history that interferes with this resurrectionary stutter, in a recognition of 'the necessity as well as the borderlines' of 'rhetorical deconstruction' (498) leading to the 'most interesting occurrence of all': 'the reemergence [of] the question of history and of ethics' (498–99) in the shape of 'new problems' no longer predicated on 'the genetic and monumental patterns that are commonly associated with Romanticism' (499)—an occurrence that 'it is exhilarating to capture.'

But how can this postrepetitive occurrence be said to take place? Perhaps by placing it as a premature thing of the past:

> It would be preposterous to try to state succinctly, in paraphrase, how this reemergence of history at the far side of rhetoric can be said to take place, as if one could save oneself the labor of reading.

As if I could invoke the labor of reading as an article of foreknowledge whose *Auslegung* would be the identity of the pastness of art and its existence as the beautiful sensible manifestation of the idea, an identity always disrupted by art's forgetful 'material[ ] inscri[ption]' of its 'ideal content' ('SS' 773–74). As if I could celebrate this disruption as the finally truly historical disfigurement of the tropological genesis of 'serenity' ('AT' 244; 'PMK' 139).[16] As if I could simply avoid appealing to a foreknowledge whose totality—the decisive 'occurrence' ('CJ' 21) of the *historical* modes of language power' ('AT' 262) that truly interfere with the total formalization of the Aesthetic Ideology in the mutual undoing of 'formal' and 'historical materialism'[17]—would spell a transcendental justification of the end of this history: reading from serenity to apathy.[18] As if I could allow the turn to be the sovereign trope of *désinvolture*.

And yet. If this prospective appeal to a conclusive coherence of genesis and revelation cannot simply be avoided, the least we must do is complicate this inevitable promise by reading the figure it imposes on de Man's further writing. If the trope is 'a change not only in terminology and in tone but in substance' ('FBI 1983' xii), we are compelled to expect the writing that follows it—roughly, *Allegories of Reading* and after—to turn away not only from 'the thematic vocabulary of consciousness and temporality' but also from the historical substance of Romanticism that determines de Man's concern with this 'thematic' apparatus in the 1960s. Reading the figure imposed by the promise of an ending, therefore, requires a sustained reflection on the afterlife of Romanticism in the wake of the trope.

One way to begin questioning this specter—the point of departure for the conclusion to this study—is by repeating de Man's thesis, in 1983, that '[e]xcept for a few passing allusions, *Allegories of Reading* is in no way a book about romanticism or its heritage' ('PRR' vii). The tension between the hesitant acknowledgment of 'passing allusions' and the determined insistence in the face of this acknowledgment that these allusions 'in no way' make *Allegories of Reading* a book concerned with Romanticism is already arresting in its own right, but its critical impact is further increased when this tension is recognized as a remarkable echo of these 'passing allusions' themselves. On any commonsensical reading, a book 'about romanticism or its heritage' partakes of the historiography of Romanticism, and the very notion of 'heritage' highlights the genetic pattern of history for which Romanticism is both a canonical case in point and a privileged source. However, if Romanticism, as de Man suggests in one of the first of the essays eventually collected in *Allegories of Reading*, far from being the origin and the end of the genetic canon, is fundamentally 'the movement that challenges the genetic principle which ultimately underlies all historical narrative' ('NG' 82), then his failure to live up to his retrospectively stated intent to make *Allegories of Reading*, precisely, 'a historical reflection on Romanticism' ('PAR' ix), would itself be a lasting allusion to his having succeeded in writing a 'book about romanticism and its heritage' after all. If '[t]he ultimate test or "proof" of the fact that Romanticism puts the genetic pattern of history in question would . . . be the impossibility of writing a history of Romanticism' ('NG' 82), then *Allegories of Reading* might well be that "proof" in passing that test, precisely in its constitutive inability to erase the massive impact of its passing allusions to what it nonetheless is not about.

In its tentative identifications of 'exemplary model[s]' with which 'to understand the aberrant interpretation of Romanticism that shapes the genealogy of our present-day historical consciousness' ('NG' 102), *Allegories of Reading* is emphatically marked by the 'earlier and unresolved obsession' the trope reproduces even as it exposes the Titanic light of Romanticism 'to the clarity of a new ironic light' ('NG' 102). 'Light covers light . . . and creates conditions of optical confusion that resemble nothing as much as the experience of trying to read [de Man's work], as its meaning glimmers, hovers, and wavers, but refuses to yield the clarity it keeps announcing' ('SD' 106). 'Nothing more obscure . . . than this clarity' ('MB' 547; O.V., 63). In the face of the temptation to translate this profoundest obscurity as itself the serene light of de Man's clarity—a clarity we do not have to fear because we have already blindly understood its power ('ROB' 106) as the very pulse of the machine—our task, perhaps, is to prevent de Man's historical concern with Romanticism from being forgotten in the cause of Reading. Even if the trope turns away from the predicament of the post-Romantic, its Titanic light must perhaps be allowed to exist in de Man's work, be it under the most tenuous of conditions ('SD' 111). What shines through this violent light is the resistance of de Man's history.

Notes

PREFACE

1. These pages occur in 'Image and Emblem,' the first part of the section on Yeats—the only portion of the dissertation available in print ('WBY' 145–238). In the published version of this section, the pages from 'IS' were deleted (the essay itself is also featured in the same volume), but the original can be roughly restored by inserting the relevant portion of 'IS' (from 'In a famous poem . . .' [2] to '. . . spiral of the dialectic.' [6]) before the paragraph beginning 'Yeats's early poetry . . .' in 'WBY' (151).
2. Letter to Harry Levin, 10 October 1951 (quoted in Waters 1989, lxiv–lxv n.4).
3. 'PN' o.v., 75. Richard Howard, the translator of the essay for the posthumous collection *Critical Writings*, distorts the reference by replacing it with the anachronistic bibliographic entry for the dissertation as it was eventually presented ('PN' 29 n.5).
4. Whatever happened to Stefan George? In his essays of the 1950s, de Man mentions him in passing only (see, e.g., 'DA' 153; 'IIE' 255; 'F' 89 n.22)—with one salient exception to which we shall turn later on. In the introduction to his dissertation, de Man still announces a more detailed study of George's work 'in its totality, as a dramatization of the problem of the image, carried to its most extreme consequences' ('PHDI' iv). It appears that portions of this study are preserved in manuscript form, but I have not been able to obtain copies. George's afterlife in de Man's writing of the 1960s will be briefly touched upon in the course of this book.
5. Such a change does occur, but this happens already in the early fifties, as I shall document later on.
6. A succinct account of the inevitable pitfalls of this undertaking—de

Man's translation as well as my paraphrase of its dynamic—can be found in Newmark 1988.

7. I paraphrase de Man's own understanding of Harold Bloom's project in *The Visionary Company*, though Bloom's 'a priori belief' is 'illustrated by far too wide a choice of texts' ('HB' 92).

8. The essays I have had the occasion to consult include three substantial pieces—'Taine and Baudelaire' (August 1953), 'Bachelard and Burke' (January 1954), and 'Yeats and the German Romantic Tradition' (June 1954)—and two shorter texts, both undated—'"Achill" by Friedrich Hölderlin' (a translation with commentary), and an untitled essay ('[Keats]') in which de Man attempts to distinguish symbolism from Romanticism by way of a comparative reading of Keats and Mallarmé. For good measure, I should add that, as Kevin Newmark tells me, there are several other papers from the same general period awaiting transcription; that the transcriptions I have used are in various stages of editing; and that there is no way to ascertain how complete the manuscripts themselves are. I cannot avoid running the risk of this contingency—which, incidentally, de Man has described in some detail in 'Dialogue and Dialogism' ('DD' 107–8) and, with different emphasis, in 'Shelley Disfigured' ('SD' 120–23).

CHAPTER ONE

1. Though de Man adds that 'a single and possible exception' to this absence of concrete examples could be found 'in certain poems of Hölderlin just prior to his madness' ('IS' o.v., 83)—the later, revised version of the essay drops this formal acknowledgment. See also 'YRT' 25.

2. Part 1, Letter 23 (Rousseau 1964, 77–78).

3. The point is evidently not that a true objective correlative should in fact be understood as coincident with the exterior object: to say that the objective correlative cannot be wholly independent of the exterior object is not to say that no relation other than coincidence obtains between them.

4. Rousseau 1964, 78.

5. In the 1970 (English) version of the essay, de Man does rehearse the absence of the acrid but leaves it untranslated and thereby subsumes it under the category of the sensuous: 'Rousseau stressed that there was nothing sensuous ("rien d'âcre et de sensuel") in Saint-Preux's moment of illumination' ('IS' 16). The effect is the same as in the original

French version: if *sensuous* summarizes both *âcre* and *sensuel*, it can only be neutrally read as 'relating to the senses.' I may point out here that throughout this book my translation for de Man's French *sensible*, understood as 'relating to the senses,' will be *sensible* rather than *sensuous*.
6. Rousseau 1964, 78.
7. Ibid., 79.
8. The characterization is Bernard Guyon's, from the notes to the *Pléiade* edition (Rousseau 1964, 1389). For an illuminating contrast between this celebration and Hegel's demystification of mountain virtue (particulary instructive in the light of de Man's later development of the political face of Rousseau's writing), see Legros 1991, 106–7.
9. The impression of nonreading is even stronger in the English version of the essay, where the long passage from Rousseau stands out untranslated as an ignored obstacle to the argument.
10. For some further suggestive reflections on this cut, see Terada 1993.
11. A programmatic statement of this poetics of the naive, the heroic, and the ideal can be read in the unfinished text known, after Beißner, as 'Über den Unterschied der Dichtarten' ('On the Difference of Poetic Modes') (in Hölderlin 1979, 343–72).
12. This term is often translated as 'idealist' or even 'idealistic' (see, e.g., Thomas Pfau's translation in Hölderlin 1988, 83), words that, however, are too tightly associated with the ideological term *idealism* and are better reserved to translate the German *idealistisch*. It is worthwhile bearing this in mind since what will concern us is precisely the ease (perhaps even the inevitability) with which *idealisch* slips into *idealistisch*.
13. De Waelhens 1971, 92.
14. It is in the middle of this turn that 'Hölderlin and the Romantic Tradition' breaks off.
15. As could already be noted in de Man's initial definition of the demigods, quoted above, which appears to allow only for objective, natural behavior and inner consciousness, not for action ('IR' 32).
16. This implies that the swerve of the Rhine, too, must be seen as a consequence of divine intervention—a point de Man makes in so many words in the final fragment of 'Hölderlin and the Romantic Tradition' ('HRT' 136). We shall turn to the implications of this complication later on.

17. It is clear that *pastoral* is used here (and in 'HRT' 130) in a different, more traditional sense than in de Man's earlier comments on Empson ('DF' 239), on which see de Graef 1993a, 140–41.
18. Rousseau 1959, 1040.
19. Hölderlin 1951, 145. De Man quotes the second sentence ('IR' 38) but omits the final line and the 'almost ironically coloured conditional clause' (Nägele 1985, 201)—we shall return to this.
20. It is a crucial index of the shift in de Man's thought that (Rousseau's) consciousness should now be credited with the one ability *(se fonder)* whose irremediable absence was the 'infinitely sorrowful' source of true pastoral before ('DF' 237).
21. It is important to mark the distinction between this temptation and that identified in, for instance, 'The Temptation of Permanence': whereas the earlier temptation was thought of as an attraction exerted by ontologically superior natural being, the present temptation consists precisely in the deceptively attractive gesture of conferring ontological priority upon natural being in the first place.
22. The critical note addressed to Heidegger is barely veiled (see also Haverkamp 1985, 247–48, and Rosiek 1992, 94), though its point can hardly be called clear. At the most obvious level, it rehearses de Man's earlier statement that being ('l'être' or 'le sacré'), having never been known to us, can consequently not be remembered, let alone forgotten. In a slightly more complicated sense, the point of the remark could be that although it marks a *rapprochement* to Heidegger in that natural being is no longer conceived of as ontologically superior to consciousness (de Man's questionable "equivalent" for *Dasein*), it at the same time preserves a trace of an unwillingness to conceive of consciousness as the privileged focal point of Being. The fact that this unwillingness is at odds with the overall purport of de Man's argument invites its being read as an involuntary but timely promise resisting this argument.
23. This qualification is of primary importance. I leave its implications undeveloped for the moment, but we may already notice the resonance of de Man's 'il faut' here with Hölderlin's 'Muß' in the lines from 'Der Rhein' quoted above and with the 'il faut' in de Man's earlier comments on Heidegger's reading of Hölderlin, where it signaled the demand ascribed to Heidegger that Being be said (by Hölderlin, his 'witness')—a demand subsequently shown to be in error ('HE' 235).
24. Rousseau 1959, 1045.
25. Though it is better than what Jan Rosiek makes of it (1989, 86–89; see

also 1992, 97–99). Rosiek's account of de Man's distortions of Heidegger from a naively Cartesian perspective is challenging but it is marred by his refusal to acknowledge de Man's repeated and explicit rejection of dualism as well as, be it said in passing, by his unqualified faith in Heidegger's having effectively abandoned the Cartesian paradigm (on which see Gasché 1986, 84). De Man's categorical rejection of dualism is, as I said, not good enough, but as an act in his argument, it at least ought to be read—particularly since, as I intend to show, it is a vital component in the historical determination of his thought.

26. An interesting symptom of the import of this question for the interpretation of de Man's work is the disagreement over the appropriateness of his equation of Hölderlin's 'earth' to Heidegger's *In-der-Welt-sein* ('IR' 40)—see Rosiek 1989, 88–89 and Gabriel 1989, 121–22.
27. Cf. Hegel 1988, 66; 1977, 55.
28. For the sake of clarity, I should point out that Timothy Bahti's English translation deletes the exclamation mark in this sentence.
29. Rousseau 1959, 1045.
30. Rousseau 1964, 78.
31. See Godzich 1986, xii.
32. The phrase (which, as we saw, was also quoted in 'Intentional Structure') is taken from §15 of the Fifth *Rêverie;* the passage on the fixed senses is §9. We shall return to this.
33. Rousseau does mention his boat, but this occurs in a later scene. The slip is probably a result of a short-circuit between the catachretic verb *berçoit* in §9 of the Fifth *Rêverie* and the image of a boat rocked by the lake quoted by de Man from the third version of Hölderlin's 'Mnemosyne,' which can be read as a gloss on the former text (cf 'IR' 23; 45).
34. Rousseau writes that for the ideal 'sentiment de l'existence' to arise, there must be a balanced 'disposition' in the subject of the experience and in the 'assistance of the surrounding objects': neither an 'absolute repose' nor an 'excess of agitation' but 'a uniform and moderate movement without shocks or intervals.' Too much movement 'awakens' the subject and, 'recalling us to the surrounding objects, destroys the charm of the reverie'; 'absolute silence,' on the other hand, 'leads to sadness' and 'offers an image of death.' It is in this latter case that a 'smiling [*riant*] imagination' is a necessary help: 'The movement that does not come from outside can then arise inside us.' He adds, 'This kind of reverie can be appreciated [*se goûter*] wherever one can be tran-

quil, and I have often thought that in the Bastille or even in a cachot where no object would reach my sight [*où nul objet n'eut frappé ma vue*], I would still have been able to dream [*rêver*] agreeably.' It is characteristic of Rousseau's trivial but admirable candor that he immediately qualifies this hypothesis by admitting that, nonetheless, such pleasant dreaming can be much more easily and agreeably performed in an appropriate location such as the Isle de Saint Pierre, where the subject of the reverie can accommodate 'all that really strikes his senses [*tout ce qui frappoit reellement ses sens*]' Rousseau 1959, 1047–48.

35. Wahl 1962, 66; also quoted in Rousseau 1959, 1800.

36. One such paradox can be sensed when we try to think what precisely is involved when exterior sound is said to substitute for inner movements that are themselves extinguished by the—presumably interior (this is the crux)—reverie. Admittedly, Rousseau's verb 'suppléer' can also mean 'compléter' rather than 'remplacer,' but the notion of 'extinguishing [*éteigner*]' it is paired to seems to favor the first option. If such favoring is at all appropriate: as Derrida's readings of Rousseau in *De la grammatologie* have argued, the logic of supplementarity cannot be exhausted in a decisive choice. As for the *ostranenie* of catachresis, it occurs not only in the striking fix of striking (*frapper*)—one of the more insistent words in the *Rêverie*—and fixing, but also in the concretization of a movement heard and seen as a force that rocks (*berçoit*) the perceiving subject (this latter figure, as we saw, is appropriately misconstrued by de Man). For an articulation of the analytics of sensation in Pater that is highly relevant for our discusssion here, see Loesberg 1991, 19.

CHAPTER TWO

1. De Man entertains the possibility of calling this union 'music,' but, in keeping with his nonsensory reading of Rousseau's water, abandons this notion on the grounds that 'we have an almost irresistible tendency to think of sound as sense perception and identify music with the sensuous Muse of harmony' ('IR' 40). One of the things I cannot do in this book is consider in more detail de Man's complicated perception of music. Such a study should at least involve the development of the present suggestion of an other-than-sensory reading of music (if not sound) in his commentary on the equation of music with language in Rousseau's *Essay on the Origin of Languages* ('ROB' 125–33) and his critique of 'the Dionysian truth of music as "Ding an sich"' in

Nietzsche's *Birth of Tragedy* ('NG' 97). See also Derrida 1985, 16; Norris 1988b; and Hart Nibbrig 1990.
2. This is the second, and I believe last, appearance of this term in de Man's writing. For a discussion of the first occurrence ('DF' 242), see de Graef 1993a, 149–52. I will consider the effect of this connection at a later stage in my argument.
3. Hyppolite 1946, 289–90; 1974, 299. On the *Ding an Sich* in this connection, see also Hegel 1988, 271. A doubly irreverent twist of one of Nietzsche's sneers at 'der grosse Chinese von Königsberg' (later ideologically renamed Kaliningrad, and as I am writing still awaiting its ideological unrenaming) is hard to suppress here: '[So werdet] das "Ding an sich"... auch eine sehr lächerliche Sache!' *Fröhliche Wissenschaft*, nr. 335 (Nietzsche 1980, vol. 3, 562).
4. I borrow my emphasis from a case, similar to the one I make here, in Redfield 1989, 41. See also Culler 1990, 268–70.
5. Norris 1988a, 23.
6. Ibid., 26. Norris's failure to appreciate this point—puzzling enough as he quotes from the very sentence that makes it—is doubly striking in light of the fact that it is precisely the avowed purpose of the entire essay to counter the 'enlightened but negative verdict on Rousseau' influentially formulated in Schiller's critique of the 'break pure and simple' between 'inwardness' and 'historical action' ('IR' 22; see also 'RTS' 31). De Man's definitive delimitation of this verdict can be read in the chapters on the *Second Discourse* and on *Julie* in *Allegories of Reading*.
7. Norris 1988a, 23.
8. Rosiek 1992, 104.
9. An instructive short circuit between this passage and de Man's later reading of Rousseau is engineered in Mizumura 1985, 93.
10. We shall always return to Montaigne later on.
11. Norris 1988a, 24.
12. Redfield 1989, 41.
13. This ahistorical use of the first person plural stands in need of correction—as I shall try to show, such a correction is arguably de Man's primary concern in his writings in the 1960s. For the moment, we can still use it with strategical naivety.
14. Rousseau 1959, 1047.
15. 'A Poet's Epitaph,' ll. 27–32 (Wordsworth 1989, 151).
16. Rousseau 1959, 1045.
17. Ibid., 1046.

18. Ibid.
19. Ibid., 1046–47. It is tempting to read the 'ruisseau murmurant' in this fragment as a slip toward 'Rousseau murmurant,' especially since, as the editor's notes to the passage point out, there is no such rivulet on the Isle de Saint Pierre. This might seem to confirm de Man's suggestion that Rousseau is not concerned with the perceptible environment of his inward murmuring, and instead wholly gives in to the interior movements of his 'sentiment.' However, this would miss the point that such a projection of a name (and particularly one's own) onto a natural entity is precisely the type of analogizing gesture de Man considers to have been radically left behind in the sublation of sensation he ascribes to Rousseau.
20. 'Forgetting' is the appropriate term here, for it cannot be said that Rousseau's text radically rejects the source previously praised. In fact, even 'forgetting' would be too strong if we read it as a conclusive erasure of prior traces—the mode of forgetting in the present text is more subtle and less decidable.
21. Rousseau 1959, 1046. Ian Balfour has rightly remarked that 'it is difficult to imagine a concept that de Man would find more mystified than that of the eternal present' and that one 'can look almost anywhere in de Man to find refutations of the possibility of an eternal present' (1989, 12), but it is necessary to add that the logic of this demystification is not simply one—as Balfour would no doubt admit.
22. Ibid., 1046–47. The circumscription of the 'difficult, unresolved realm of time' is not Rousseau's—though it would not have been out of place in the *Rêverie*—but de Man's. It is taken from his 1964 review of the 'spacecritics' J. Hillis Miller and Joseph Frank ('SC' 113), where it identifies the chastened awareness that has come to terms with 'the illusory character of spatial analogies' (114)—an awareness de Man further claims to have been voiced in an eminently 'radical and consistent manner' in Romanticism. Our point is that the *Rêverie* could indeed have contained this 'realm' but only as the name of the 'fugitive state' to be abandoned. To the extent that this is the case, Romanticism's renunciation of 'the will-toward-space,' which is also its separation from the 'illusion' of 'nature beyond time,' is never simply the readably radical and consistent revelation de Man requires.
23. The phrase 'poetically transfigured [*dichterisch verklärt*]' as applied to Hölderlin's Rousseau is Bernard Böschenstein's (quoted in Philipsen 1990, 178).

24. In his 1957 comparative commentary on Keats and Hölderlin, de Man also refers to this final letter to insist on the total transcendence achieved through 'the inward movement of a soul that, up till then, had conducted its search for unity in a world that lies outside of itself' ('KH' 48).
25. Hölderlin 1982b, 781.
26. Hölderlin 1982a, 47. For de Man's own earlier reading of this 'law of gradual growth,' see 'KH' 46.
27. Hölderlin 1982a, 47. Another version of this epitaph ('Non coerceri maximo, contineri minimo, divinum est' [Not to be coerced by the greatest, yet to be contained in the smallest, is divine]) figures as the epigraph to the first volume of the final version of *Hyperion*. For the original epitaph, see the editorial matter in Hölderlin 1969b, 176.
28. 'Rousseau,' stanzas 4 to 6 (Hölderlin 1951, 12). For a powerful reading of these lines, see Nägele 1985, 176–77.
29. Shelley 1963, 163.
30. We shall return in more detail to the hermeneutic circle in a later section—for the time being, I would just indicate that as witness the paragraph of *Sein und Zeit* de Man refers to, Heidegger is not without his defenses against the (naive but not therefore irrelevant) objection to the analogical status of his circle (see Heidegger 1977, 204).
31. In this connection, see Haverkamp 1985, 245.
32. 'Rousseau,' stanzas 8 through 10 (Hölderlin 1951, 13). The German version is taken from the Beißner-edition, which de Man probably also used. The more recent authoritative edition edited by Michael Knaup and D. E. Sattler offers an even more fragmented reconstruction of the text (Hölderlin 1984, 787). On these lines, see also Nägele 1985, 179–80.
33. The lines from 'Mnemosyne' (48–50) can be translated as follows: 'For the heavenly are / Unwilling, when one has not, protecting the soul, / Recollected himself, yet he must.'
34. An excellent account of the complicated anatomy of 'Divination' in Schleiermacher's hermeneutics is Hamacher 1979.
35. Such is at least de Man's profession of reading in his 1980 interview with Robert Moynihan ('INT 1980,' 586).
36. Hegel 1967, 30.
37. Ibid., 28–29.
38. Ibid., 132.
39. Hegel 1970, 141. On the argument from which this fragment is taken,

and which also involves the 'return to the self' central to our discussion, see Derrida 1972.

40. 'More before long': the final words of the last version of *Hyperion* (also quoted by de Man in 'KH' 48). The final letter we might almost have quoted in full is not final—not only in the sense that no letter is, but more pointedly, in the sense that its closing words have a specific afterlife of their own in the consciously abandoned project of a hypothetical 'eschatological "rounding of"' ['*Abrundung*']' (Philipsen 1994, 191). As we shall see, everything depends on whether this projected finish can come full circle.

CHAPTER THREE

1. Don Bialostosky correctly notes that 'Intentional Structure' 'entertains the possibility that the potentially explosive violence might be appeased or the hope that poetry could escape the dialectical opposition of mind and nature into a poetry of pure mind,' but his suggestion that this is 'the last place' in de Man's work in which such a projection figures is misleading at best (Bialostosky 1992, 157). Similarly, Tilottama Rajan's observation that the 'deferred restoration' of an 'affirmative reading' of Romanticism 'as project rather than fact' with which 'Intentional Structure' ends is a projection that 'will not be repeated' in de Man's work (Rajan 1985, 455) is valid only when read as indicating that in the later 'Image of Rousseau' this 'affirmative reading' is referred as fact into the future of the (Romantic) past—the deferral/referral itself figuring as the affirmation.

2. See also de Graef 1993a, 111–15.

3. Kojève 1985, 149.

4. De Man's comments on this poem can be found in 'HEW' 76–82; 'WWH' 141–43; and 'THW' 76–82. The three readings are almost identical, so I shall not cross-reference my commentary, which draws primarily on the first version. For a critical commentary on de Man's distortive reading here, see Servotte 1990 and Christensen 1990. Christensen recalls Thomas De Quincey's comments on 'There Was a Boy' and diagnoses the use made of the poem by 'De Man and de Manians' as an instance of their 'regressing from the full rhetoricity of De Quincey's example, which recapitulates Wordsworth's poetic language within a critical practice that effectively suspends, as de Man's does not, Wordsworthian correspondences' (442; see also 'SD' 123). In what follows

I shall try to show how in de Man's writing of the mid-1960s, the impossibility of a supposedly 'regressive' capitulation to 'the pleasures of identification with the Wordsworthian subject' (Christensen 1990, 443) figures precisely as the historical index of 'our' regression from Romantic insight, and how the simultaneous performance of this identification indicates a crisis of de Man's historical sense, which Christensen's argument, in taking recourse to the ahistorical shorthand reduction of 'De Man and de Manians,' fails to allow for.

5. On rereading I must note that placing de Man in 'the best philological tradition' is not quite defensible: contrary to what de Man writes, Wordsworth's disquisition on the poetics of 'hanging' figures not in the 'second' or '1815 Preface to the *Lyrical Ballads*' ('WWH' 52; 'HEW' 142)—there is no such text—but, as de Man does note elsewhere, in the 1815 Preface to *Poems* ('THW' 79). Similarly, the statement on the essential specular adaptation of mind and nature does not strictly speaking occur in the 'first' or '1800 Preface to the *Lyrical Ballads*' as de Man has it ('HEW' 141; 'WWH' 51–52) but, as the editors of *RCC* also note, in one of the paragraphs added by Wordsworth in 1802 ('THW' 200 n.4).

6. I quote de Man's quotation but shall return to Hölderlin's own text in the next section.

7. Though Ruskin would have to reject the ontology it espouses as a 'tiresome and absurd' specimen of 'German dulness' all too germane to 'English affectation': as he explicitly tells us, parts of the natural world—say, a waterfall—can only be allowed 'to hang listening' when perceived by weak characters as imagined by strong poets, these latter undeluded about the 'mystification, egotism, selfishness, shallowness, and impertinence' of philosophers believing 'that everything in the world depends upon [their] seeing or thinking of it' (Ruskin 1963, §§ 4, 1, 15).

8. Wordsworth 1974, 31.

9. Neither would this latter option be an adequate characterization of Fancy, as de Man seems to imply: rather, it would apply to the least prestigious faculty on Wordsworth's list of 'powers requisite for the production of poetry,' i.e. 'Observation and Description'—a faculty that itself, we may add, is invitingly complicated by Wordsworth's comparison of its process with that of translation (Wordsworth 1974, 26).

10. A minor inaccuracy in the edited version of de Man's essay locates this

passage in the opening pages of the final version of *Hyperion*, whereas in fact it occurs in the project for the 'Metrical Version' (Hölderlin 1982a, 106).
11. Hölderlin 1982a, 106.
12. Ibid. I emphasize the clause deleted by de Man.
13. Ibid., 106–7.
14. Ibid., 107.
15. 'It was the voice of the noblest of rivers, the free-born Rhine,' 'Der Rhein,' stanza 3 (Hölderlin 1951, 143).
16. 1805 *Prelude*, Book Five, 395–96 (Wordsworth 1959, 196).
17. The original German speaks of a correspondence between 'die Bewegung unseres Wünschens' and 'jener der Zeit.' Timothy Bahti renders 'der Zeit' as 'the age' ('WWH' 55), which, although undeniably more elegant than my own suggestion, disambiguates the original at the expense of the reading that is most pertinent to the argument.
18. Benjamin 1977b, 259.
19. The phrase, which de Man slightly modifies in the present essay, is taken from Hölderlin's 'Grund zum Empedokles' (Hölderlin 1969a, 570).
20. De Man's reading follows an interpretative tradition going back at least to Beißner by adding 'sterben' to 'er muß doch,' but he also acknowledges the apparently more obvious reading relating 'muß' to 'sich zusammengenommen.' On the further crux involved in reading 'dem gleich fehlet die Trauer,' see Haverkamp 1985.
21. The explanatory parentheses are inserted in Montaigne's text by Richard Howard, the English translator of de Man's essay. For the original, see Montaigne 1988, 119–20 (Book 1, no. 23). I may perhaps point out here that de Man erroneously identifies another passage from Montaigne he quotes earlier on as coming from the same essay (Book 1, no. 23) whereas in fact it is taken from the 'Apologie de Raimond Sebond' (Montaigne 1988, 579 [Book 2, no. 12]). Richard Howard copies the error ('MT' 8). In rereading de Man's use of Montaigne, I have benefited from Starobinski 1982 and Schaefer 1990.
22. On this policing of de Man's past into total meaning, see Derrida 1989, 152.
23. In *Serenity in Crisis* I have already offered some minimal commentary on de Man's formal invocation of Montaigne's revolt; here I wish to give this minimal form some virtual substance. In the process of forming this substance, I have come across Shoshana Felman's recent attempt

to establish another juxtaposition of de Man and Camus (Felman & Laub 1992, xviii–xix). Felman's reading is more ambitious than the one I try to sketch, but it has helped me to convince myself that some connection is there to be read.

24. Camus 1977, 423. It is worth noting that this double performance formally prefigures the 'simultaneous Yes and No' of Heidegger's *Gelasssenheit* in the face of technology (Heidegger 1959, 26)—the substance that complicates this important formal resemblance cannot be summarily sketched here, but from our perspective it must at least involve de Man's 1955 comments on history and technology ('TP' 30–31) and his 1958 comments on the course of the Rhine: 'If the movement toward Greece had continued, it would have grown from mere rebellion into pure *hubris*. It is violent and destructive, as the stream near its source is savage, undaunted. In its desperate desire to possess a nature which it can never reach, it tears and destroys (much as the technology of our day tears and destroys)' ('HRT' 135). See also de Graef 1993a, 174–78.
25. Camus 1977, 431.
26. Ibid., 437.
27. Ibid., 545.
28. Ibid., 550.
29. Ibid., 554.
30. Ibid., 647.
31. Ibid., 649.
32. Ibid., 420.
33. Ibid., 652.
34. Ibid., 707.
35. Ibid., 653. For some indications of possible affinities between Hölderlin and Camus, see Stucky 1980.
36. Some aspects of the genesis and context of this polemic are helpfully sketched in Quilliot's comments in the *Pléiade* edition (Camus 1977) and in Lottman 1981, 523–25; McCarthy 1982, 235–59; Chebel d'Appollonia 1991b, 149–53; and Felman & Laub 1992, 172–91. For punitive hindsight on and reactive nostalgia for the larger context of these matters, see Judt 1992.
37. Jeanson 1952a, 2086.
38. Camus 1977, 437.
39. Jeanson 1952a, 2077.
40. Ibid., 2086.

41. Ibid., 2088. I translate the entire quotation as given by Jeanson (itself taken from Hyppolite's 1941 translation of the *Phenomenology* [Hegel 1941, vol. 2, 189]) but have corrected the revealing misprint that has *infériorité* instead of *intériorite (Innern)*. For the original, see Hegel 1988, 432–33; 1977, 400.
42. Jeanson 1952a, 2072.
43. Sartre 1952, 338. Sartre makes his point in a rhetorical question: 'La République des Belles-Ames vous aurait-elle nommé son accusateur public?' The translation must needs miss the point that in present-day French the term for 'public prosecutor' is 'procureur (général)': 'accusateur public' was the name for this office during the French Revolution, and Sartre profits from its being tainted by the memories of the Revolutionary Tribunal during the Terror to score an ironic turn.
44. Ibid., 347.
45. Ibid., 353.
46. See Camus 1977, 213–43.
47. Sartre 1952, 347.
48. Ibid., 335.
49. Ibid., 347.
50. Jeanson 1952a, 2090.
51. Camus 1952, 328.
52. See Lottman 1981, 510; Chebel d'Appollonia 1991b, 154–55; and Judt 1992, 128, 136–41.
53. Camus 1952, 326.
54. Ibid., 328–29.
55. Ibid., 330–31.
56. Camus hints at this practice by invoking—in order to refute it—the objection Sartre and Jeanson could make to his denunciation of Stalinist terror: 'Nous balayons d'abord devant notre porte: le Malgache avant le Kirghize' (1952, 328). On the forced settlement of the Kirghiz and other non-Russian nationalities, see Simon 1991, 107.
57. 'On January 13, 1953, *Pravda* reported that a "terrorist group of doctors" had "been discovered" who had already murdered several Soviet leaders by giving them the wrong medical treatment and who planned further assassinations. Seven of the nine doctors named were Jewish. This so-called doctors' plot not only signalled an imminent new great wave of purges, but must also be seen as a preview of the mass deportation of Jews, which Soviet authorities had already planned concretely and in detail. Stalin's death saved the Jews from meeting the same fate

as Soviet Germans, Crimean Tatars, and the other deported peoples' (Simon 1991, 209). On the French perception of Soviet anti-Semitism at the time, see Judt 1992, 220–24.
58. In 'Le Yogi et le prolétaire' (first published in *Les temps modernes* and soon after reprinted as the final chapter of his disturbing 1947 'essay on the communist problem,' *Humanisme et terreur*), Maurice Merleau-Ponty castigates Arthur Koestler's account of his conversion away from communism as a suspicious about-face toward 'brand new beautiful sentiments' by appealing to Montaigne's critical comment on the 'singular harmony' between 'super-celestial opinions' and 'subterranean morals,' thereby condemning a 'secret affinity' between Koestler's 'ostentatious cult of values, of moral purity, of inward man' and 'violence, hatred and fanaticism' (Merleau-Ponty 1980, 284). If *Humanisme et terreur* is read as a justification, however circuitous, of the Stalinist purges, this reference to Montaigne can perhaps stand as a referent for de Man's allusion. I am not convinced myself: the point may stand only as a symptom of my rage for reference. For the original quotation from Montaigne (also quoted in Merleau-Ponty's 'Lecture de Montaigne' [1947, 1050] to which de Man does refer ['MT' 3, 11]), see Montaigne 1988, 1115 (Book 3, no 23). On Merleau-Ponty's attack on Koestler as a parallel to the conflict between Camus and Sartre eventually leading to their rupture in 1952, see McCarthy 1982, 218.
59. Camus 1952, 317.
60. Jeanson 1952b, 382.
61. Camus 1977, 585.
62. An experience similar to the one de Man effectively imagines for himself in his 6 June 1955 letter to Harry Levin. Commenting on the 'ceaseless mood of polemics and "prises de position"' among Parisian intellectuals, he writes: 'The main obsession remains, of course, political, but in a way, which, after the United States, seems rather childish. The long and painful soul-searching of those who, like myself, come from the left and from the happy days of the *Front populaire,* seems to have made less headway than in the States' (quoted in Waters 1989, lxv n.5). The letter goes on to specify this 'soul-searching' as taking the form of 'an embarrassed and apologetic criticism of orthodox Marxism, in terms of which everyone, including the communists themselves, would readily agree,' and names Merleau-Ponty, on the grounds of his 1955 *Les aventures de la dialectique,* 'in which he breaks at last openly and publicly with Sartre,' as the 'last case in point': 'So

Camus and Merleau-Ponty find themselves together as the last heretics of note.' Rewriting and relocating his limited leftist past in the Cercle du Libre Examen as an involvement in the Front populaire, and eliding his wartime involvements, de Man constructs an understanding of his own past (and that of his newly invented fellow Americans) that not merely repeats the itinerary of a Camus or a Merleau-Ponty but in fact gives him the ascendancy over—such is the implication—these slower minds. In 'Montaigne et la transcendance,' the pattern is far less crude, but it does leave its marks.

63. Derrida 1989, 152.
64. Montaigne 1988, 119–20 (Book 1, no. 23). Judt, in his succint imitation of the received comparison of both the Moscow trials (as 'justified' by Merleau-Ponty) and the French postwar purges with the 1793–94 Terror (for other versions of this comparison, see, e.g., Assouline 1990, 8, 131), offers a symptomatic variation on the form of Montaigne's concession when he argues that, in contradistinction to these twentieth-century reactions to 'treason,' 'l'intransigence d'un Saint-Just, les arguments d'un Robespierre, qui relevaient de la démocratie totalitaire, avaient le mérite de l'originalité' (1992, 91). The pattern is further complicated when superimposed on Judt's gratuitous epilogue, in which the sadly deluded followers of 'la seconde génération d'intellectuels parisiens de l'après-guerre' ('Lacan, Foucault, Derrida, Barthes, Lyotard, Bourdieu, Baudrillard et autres') in 'anglophone' universities are contrasted with the genuine 'intellectuels français' of days gone-by who, despite their lack of originality when compared to Saint-Just and Robespierre, still 'counted' (354). As I have no doubt Judt wishes he would too—and perhaps quoting him in French is a start.
65. Montaigne 1988, 117–18 (Book 1, no. 23). On the 'revolutionary thrust' of Montaigne's politics in this connection, see Schaefer 1990, 168.
66. We may recall here the wartime version of this analogy self-servingly used by Hendrik de Man in his *Cahiers de ma montagne* (1944, 21–22). See de Graef 1993a, 37.
67. Of particular interest to the present constellation is Camus's change of mind in this respect, moving from a direct call for 'terrible' justice to avenge 'the destruction of the soul' ('Le temps du mépris,' *Combat*, 30 August 1944; Camus 1977, 258–59) to a recognition that the *Epuration* had foundered (e.g., *Combat*, 30 August 1945; Camus 1977,

289–91)—a change of mind whose terms prefigure the dynamics of revolt into revolution he would more fully develop later. Useful synopses of and/or comments on the history of the *Epuration* can be found in Lottman 1981, 421–44; Assouline 1990; Chebel d'Appollonia 1991a, 69–97; and Judt 1992, 56–92. See also Derrida 1989, 138.

68. In the letter to Harry Levin I have quoted from above, de Man diagnoses the 'obvious mistake' that dominates French thought in 1955: 'that every intellectual thinks he should stand and express himself on Algeria, Tito, Mendès, the baccalariat, etc. Coming back to these exchanges after a long time is pleasant enough, especially with the prospect of not having to spend one's life among them' (quoted in Waters 1989, lxv n. 5). Such judgment opens his own rebellious stand in 'Montaigne et la transcendance' to charges of considerable bad faith (to use that shorthand notation), in the sense that he, too, claims the authority to take such positions but refuses to give them substance, thereby remaining open, like Montaigne, 'to every wind that blows' ('MT' 11). It is only fair to add that in thus mobilizing Montaigne as a privileged point of reference for purposes of formal political innuendo, de Man is not alone. Consider, for instance, Jeanson's 1951 suggestion of the formal possibility of a retrospective understanding of Montaigne's 'extreme *conservatism*': 'Beyond the simplistic identifications, certain analogies between his situation and that of a European of today could be drawn out which would no doubt be favourable to an understanding of his attitude.' (64). Which identifications? What analogies? Whose understanding?

69. Hegel 1988, 433; 1977, 400. For a succinct account of Hegel's Beautiful Soul, see Hyppolite 1974, 512–17; and Taylor 1975, 194–95.

70. Hegel 1988, 521; 1977, 483.

71. Hegel 1988, 432; cf. 1977, 400.

72. To read this claim to seriousness that links the practice of poetry to the writing of history as an attempt 'to assure the historian that no one else is having any fun' (Bialostosky 1992, 163) is, in the light of the reading I try to argue here, not only silly but strictly revolting.

CHAPTER FOUR

1. As de Man half-ironically recognizes when he states that it would not be a 'great exaggeration' to say that the institution of comparative literary history in America as a whole is a response to Lovejoy's notorious call to erase the very word 'romantic' on grounds of meaninglessness

('WWH' 48–49; see also 'DA' 147 and 'F' 80–83). On this count, see also Warminski 1984.

2. For a challenging commentary on this passage, see Chase 1991, 352.
3. As Wlad Godzich (1986) has documented, de Man himself authorized this retrospective heuristic 'organization of his writings' in roughly four phases, thereby apparently sublating his earlier remark that many of the *'theoretical'* (Godzich 1986, x) essays gathered in *Blindness and Insight* 'are by-products of a more extensive study of romantic and post-romantic literature that does not deal with criticism' ('FBI 1970' vii). My suggestions in what follows, benefiting—as Godzich's could not—from the critical articulation central to de Man's 1967 Gauss lectures, should lead to a recognition of the point that the resistance to Romanticism the later scheme displays is of primordial importance for a sustained reading of de Man's work. A more focused account of this resistance will be the subject of the sequel to the present volume.
4. For reasons of discursive economy, and in response to the diverse genres of de Man's writing in this period (ranging from book reviews to highly condensed critical reflections), I shall sketch this pseudosynthesis in a manner that moves further away from expository exegesis of isolated texts than has been the case in the previous chapters. This strategy obviously runs the risk of erasing the logic of the original in a superimposition of alternative coherence carried by citational overkill, but I am not in a position to judge whether that is not too high a price to pay.
5. A measure of this absurdity is the ease with which these formal propositions can be modified, irrespective of the pertinence of the proposition itself: for one can always blame Rousseau for the Terror (as Hegel did [see, e.g., D'Hondt 1991, 81]) and praise Nietzsche for—or perhaps not Nietzsche . . . (see Derrida 1988, 19–38). For further recent historico-philosophical variations on the conflicting views involving Rousseau and the Revolution, see Philonenko 1991 and (or versus) Barny 1991.
6. A further complication of this pattern arises in relation to de Man's 1962 recognition of Wordsworth's style as a 'delicate balance between perception and imagination' ('SL' 143) grounded in 'the complex act of pure vision,' which 'obeys the logic of the eye' (133) rather than the logic of postperceptual emancipated Imagination celebrated in the later analysis of the Winander Boy and in the allegorizing reading of a sonnet from the *River Duddon* cycle ('THW' 84–92). The tension be-

tween these two logics is a version of the tension between a poetry of substance and a poetry of consciousness, between the image and the emblem in Yeats, or between symbol and allegory in general. Though this tension is evidently one of de Man's persistent concerns, I have opted here for an alternative guiding perspective—the grounds for this choice will, I hope, become gradually clearer.

7. The original version of the essay was published in *Arion* in 1967; the Gauss lecture on 'Romanticism and Demystification' (renamed as 'The Contemporary Criticism of Romanticism') was published for the first time in 1993. For helpful comments on part of this publishing history, see the editors' preface and the editorial matter in *RCC*.
8. This phrase ('CC' o.v., 56) does not occur in the republication of the essay in *BI*, where most of the other sweeping references to 'structuralism' are also replaced by phrases such as 'contemporary criticism' or 'Continental criticism.'
9. Klein 1973, 35.
10. And will continue to be about: 'Sanity can exist only because we are willing to function within the conventions of duplicity and dissimulation, just as social language dissimulates the inherent violence of the actual relationships between human beings' ('ROT' 215–16).
11. I emphasize that the 'radical relativism' de Man here ascribes to Lévi-Strauss is emphatically neither de Man's 'solution to the crisis' nor an instance of 'deconstructive credo' (Lehman 1991, 153). Not because I hope to show David Lehman the error of his ways (I have no desire to welcome him into the dark fold of de Man devotion [163]), but because the same mistake is sometimes made by readers turning to *Blindness and Insight* for deconstructive insight in good faith. A good instance is Ronald Shusterman's misguided attempt to canonize I. A. Richards as something of a deconstructor himself by likening de Man's account of 'radical relativism' to the birth of relativism in Richards's thought (1988, 396–97). For a less straightforward instance of this confusion, see Cebulla 1992, 88.
12. The original version of 'The Crisis of Contemporary Criticism' has a reference to this colloquium as a sign of the times: 'I have recently taken part in congresses entitled "Literary Criticism and Psychoanalysis," "Literary Criticism and Sociology," and, most recently, "The Language [*sic*] of Criticism and the Sciences of Man," and I can testify that, in these meetings, nothing was said that had the remotest connection with literature' ('CC' o.v., 45). We shall return to this specific historical

diagnosis later on. For de Man's own participation in this symposium, see 'c.'
13. Derrida 1967, 417.
14. As far as I know, this is the first record in print of the encounter between Derrida and de Man (see also 'INT 1983,' 117, and Derrida 1986, 127). The first irony of this encounter, aptly underscored in the materiality of the misspelt name, was that de Man swiftly decided that 'Deridda,' too, was a structuralist by implication, despite the fact that 'Structure, Sign and Play' (the essay in question here) is one of the first truly critical arguments with structuralism. The 1967 version of de Man's argument repeats the mistake (but corrects the name, at least in the editors' transcription ['CCR' 11]), whereas the definitive version of the essay replaces the final sentence of the passage just quoted with the phrase 'and the problem is made more complex when it involves the disappearance of the self as a constitutive subject' ('CC' 11). Meanwhile, de Man had carefully read *De la grammatologie* and had recognized 'Derrida's work [as] one of the places where the future possibility of literary criticism is decided' ('ROB' 111) over and against its structuralist recuperation as just another kind of science. In any event, this initially missed crossing should make it clear that the essays collected in *Blindness and Insight* can hardly be accurately characterized as 'a powerful application of Derridean ideas to the rhetoric of modern poetics' (Norris 1982, 22). A good reading of the friction between Derrida and de Man in this connection is Loesberg 1991, 110–14.
15. De Man also briefly considers this text in 'FG' 97–98. Exemplary ways to read these passages are sketched in Weber 1989, 407–9; and in Esch 1990, 33–37.
16. Husserl 1976, 346.
17. Ibid., 347.
18. Ibid., 346.
19. In a preceding passage from the text, de Man oddly insists that Husserl even goes so far as to literally ground this consciousness in a 'concrete,' 'geographical expansion' that has stopped 'once and for ever, at the Atlantic Ocean and the Caucasus' (15). Husserl does no such thing (at least not in these terms), insisting instead that, for instance, the United States and the English Dominions also belong to the 'unity of the spiritual *Gestalt*' that is Europe—an honor which, however, is not extended to Eskimos, Indians, or Gypsies (1976, 318–19), who, in de Man's harsh articulation of Husserl's typology, are 'primitive,

pre-scientific and pre-philosophical, myth-dominated and congenitally incapable of the disinterested distance without which there can be no philosophical meditation' (15). As this exclusion illustrates, de Man's point about Husserl's Eurocentrism stands irrespective of its particular geographical grounding, but we shall see how his misreference to this 'empirical' issue here indicates a tension of a more general nature.

20. The transcription of a slightly later text reads: 'Thought that occurs in a state of crisis. . . states its own birth in the mode of error' ('RTS' 26), but it is hard to say whether this is a true variation or an error. See also 'CCR' 23.

21. On the highly similar pattern of the structuralist *bricoleur*'s invention of his other, the *ingénieur,* see Derrida 1967, 418.

22. Jerome McGann has advanced the claim that this is simply incorrect and that in particular the language of theoretical physics in the wake of quantum mechanics demystifies de Man's privileging of literature at the expense of a reductive understanding of science (1988, 102–3; in this connection see also Cebulla 1992, 3–4). If we must use Stanley Corngold's distinction between error and mistake (as McGann urges us to do [101]) I would suggest that this moment in de Man's thought is an error only as a result of its being a historically overdetermined mistake. The remainder of this book should further complicate this dubious distinction.

23. The afterlife of this confusion as a conceptual frame in de Man's work involves his definition of ideology as 'the confusion of linguistic with natural reality, of reference with phenomenalism' ('RT' 11) and his material commentary on the difference between transcendental and metaphysical principles in Kant ('PMK' 121–25). I shall not try to further justify my blank imposition of this afterlife here, but I am convinced (and hope to show in a third volume) that a reading of de Man's 'historical materialism' (Warminski forthcoming) must *also* begin here.

24. The phrase is a favorite point of reference for de Man—it occurs in 'CC' 17; 'FI' o.v., 36; 'PT' 50; 'AIB' 117; 'ROB' 131; 'GP' 88; and 'RJ' 198.

25. Another short-circuit here: 'We do not see what we love but we love in the hope of confirming the illusion that we are indeed seeing anything at all' ('MR' 53 n.23).

26. In the revised version of this passage, de Man has replaced 'his own being' with 'itself'—the change is not only politically correct but also filters out the (in terms of de Man's argument) incongruous specification of the self in terms of sexual, natural, empirical, ontic difference.

27. As it is not in 'minor works' like *Pygmalion* ('PT' 50), though we must register here that in his earlier comments on this play, de Man claims a saving authenticity for this 'failure' as itself a mode of demystification ('RTS' 49). An elaboration of this apparent inconsistency—which repeats a systematic inconsistency in de Man's rhetoric of crisis—should move through his reading of *Pygmalion* in *Allegories of Reading* ('RNP').
28. Whether this 'disinterestedness' opens a scene of recognition where de Man would join the 'Arnoldian Concordat' (Hartman 1980, 253) is another matter.
29. De Man delivered the essay from which the preceding phrases are lifted ('Ludwig Binswanger et le problème du moi poétique,' later translated and slightly revised as 'Ludwig Binswanger and the Sublimation of the Self') at the September 1966 symposium in Cerisy-la-Salle on 'Les Tendances actuelles de la critique.' Ostensibly primarily devoted to a critical analysis of Binswanger's failure to live up to the rigors of the ontological project, its main adversary is Michel Foucault, whose archaeological enterprise in *Les mots et les choses* de Man characterizes as 'a description of the signs of the transformative action of consciousness as these invade the manifest and observable realms of existence,' i.e., a description of 'the structures that exist on the level of empirical and concrete functions,' which substitutes itself for the failed attempts to understand the 'initial phenomenon of consciousness as a constitutive power' by the method through which ' "thought tries to grasp itself at the root of its own history" ' ('LB' 37; O.V., 64).

Roughly, de Man's argument with Foucault is that having registered the 'permanent crisis of phenomenological thought,' he misunderstands this crisis as a conflict between phenomenology and ontology rather than as a symptom of the difficulty of maintaining the essentially compatible perspectives of fundamental ontology and transcendental phenomenology in the face of empirical seduction (49; O.V., 77). Binswanger, in failing to brave this difficulty, exemplifies the 'danger' Heidegger and Husserl had already 'denounced and interpreted,' but to conclude from this, as does Foucault according to de Man, that the entire task had better be abandoned is to give up prematurely (49; O.V., 77–78). The essay does not mention Romanticism, though it is clear that Foucault here figures as one more representative of structuralist—and therefore, by implication, anti-Romantic—demystification. The fact that parts of the essay also appear in the last of de Man's Gauss lectures ('AIB' 101–2, 109–10), which is concerned with an understanding of Baudelaire's relation to Romanticism and in its turn contains passages that will later reappear in 'The Rhetoric of Temporality,' indicates the persistence of de Man's Romantic concerns in his reading of contemporary criticism.

30. Cynthia Chase has suggested another way to read 'de Man's writing as the *translating* of Romantic texts' (1991, 353), but she focuses primarily on de Man's later work and thereby, admirably, activates a notion of translation which is critically different from the one I here try to read in de Man's reflections on Romanticism dating from the second half of the 1960s.
31. For the original terms of this inversion, see Hölderlin 1969a, 788.
32. This particular phrase is applied by de Man to Sartre ('JPS' 122), but, as we have seen, anti-Romanticism is the condition of most—if not all—forms of genuinely critical contemporary thought.
33. See de Graef 1993a, 23–26.
34. Rousseau 1959, 1046.
35. 'Mnemosyne [Dritte Fassung],' stanza 3.
36. 1805 *Prelude,* Book Five, 545–46 (Wordsworth 1959, 210).
37. The less than elegant translation of this last phrase—taken from de Man's slightly later bibliographical notice of the same book reviewed in *Le Soir*—tries to preserve the slight ambiguity as to the antecedent of 'dont' in 'mais dont nous tenons cependant à nous souvenir de temps en temps': either 'une époque révolue' or 'une œuvre qui reste parmi les plus marquantes.' The point of de Man's argument being the coincidence of both antecedents.
38. Contrary to what de Man's comments seem to imply, both quotations from Spinoza are given by Rolland himself, who explicitly promotes Spinoza as a figure whose 'realism' has been rendered invisible by 'the heavy verbalism of professional philosophers': 'How could they not have grasped, at first sight, this gaze, this voice, intoxicated with the Real [*ivres du Réel*]!' (Rolland 1942, 43). In shorthand (and much more could be said about this, even if only because Rolland's book is dedicated to a walnut tree): the problem with Rolland's eulogy of Spinoza is that it presents a threat to de Man's own realism by transgressing precisely the boundaries he tries to establish between the Real and the order of intoxication in order to arrive at a realistic appreciation of the reality of the 'spirit of the age' (as he calls it in a review published one week later [*LS,* April 1942, 227]), a spirit that itself heralds 'a period of faith and belief, with all that this entails in suffering, exaltation

and intoxication [*ivresse*]' (see also de Graef 1993a, 16–20): Rolland's Spinoza's 'hallucinated realism [*réalisme halluciné*]' (Rolland 1942, 44) scrambles the terms with which de Man proposes to establish a 'sober' (*HVL*, March 1942, 300) account of the real impact of the 'mystical' (*LS*, April 1942, 227) forces on the nonmystical Real. This threat to the system has to be exorcized. (I have translated the Spinoza quotations from the French in de Man's quotations from Rolland. The passages in question are taken from the *Treatise on the Correction of the Understanding*, §§ 99–100. For a direct English translation, see, e.g., Spinoza 1977, 259–60. The epigraph to the present section is taken from T. S. Gregory's introduction to this translation [xi, xiv], first published in 1910.)

39. A typesetting error slightly complicates this passage in de Man's text: 'Instead of turning itself to reality, his foggy reverie chooses the abstract emanations of thought and the imagination *surrounding world which in no way reflects* science become for him ethical values and, consequently, the artists transform themselves into directors of conscience' (*LS*, April 1942, 224; emphasis added). The line of print I have italicized is an erroneous repetition of a line that had already occurred in the earlier passage on the crisis of adolescence (quoted above). Judging from the context of the argument, we might hypohetically reconstruct the missing phrase as 'which is to say that art and,' but the point of the passage is sufficiently clear even without this correction.

40. For an account of this insurgence of the literary supplement, to which I will return below, see de Graef 1993a, 23–26.

41. For a bibliographic remark on this and other unpublished texts, see the preface. My comments on these writings will be minimal and predictable, and this largely for the reason that they fit the hypothetical reconstruction of de Man's thought I have been trying to articulate. Such hermeneutico-scientific gratification risks stabilizing a preemptive understanding (that is, a nonreading) of these texts: I cannot pretend not to be implicated in this pattern.

42. The transcription gives the Latin original (Proposition 7 of the second part of the *Ethica ordine geometrico demonstrata*) as an endnote, whereas the main text gives an English translation from 1982 supplied by the editors. De Man probably quoted the Latin only.

43. This is not the place to enter into a discussion of the merits of de Man's commentary as a reading of Spinoza—or Taine, for that matter. The reference to Negri is merely to indicate the power of resurrec-

tionary patterns stretching across the ideological spectrum of modernity—more recent instances would include Allan Bloom's and Camille Paglia's nostalgia for the German University (Bloom 1988, 272; Paglia 1991, 1, 29), Stephen Toulmin's monumentalization of Montaigne (Toulmin 1990), and Charles Taylor's search for the sources of the modern self (Taylor 1989). I have commented on this pattern as it involves the self-determination of the American subject (a simulacrum of which can be found in de Man's 'The Temptation of Permanence') in de Graef 1992.

44. For an interesting self-definition of Taine's socioscientific descriptive method, see Lepenies 1988, 5; see also 60 and 67–68 for further salient commentary on Taine.

45. The *Fremdkörper* of this *désinvolture*, a favorite stance of Ernst Jünger, indicates and complicates a further point of reference we shall turn to below. See also de Graef 1990, 63.

46. See also de Graef 1993a, 24–25.

47. De Man's verdict on Burke is significantly harsher than that on Bachelard, though he does suggest toward the end of his presentation that the last chapter of *A Rhetoric of Motives* may promise a 'new beginning' ('BB' 30). Toward the end of his life, de Man planned to return to Burke (see Godzich 1986, xi) but had to leave the project behind. This missed encounter has meanwhile taken on a life of its own—see, e.g., Lentricchia 1983; Bretzius 1987; and Kennedy 1990, x.

48. We should note here that Burke's 'extravagantly naive claims' resonate in de Man's later suggestion (via Empson) that Marxism is an impatient version of pastoral ('DF' 240) and in the 'fantastically high claims' ascribed to Mallarmé ('PHDM' 4): for de Man, the quality of these claims is a measure of their metaphysical patience with form, but how such patience itself should be historically measured (as distinct from merely denied or granted) is another matter.

49. A stark illustration of the important change in de Man's mind in this connection can be given by juxtaposing this passage to the following lines from his early essay on Keats and Mallarmé (the essay is undated but was probably written in the early 1950s). The target of de Man's attack in these lines is Earl Wasserman, who has made the mistake of reading 'the "Ode on a Grecian Urn" as if Keats were Mallarmé' ('K' 10): 'This kind of fallacy might well be called the symbolist fallacy: the reading of all poetry, particularly romantic poetry, as if it were written with the same self-consciousness as the later symbolist

works. The difference between romanticism and symbolism starts precisely here: for the romantics, the failure of the aesthetic was at most a diffuse and vague awareness that pervades their work as an overhanging mood, but remains much too remote from their consciousness to find concrete formal expression' (11). Renaming this symbolist fallacy as the truth of Romanticism is, again, one central name for de Man's mission.

50. Hegel 1988, 433; 1977, 400.
51. For a particularly rigid, but in the present context, highly pertinent rehearsal of such a diagnosis, see Verene 1985, 99–103. For a reproduction of Hegel's virtual portrait of Rousseau in similar terms, see Philonenko 1991, 28–34.
52. Hegel 1988, 433; 1977, 400. I have translated Hegel's German myself in order to retain a measure of its vertigo, which is smoothened out to some degree in Miller's translation.
53. 'There was a man who, in reaffirming the ontological priority of consciousness. . . . This man is called Rousseau' ('IR' 45; translation modified). To the extent that this man also incarnated the Beautiful Soul, he falls short of the Absolute Spirit—as does, necessarily, the prefiguration of the Beautiful Soul in the Spiritual Animal of *das geistige Tierreich*. Yet, in Hegel's afterlife, both the Beautiful Soul and the Spiritual Animal resist sublation. What awaits further reading is the juxtaposition of two strong rereadings of Hegel's *personae:* de Man's Beautiful Soul and Blanchot's 'littérateur': 'It would be wrong to hold the powerful contemporary movements of negation responsible for this volatile force literature seems to have become. Approximately a hundred and fifty years ago, there was a man who had the highest possible idea of art that one could form,—since he saw how art can become religion and religion art—, this man (called Hegel) has described all the movements by which he who chooses to become a *littérateur* condemns himself to being part of the "animal reign of the spirit"' (Blanchot 1949, 307).
54. Hyppolite 1974, 12.
55. Kojève 1985, 151.
56. Ibid., 151–52.
57. Ibid., 152.
58. Ibid., 154.
59. Rousseau 1964, 967 (Preface to *Narcisse, ou L'Amant de lui-même*).

60. I quote Shelley's phrase via Charles Taylor's appeal (via Earl Wasserman) to understand its Romantic context as a privileged source of the self (Taylor 1989, 381; 1991, 85), the 'sentiment de l'existence' (1991, 27, 91) we should reestablish contact with in order to adequately face the malaise of modernity. Richard Rorty's modulation of this appeal is particularly suggestive here: 'Perhaps we philosophers, even Taylor himself, are still working with pre-Romantic ideas, ideas which those poets hoped to make obsolete. Perhaps we have not yet caught up with those poets, not yet glimpsed the horizon of significance within which they wrote' (Rorty 1993, 3). A more extensive discussion of the radical dissonances between de Man's and Taylor's rhetorics of crisis cannot be sketched here, but it is important to bear in mind that de Man's is a thing of the past and that Taylor's assumes that the passage to a different reading (of Romanticism) as suggested by—among others—de Man in his later work has never really happened (1989, 580 n.9 and 573 n.26). For critical comments on Taylor's Romantic turn, see Lemmens 1994.
61. One internal diagnosis of this condition is Merleau-Ponty's observation that 'in the history of political thought, the Hegelian compromise had more future than the radicalism of Hölderlin' (1980, 170).
62. De Man points out that he 'happen[s] to be familiar with [the] case ... of Flemish nineteenth-century literature within the Belgian state, where the cultural language was French' ('YRT' 5). There is a germ for a mock-ironic family saga in this familiarity: In 1870, Jan van Beers (1821–88), de Man's great-grandfather, composed a poetic address to his 'boys,' 'Aan mijne Jongens' (Van Beers 1921, 335–39), in which he implores them—if they *must* be artists—not to 'take up the poet's pen': for Poetry, though it is the 'supreme art,' cannot flourish in the Flemish language, which, like a 'New Cinderella,' has been deprived of its birthright by its 'stepsister,' French. Historical circumstances have shattered the dream of a unified Netherlandic culture that, 'like another Greece,' might have become 'Europe's light and pride'—as it is, van Beers repeats, the 'demon of art' haunting the 'soul' of his offspring had better be accommodated through other arts, such as sculpture or painting. Unless the cause he strove for—'In Flanders Flemish'—would find a realization in the future after all: for in that case, van Beers muses, 'if among my sons and grandsons there be one / In whose heart the hereditary holy fire sparkles, / Put my lyre in his arms.' The poem

ends on a wistful retraction of this fond hope, expressing instead the faint desire that the memory of the poet's national enterprise may not entirely fade. *Sapienti sat.*

63. The best way not to read this methodological privileging of German poetry and thought is by recognizing it as the supremely familiar figure it undoubtedly is. For a critical investigation of de Man's 'necessarily troubled admiration of German poets and philosophers,' Harrier 1993 is an entertaining footnote. For a reply to Harrier, see de Graef 1993b. Further reflections on the language of this admiration should engage with Kaplan 1993.

64. Yeats, for his part, only 'comes close to being able to name reality again as it is,' and the price he has to pay is consequently lower, though it is still no less than 'serenity' ('YRT' 25). I bracket de Man's further commentary on Yeats and am aware that this is becoming a questionable habit—though not, I hope, for the reasons advanced by Andrzej Warminski in his advice that we read de Man's writing on Yeats (1994).

65. This judgment, it will be noted, echoes de Man's earlier statements on modern conservative blanket condemnations of 'the political and aesthetic beliefs of the twenties' ('IG' 14).

66. Wolfgang Lepenies's remarks on George's culture of the prophetic are, as ever, highly pertinent in this connection (1988, 279–96).

67. I realize that in borrowing this shibboleth from Philippe Lacoue-Labarthe's *La fiction du politique* (1987), I risk translating its acute specificity into the bland diction of received ideas: my only excuse is that de Man's forbidding formulas here do not yet allow for a more critical translation. For suggestions as to what might happen in the course of such a more critical translation, see especially Chase 1989 and Redfield 1990. The latter essay contains a discussion—touching, in passing, but significantly, on the Beautiful Soul—of de Man's quotations (in 'Kant and Schiller') from Goebbels's *Michael*, as a case in point for the aesthetic ideology. Lacoue-Labarthe also signals de Man's references to *Michael* (1987, 94 n.2) but misplaces them in 'Hegel on the Sublime'—where, of course, they are very much in place. See also Johnson 1990, 9–10.

68. A post-Hellenic version, perhaps, of the 'noble lie' 'contrived' in Plato's *Republic* (Book 3, 414b–c). Paul Shorey's translation adds an inviting note to these 'opportune falsehoods': 'The concept $\mu\eta\chi\alpha\nu\eta$ or ingenious device employed by a superior intelligence to circumvent necessity or play providence with the vulgar holds a prominent place

in Plato's physics, and is for Rousseau-minded readers one of the dangerous features of his political and educational philosophy' (Plato 1937, 300–301). Desmond Lee gilds the *pharmakon* by translating the 'opportune falsehood' as a 'convenient story' and the 'noble lie' as a 'magnificent myth' (Plato 1987, 181). On these myths, see Nancy 1990.
69. As I have already indicated, de Man's dissertation was to have been completed into a book with a further chapter on George, but I have not been able to read this suspended conclusion. For de Man's last words on George and the messianic conception of poetry, see 'WB.' See also Klein 1989, 296 n.11.
70. 'A Poet's Epitaph,' ll. 17–21 (Wordsworth 1989, 151).
71. In 'The Crisis of Contemporary Criticism,' de Man writes that 'it would be a great deal more complex to demonstrate the self-mystification of as ironical a man as Mallarmé than of as admirably honest a man as Husserl' ('CC' 16), thereby alluding to the complex demonstration of Mallarmé's 'philosophical blindness' he had already undertaken in 'La circularité de l'interprétation dans l'œuvre de Maurice Blanchot,' published in June 1966. We shall briefly return to this rereading later.
72. For a recent rehearsal of a similar warning from different quarters, see Putnam 1983. Putnam's suggestion (which is not just his) that the only metaphysical picture that survives today is the dangerous and untenable hybrid of materialist metaphysics—naturalized philosophy, or 'metaphysics within the bounds of science' (210)—would bear developing here. I am grateful to Stefaan E. Cuypers for his clear delineation of the terms of this problem in contemporary analytical philosophy.
73. For later diagnoses of this disruption of 'serene speculation' and 'serene methodological self-assurance,' see 'RT' 12 and 'MR' 28.

CHAPTER FIVE

1. Rousseau 1964, 972.
2. Ibid., 972–73. The *Trésor de la langue française* lists various circumscriptions of the term 'police' as it was used in eighteenth-century French. The common denominator of these definitions is 'organization,' but I have chosen for the more focused alternative *discipline* to catch what I take to be Rousseau's point. The *Trésor* also documents its definitions with a 1792 quotation from Robespierre that is hard to suppress here: 'Souviens-toi de la police maintenue jusques ici, sans baïonnettes, par la seule vertu populaire.'

3. Ibid., 972n.
4. Ibid., 970.
5. Ibid., 973.
6. Ibid. The fact that the piece had in fact been relatively successful and that Rousseau himself was its most dismissive critic complicates the experiment considerably, but we cannot develop this point here. On Rousseau's 'volonté d'échouer' in this connection, see Jacques Scherer's introduction to the *Pléiade*-edition (especially Rousseau 1964, lxxxvi–ix).
7. Ibid., 974. It is not entirely clear whether the phrase 'ce discours' applies to the preceding preface or to the verdict of the future—as is only appropriate.
8. The poem de Man comments on is Hölderlin's 'Feiertags-Hymne,' and his principal interlocutor is, as suggested, Heidegger. De Man's commentary—which he not insignificantly qualifies as a 'us[ing of Hölderlin's poem] for more general considerations' rather than as a '"reading"' ('PT' 59)—is largely a hermeneutically articulated form-oriented sophistication of his criticism of Heidegger in 'HE' (see de Graef 1993a, 95–98). The relation of source and *telos* on which this commentary turns is one of the governing concerns of all de Man's Gauss lectures, most prominently (next to the present lecture) in his remarks on Girard ('CCR' 14–24) and on Wordsworth's 'origin and tendency' ('THW' 83–94). Since the first publication of this latter lecture in 1987, the figural effacement of this very relation in de Man's later 'actual "reading"' of Wordsworth (202 n.11), as affirmed in the 1971–72 revision of the lecture, has itself become something of an *archè* for readers of de Man's later work. (Another point of reference that must complicate this reading is de Man's commentary on the 'point of departure' in the work of Georges Poulet ['GP'].) At any rate, in the lecture on the 'Feiertags-Hymne,' the relation of beginning and end is explicitated in terms of Hölderlin's *Wechsel der Töne,* whose 'paratactic' discontinuity is understood as wholly contained in the poem's 'ontological principle of totalization' ('PT' 72). De Man's explicit enlistment of Adorno's notion of parataxis in the project of ontological hermeneutics is less than promising, except insofar as it promises its own future breakdown (retrospectively recognized by de Man in 1983) in a '"reading"' of the corpus in connection with which Adorno 'established' his 'claim . . . for the exemplary character of parataxis' ('PRR'

ix): 'the poetry of Hölderlin, the obvious stumbling block of my own enterprise.'

9. Blanchot 1955, 257–58. The passage is quoted (in the original French) in 'MB' o.v., 548; de Man's translation in the English version of the essay (63) adds and takes away some turns of the original; the translation I have given here remains closer to Blanchot. Note the similarity between the work's self-affirmation as allowed by Blanchot and de Man's 1953 characterization of the 'ontological intent' of 'form': 'These proportions *are*, and that is the end of it' ('TB' 5).

10. In a footnote de Man acknowledges Levinas's 'Le regard du poète,' from which I have taken the epigraph to this chapter, as the source for his understanding of this swerve.

11. In his English translation of this essay, de Man qualifies his confidence in this verification: 'At most, the circularity proves the authenticity of our intent' ('MB' 77). This is as good a place as any to underscore that de Man's revisions (by way of translation or not) of the essays in *BI* are not quite as 'minor' as he suggests ('FBI 1970' vii). A more exhaustive comparative analysis of the different versions of these essays lies ahead, in the repetition of the project of which the present volume is one instance.

12. For the account of *Dasein*'s triple *Vorrang* (ontic, ontological and ontico-ontological), see *Sein und Zeit*, § 4 (Heidegger 1977, 18). De Man's use of the concept of 'ontological priority' is not marked by Heidegger's analytical distinctions: in the present account of circularity, it resembles Heidegger's first, ontic *Vorrang*; in 'The Image of Rousseau,' it also involves the second and the third.

13. On this 'constru[al] as value' of the 'insistent thematization and performance of the [ontological] question,' see Chase 1986, 216–17 n.36.

14. On avoiding the coincidence of truth and authenticity as a means of leaving Heidegger behind, see Levinas 1975, 20.

15. It is an index of de Man's comprehensive intent that the conclusion to this essay already announces the argument against structuralism developed in 'The Crisis in Contemporary Criticism' ('FI' 32–33; o.v. 35–36). As Cyrus Hamlin has pointed out, the first version of the essay was delivered at Yale in 1965, and this to the understandable dismay of William Wimsatt, 'who walked out rather conspicuously in the middle' (Hamlin 1989, 143–44). The first publication of the essay was in the October 1966 issue of the French journal *Preuves*; the final English re-

vision became the second essay in *Blindness and Insight*. For reasons that should be clear (both from the essay itself and from what follows) we are not concerned here with the fairness of de Man's commentary on Stephen Ullmann, William Wimsatt, or Northrop Frye (some remarks in this connection can be found in Culler 1971; Fletcher 1972; Raval 1981, 205; Arac 1983, 180; and Bové 1983, 8), and the phrase 'American formalism' I shall be using in the following pages designates de Man's enabling construction of a composite figure of blindness (a slightly more naive counterpart to 'the structuralist aberration') rather than a particular critical practice. For further dismissive statements on 'American formalism' in de Man, see, e.g., 'SC' 107, 110.

16. Cf. also 'FI' O.V., 30: 'this continuity [between the initial subjective experience of the writer and the exterior characteristics of language] implies an ontological presupposition about the nature of literary language.' We recall that some ten years earlier, I. A. Richards (also identified as one of the central mediators of delusion in the present essay) had already been taken to task for the 'questionable ontological presuppositions' of his postulate of 'a perfect continuity between the sign and the thing signified' ('DF' 232). In fact, the present essay for a large part repeats the argument made in 'Impasse de la critique formaliste,' but rather than to exhaustively document this similarity I shall focus in what follows on the modification of de Man's dialectical frame of reference in terms of a hermeneutics of form.

17. Appealing to Meyer Abrams and Georges Poulet, de Man also hastens to qualify the affiliation of this natural analogism, through Coleridge, to Romanticism by insisting that even for Coleridge the '"esemplastic" power of the imagination was not founded on a direct participation of consciousness in the natural energy of the cosmos,' but rather decisively involved the conscious intervention of the free will ('FI' 28; O.V. 33).

18. For one of several later diagnoses of New Critical self-inversion in de Man's work, see 'MK' 182.

19. The primary text for this development (as de Man also indicates in 'IR' 294 n.28) is *Sein und Zeit*, § 32 (Heidegger 1977, 197–204). For a further understanding of this circle, either in its Schleiermacherian or Heideggerian form, I have found useful support in Gelley 1962 (an essay that politely suspends judgment [196 n.4] on the validity of de Man's critique of Heidegger in 'HE' and referred to also by de Man

['IR' 294 n.28]); Gadamer 1965, 250–83; Hoy 1978; Hamacher 1979; Nancy 1982; Silverman and Ihde 1985; and De Schutter 1988. Spanos (1976, 487–88 and 1977, 447–49) uses this notion to trash de Man's (and Derrida's) reading of (among other things) Heidegger.
20. Heidegger 1977, 202; 1978, 194.
21. In the English version of 'New criticism' de Man phonetically misspells *Vorhabe* as *Forhabe* ('FI' 30).
22. Heidegger 1976, 19; 1978, 188–89.
23. In fact, Heidegger points out that 'philological Interpretation [*Interpretation*]' (1976, 202; 1978, 194)—or the 'particular concrete kind of interpretation, in the sense of exact textual Interpretation [*die besondere Konkretion der Auslegung im Sinne der exakten Textinterpretation*]' (1976, 200; 1978, 192), the closest his text here comes to engaging with textuality—is itself a 'derivative way of understanding [*Verstehen*] and interpretation [*Auslegung*]' which properly belongs 'within the range of scientific knowledge' (1976, 202; 1978, 194). The point is instructive in that de Man, in the English version of the present essay, quotes in English half a page of Heidegger, beginning with the passage in which this suggestion occurs, but significantly masks Heidegger's distinction between *Auslegung* and *Interpretation* as he does so. For the sake of clarity: Heidegger's German reads 'Man hat diese Tatsache immer schon bemerkt, wenn auch nur im Gebiet der abgeleiteten Weisen von Verstehen und Auslegung, in der philologischen Interpretation. Diese gehört in den Umkreis wissenschaftlichen Erkennens. Dergleichen Erkenntniss verlangt die Strenge der begründenden Ausweisung' (1976, 202); Macquarrie and Robinson's 1962 translation renders this as: 'This is a fact that has always been remarked, even if only in the area of derivative ways of understanding and interpretation such as philological Interpretation. The latter belongs within the range of scientific knowledge. Such knowledge demands the rigour of a demonstration to provide grounds for it' (1978, 194); de Man's version runs: 'This is a fact that has always been remarked, even if only in the area of derivative ways of understanding and interpretation such as philological interpretation. . . . [de Man's elision marks, followed by a new, indented paragraph] Scientific knowledge demands the rigors of a demonstration for its justification' ('FI' 30). Macquarrie and Robinson's practice throughout their translation is to render *Auslegung*—which they qualify as 'any activity in which we interpret

something "as" something'—as 'interpretation,' and *Interpretation*— 'interpretations which are more theoretical or systematic, as in the exegesis of a text'—as (capitalized) 'Interpretation' (1978, 19 n.4).

24. As has already been indicated, the relation of Heidegger's *Auslegung* to the linguistic explicitation of linguistic understanding is problematic at best. This is not the appropriate place to explore this relation in a reading of Heidegger's text (in this connection, see Nancy 1982, 31), but we may perhaps underscore that, for Heidegger, the *Auslegung* emphatically does not have its original being in 'an assertion which definitely characterizes [*bestimmende Aussage*]' (Heidegger 1976, 198; 1978, 189). To the contrary, if such a (thematic) expression is at all possible, this is because what it expresses is already available *(vorliegt)* 'as something expressible [*als Aussprechbares*],' in precisely the 'mere pre-predicative seeing [*vorprädikative schlichte Sehen*]' of the *Auslegung*. To register this moment in Heidegger is also to identify a significant difference between *Dasein*'s priority (its access to an 'Understanding [*Verstehen*] of the Being of all entities of a character other than its own' [1976, 18; 1978, 34]) and de Man's suggestion that 'the word "water" is closer to the ontological essence of water than the sense perception of this element' ('IR' 40–41).

25. The later revision of the essay is marginally less confident on this score, as witness de Man's concession that '[t]he notion of the hermeneutic circle is not introduced by Heidegger in connection with poetry or the interpretation of poetry, but applied to language in general' (31). Yet, since poetry still seems to fall under the heading of 'language in general,' the rest of the argument remains unaltered. The point being, again, that Heidegger does not 'apply' this notion to 'language in general' in the first place (at least not in the sense of language as a system of predicative utterances susceptible of interpretation). This 'first place' is, as we saw, §32 of *Sein und Zeit,* and it is important to underscore here yet again that, for de Man, the later place where a 'demonstration' ('IR' 294 n.28) of hermeneutic circularity at work in (the) language (of Hölderlin's poetry) does take place, is the scene where this principle is in fact violated ('FI' 30–31). The *locus classicus* for this violation is Heidegger's programmatic but ambiguous claim for the decisive disappearance of the *Auslegung* in his 1950 foreword to the second edition of the *Erläuterungen* (1981), which de Man also quotes from ('PT' 56). One way to frame the problem would be by saying that de Man opposes the particular modality of Heidegger's transferring the structure

of *Dasein*'s *Verstehen* to the *Verstehen* articulated in the *Auslegung* of literary elucidation, but preserves the principle of such a transfer as itself entirely 'legitimate' (58). Briefly put, Heidegger's fundamental shortcoming—which 'throws light not only upon certain problems inherent in contemporary criticism but also upon the link between these problems and their origins in romanticism' (58)—is his total disregard for 'the expressive value of Hölderlin's highly deliberate formal structurization' (55) (on this count, we should further recall de Man's 1950s vacillation on the technical merits of Heidegger's exegeses—see 'TP' 36 versus 'HE' 250; cf. also de Graef 1993a, 200 n.42). The ground for this disregard is Heidegger's 'substitution of ontological for what could well be called formal dimensions of language' ('PT' 71), a short-circuit powered by his misunderstanding of poetry's ontological orientation in such a way that the poet is thought 'to act as a direct spokesman for being' (71) instead of being understood as a mediator of 'the discontinuous structure of being itself' (72). The question we are left with is whether this difference can be rigorously maintained: whether the transfer of hermeneutic circularity from *Sein und Zeit* to the realm of literature can in fact be performed (or rather: whether this performance as it does take place in de Man's hermeneutics can lay claim to a critical grounding as poetics). A good invitation to this question is Bahti 1989.

26. For other usages of this figure in de Man, see de Graef 1993a, 195 n.15.
27. On this count, see Carroll 1980 and Geldof 1992, 283–92.
28. On a possible but far from fulfilled future for this cadaver as a gigantic textual corpse mummified by deconstruction, see Felperin 1985, 145–46.
29. The English version omits the quotation from Rousseau. For another instance of de Man's impatience with Doubrovsky's happy Sartrian outlook, see the exchange at the Cerisy-la-Salle colloquium where de Man read his Binswanger-essay ('LB' o.v., 81–82; the English version does not include this question and answer session).
30. To my knowledge, this is the first substantial reference to Benjamin in de Man's writing (previously, he had only been referred to in brief introductory remarks on recent trends in criticism [e.g., 'SC' 107 and 'LN' 164]). For the original sentence, slightly modified by de Man, see Benjamin 1978, 208.
31. Less familiar is the sentence following the definition from Benjamin quoted by de Man: 'The absolute vices, as they are represented by

tyrants and schemers, are allegories [*Die absoluten Laster, wie Tyrannen und Intriganten sie vertreten, sind Allegorien*]' (1978, 208). One of the tasks indicated here is a redoubled reading of Rousseau's simulacrum of virtue as the mask of vice in the empty light of Benjamin's allegory.

32. See de Graef 1993a, 51.

CHAPTER SIX

1. Derrida 1986, 121.
2. As Derrida (1980, 491) writes of attempts to periodize the itinerary of Jacques Lacan.
3. 'The Rhetoric of Temporality' was first published in 1969, but substantial sections of it were already delivered by de Man in 'Nature Imagery and Figural Diction' and 'The Romantic Heritage: Allegory and Irony in Baudelaire,' the fifth and sixth of his Spring 1967 Gauss lectures (see also the editors' notes to [fragments of] these lectures in *RCC*, 203–5). As for the bad movies, here is a line de Man did not manage to erase: 'Death men, as we all know from Western movies, tell no tales, but the same is not true of Western romantic poetry, which knows that the only interesesting tale is to be told by a man who [sentence suspended]' ('THW' 201 n.7). The other phrases that haunt (us in reading) de Man have been extensively (though not exhaustively) quoted already—see, e.g., Goodhart 1989, 228 (though in Goodhart's quotation the 'phrases' are curiously deleted).
4. See, e.g., 'AT.'
5. Wordsworth 1974, 30.
6. On this count, see, for instance, Derrida 1972, 302 and 1978, 106 n.1; Rand 1986, 296–97; and Attridge 1987.
7. On the dramatic qualities of the Mass and the trope figuring in it, see the introductory pages in the second volume of Chambers 1963. A more recent discussion of the same matter is Wright 1988, 163–75. Chambers has some inviting reflections on the ambivalence of the Christian reception of 'the deep-rooted mimetic instinct in the folk' (1963, vol. 2, 2). The epigraph to the present chapter is his comment on the 'remarkable' event of the 'most singular new birth of the drama in the very bosom of the Church's own ritual' (2–3).
8. Chambers 1963, vol. 2, 3.
9. Quoted from ibid., 9. This, one of the oldest (if not the oldest) tropes, interprets Matthew 28:1–7, Mark 16:1–7, and/or Luke 24:1–10. John

20:1–18 renders the same matter with increased dramatic sophistication. See also Wright 1988, 170–71.
10. And not (yet) the body of (Jesus) Christ. As far as I understand, the angels' calling the three Marys *Christicolae* (itself a formation of Church Latin) is probably an anachronism: even according to the Bible's own chronology, the followers of Jesus were not called Christians before Paul and Barnabas's visit to Antioch (Acts 11:26), i.e., around 43 A.D., and it is only in the second century that the name became part of general usage. The point of this fussy note being that the angels' naming the three Marys as followers of Christ (rather than as seekers for the body of the Nazarene, itself already an inference of sorts) strengthens the interpretive grasp of their founding question. A further point that could be underscored here is that the trope does in fact allow the women to respond: in Matthew, Mark, and Luke they remain silent, but the trope forces them to actively participate in interpreting their line. The fact that this participation is, of course, necessary from a dramatic point of view in no way diminishes the importance of this modification of the gospel: the point is precisely that there is a theatrical necessity in the first place. For John matters are different, but I suspect this is already enough in the line of amateur exegesis.
11. On the hermeneutical imperative here and, especially, elsewhere, see Hamacher 1989.
12. On the mathematical—*ta mathemata*—as the order of the already known, see De Schutter 1988, 467. On the implication of 'negative pathos' (Hamacher 1989, 181) in this model, see de Man's late unreading in 'Anthropomorphism and Trope in the Lyric' ('AT' 252–62) of his own 1967 reading of Baudelaire's 'Obsession' (as sketched in 'AIB' 113–14). Kevin Newmark's 'Paul de Man's History' (1989) puts up the necessary resistance to a developmental reading of this change of mind.
13. Jameson 1992, 259.
14. On the finality of this page (far from being de Man's last word), see Jacobs 1989. For a further angle on irony close to this question, see Newmark 1992.
15. The sentence is taken from de Man's introduction to the special issue of *Studies in Romanticism* hosting papers mostly written by young scholars working with de Man on 'The Rhetoric of Romanticism.' In this tongue-in-cheek institutional genealogy (reminiscent of the original version of 'The Crisis of Contemporary Criticism'), de Man

stages a difference between, on the one hand, his own (invented) '"generation"' (498)—'those who were beginning to write on Romanticism in the nineteen fifties' (496) and whose 'persistent commitment to the historical outlook . . . keeps haunting [their] textual analyses as their bad conscience,' causing the special kind of 'nervousness which, speaking for myself, makes me feel as if someone were looking over my shoulder whenever thematic assertions can be shown to be subservient to rhetorical overdeterminations' (498)—and, on the other hand, that of the contributors to the issue (those who take their tropes apart with 'remarkable ease' and 'casual elegance'). It is tempting to read this fiction as an ironic recollection of the post-Romantic (modern) predicament aimed at the post–post-Romantic (post-modern) condition that inherited this predicament. I shall not quite do so here.

16. On the prefiguration of the genetic gesture in this hypothesis, see Newmark 1989, 133–34.
17. For seminal arguments regarding these versions of 'materialism' in de Man, see Gasché 1989 and Warminski 1994.
18. I borrow this notion from Rodolphe Gasché's impressive remarks on de Man's 'apathetic rhetorical reading' offered in a paper delivered in 1988 at a conference on de Man in Antwerp, and available in a modified form in Gasché 1989. For an acute understanding of 'the pathos of a-pathy' through de Man, see Redfield 1990, 160–61.

Bibliography

Primary Sources

The following list comprises only those items of de Man's bibliography cited in the text, with the exception of the individual items of his wartime journalism. Each item is listed with the reference for its first publication, and, whenever applicable, with the reference for its later revision or reprint in a collection of de Man's essays. Whenever possible, the items are chronologically listed according to the year of composition or, in the case of lectures, of first delivery. The most complete bibliography of de Man's post-1950 writings is Thomas Keenan's 'Bibliography of Texts by Paul de Man' (*RT,* 122–27).

BOOKS BY PAUL DE MAN

Blindness and Insight: Essays in the Rhetoric of Contemporary Criticism. New York: Oxford University Press, 1971. 2d ed., with five additional essays and an introduction by Wlad Godzich; Minneapolis: University of Minnesota Press, 1983.

Allegories of Reading: Figural Language in Rousseau, Nietzsche, Rilke and Proust. New Haven: Yale University Press, 1979.

The Rhetoric of Romanticism. New York: Columbia University Press, 1984.

The Resistance to Theory. Foreword by Wlad Godzich. Minneapolis: University of Minnesota Press, 1986.

Wartime Journalism, 1939–1943. Ed. Werner Hamacher, Neil Hertz, and Thomas Keenan. Lincoln: University of Nebraska Press, 1988.

Critical Writings, 1953–1978. Ed. and introduction by Lindsay Waters. Minneapolis: University of Minnesota Press, 1989.

Romanticism and Contemporary Criticism: The Gauss Seminar and Other Papers. Ed. E. S. Burt, Kevin Newmark, and Andrzej Warminski. Baltimore: Johns Hopkins University Press, 1993.

Aesthetic Ideology. Ed. and introduction by Andrzej Warminski. Minneapolis: University of Minnesota Press, forthcoming.

Essays and Reviews by Paul de Man

1953

'[Keats].' Transcription of unpublished manuscript, undated.
'Taine and Baudelaire.' Transcription of unpublished manuscript, dated August 1953.
'Montaigne et la transcendance.' *Critique* 79 (December 1953), 1011–22. Trans. Richard Howard as 'Montaigne and Transcendence,' CW, 3–11.

1954

'Bachelard and Burke.' Transcription of unpublished manuscript, dated January 1954.
'Yeats and the German Romantic Tradition.' Transcription of unpublished manuscript, dated June 1954.

1955

'The Double Aspect of Symbolism.' *Yale French Studies (Phantom Proxies: Symbolism and the Rhetoric of History)* 74 (1988), 3–16. Rpr. in RCC, 147–63. Transcription of manuscript probably written between 1954 and 1956.
'The Inward Generation.' *i.e., The Cambridge Review* 1:2 (Winter 1955), 41–47. Rpr. in CW, 12–17.
'Le néant poétique (commentaire d'un sonnet hermétique de Mallarmé).' *Monde nouveau* 88 (April 1955), 63–75. Trans. Richard Howard as 'Poetic Nothingness,' CW, 18–29.
'Tentation de la permanence.' *Monde nouveau* 93 (October 1955), 49–61. Trans. Dan Latimer as 'The Temptation of Permanence,' CW, 30–40.
'Les exégèses de Hölderlin par Martin Heidegger.' *Critique* 100–101 (September–October 1955), 800–19. Trans. Wlad Godzich as 'Heidegger's Exegeses of Hölderlin,' BI, 246–66.

1956

'Keats and Hölderlin.' *Comparative Literature* 8:1 (Winter 1956), 28–45. Rpr. in CW, 41–60.
'Impasse de la critique formaliste.' *Critique* 109 (June 1956), 483–500. Trans. Wlad Godzich as 'The Dead-End of Formalist Criticism,' BI, 229–45.

'Le devenir, la poésie.' *Monde nouveau* 105 (November 1956), 110–24. Trans. Kevin Newmark and Andrzej Warminski as 'Process and Poetry,' CW, 64–75.

1957

'La critique thématique devant le thème de Faust.' *Critique* 120 (May 1957), 387–404. Trans. Dan Latimer as 'Thematic Criticism and the Theme of Faust,' CW, 76–89.

1958

'Hölderlin and the Romantic Tradition.' Incomplete manuscript transcribed in RCC, 123–36.

1960

'Mallarmé, Yeats, and the Post-Romantic Predicament.' Diss., Harvard, 1960.
'Image and Emblem in Yeats.' Part of 'Mallarmé' rpr. in RR, 145–238.
'Structure intentionnelle de l'Image romantique.' *Revue internationale de philosophie* vol. 51 (1960), 68–84. Trans. and rev. Paul de Man in 1970 as 'Intentional Structure of the Romantic Image,' rpr. in RR, 1–17.

1962

'A New Vitalism.' Review of *The Visionary Company* by Harold Bloom. *The Massachusetts Review* 3:3 (Spring 1962), 618–23. Rpr. in CW, 90–96.
'Symbolic Landscape in Wordsworth and Yeats.' In *In Defense of Reading*, ed. Richard Poirier and Reuben Brower, 22–37. New York: Dutton, 1962. Rpr. in RR, 125–43.

1964

'Heidegger Reconsidered.' Review of *What is Existentialism?* by William Barrett. *New York Review of Books*, 2 April 1964, 14–16. Rpr. in CW, 102–6.
'Spacecritics.' Review of *The Disappearance of God* by J. Hillis Miller and *The Widening Gyre* by Joseph Frank. *Partisan Review* 31:4 (Fall 1964), 640–50. Rpr. in CW, 107–15.
'Sartre's Confessions.' Review of *The Words* by Jean-Paul Sartre. *New York Review of Books*, 5 November 1964, 10–13. Rpr. in CW, 116–22.

1965

'Whatever Happened to André Gide?' Review of *Marshlands* and *Prometheus Misbound* by André Gide and *André Gide: His Life and Art* by Wallace Fowlie. *New York Review of Books*, 6 May 1965, 15–17. Rpr. in *CW*, 130–36.

'What Is Modern?' Review of *The Modern Tradition*, ed. Richard Ellman and Charles Feidelson. *New York Review of Books*, 6 May 1965. Rpr. in *CW*, 130–36.

'The Mask of Albert Camus.' Review of *Notebooks, 1942–1951* by Albert Camus. *New York Review of Books*, 23 December 1965, 10–13. Rpr. in *CW*, 145–52.

'L'Image de Rousseau dans la poésie de Hölderlin.' *Deutsche Beiträge zur Geistigen Überlieferung* vol. 5 (1965), 157–83. Trans. Andrzej Warminski as 'The Image of Rousseau in the Poetry of Hölderlin,' *RR*, 19–45.

'Modern Poetics: French and German.' In *Princeton Encyclopedia of Poetry and Poetics*, ed. Alex Preminger, 518–23. Princeton: Princeton University Press, 1965. Rpr. as 'Modern Poetics in France and Germany,' *CW*, 153–60.

'Heaven and Earth in Wordsworth and Hölderlin.' Paper delivered at 1965 MLA panel on 'Romanticism and Religion,' transcribed in *RCC*, 136–46.

1966

'Wordsworth und Hölderlin.' *Schweizer Monatshefte* (March 1966), 1141–55. Trans. Timothy Bahti as 'Wordsworth and Hölderlin,' *RR*, 47–65.

'La circularité de l'interprétation dans l'œuvre de Maurice Blanchot.' *Critique* 229 (June 1966), 547–59. Trans. and rev. Paul de Man as 'Impersonality in the Criticism of Maurice Blanchot,' *BI*, 60–78.

'The Literature of Nihilism.' Review of *The Artist's Journey into the Interior* by Erich Heller and *The German Tradition in Literature, 1871–1945* by Ronald Gray. *New York Review of Books*, 23 June 1966, 16–20. Rpr. in *CW*, 161–70.

Comments at the 1966 Johns Hopkins symposium. In *The Languages of Criticism and the Sciences of Man (The Structuralist Controversy)*, ed. Richard Macksey and Eugenio Donato, 150, 184–85. Baltimore: Johns Hopkins University Press, 1970.

'New Criticism et nouvelle critique.' *Preuves* 188 (October 1966), 29–37. Trans. and rev. Paul de Man as 'Form and Intent in the American New Criticism,' *BI*, 20–35.

Introduction to *Selected Poetry* by John Keats, ed. Paul de Man, ix–xxxvi. New York: Signet, 1966. Rpr. in *CW* 179–97.

'Ludwig Binswanger et le problème du moi poétique.' In *Les Chemins actuels de la critique* (Colloque de Cerisy, 2–12 September 1966), ed. Jean Ricardou, 77–103, with further comments at 54, 121–24. Trans. by de Man as 'Ludwig Binswanger and the Sublimation of the Self,' *BI*, 36–50.

'Madame de Staël et Jean-Jacques Rousseau.' *Preuves* 190 (December 1966), 35–40. Trans. Richard Howard as 'Madame de Staël and Jean-Jacques Rousseau,' *CW*, 171–78.

'Georg Lukács's *Theory of the Novel*.' *MLN (Modern Language Notes)* 81:5 (December 1966), 527–34. Rpr. in *BI*, 51–59.

1967

'The Crisis of Contemporary Criticism.' *Arion* 6:1 (Spring 1967), 38–57. Rpr., rev. as 'Criticism and Crisis,' *BI* 3–19.

'The Contemporary Criticism of Romanticism.' First Gauss lecture, originally announced under the title 'Romanticism and Demystification,' delivered at Princeton, 6 April 1967, transcribed in *RCC*, 3–24.

'Rousseau and the Transcendence of the Self.' Second Gauss lecture, delivered at Princeton, 13 April 1967, transcribed in *RCC*, 25–49.

'Patterns of Temporality in Hölderlin's "Wie wenn am Feiertage . . . "' Third Gauss lecture, originally announced under the title 'The Problem of Aesthetic Totality in Hölderlin,' delivered at Princeton, 20 April 1967, transcribed in *RCC*, 50–73.

'Time and History in Wordsworth.' Fourth Gauss lecture, originally announced under the title 'Nature and History in Wordsworth,' delivered at Princeton, 27 April 1967, transcribed, with later revisions, in *Diacritics* 17:4 (Winter 1987), 4–17. Rpr. in *RCC*, 74–94.

Fragment of the Fifth Gauss Lecture. Originally announced under the title 'Natural Imagery and Figural Diction,' delivered at Princeton, 4 May 1967, transcribed in *RCC*, 95–100.

'Allegory and Irony in Baudelaire.' Sixth Gauss lecture, originally announced under the title 'The Romantic Heritage: Allegory and Irony in Baudelaire,' delivered at Princeton, 11 May 1967, transcribed in *RCC*, 101–19.

1969

'Vérité et méthode dans l'œuvre de Georges Poulet.' *Critique* 266 (July 1969), 608–23. Trans. Paul de Man as 'The Literary Self as Origin: The Work of Georges Poulet,' *BI*, 79–101.

'The Rhetoric of Temporality.' In *Interpretation: Theory and Practice*, ed. Charles S. Singleton, 173–209. Baltimore: Johns Hopkins University Press, 1969. Rpr. in *BI*, 187–228.

1970

'Literary History and Literary Modernity.' *Daedalus* 99:2 (Spring 1970), 284–404. Rpr. in *BI*, 142–65.

'Lyric and Modernity.' in *Forms of Lyric*, ed. Rueben A. Brower, 151–76. New York: Columbia University Press, 1970. Rpr. in *BI*, 166–86.

Foreword to *BI*, vii–x.

'The Riddle of Hölderlin.' Review of *Poems and Fragments* by Friedrich Hölderlin. *New York Review of Books*, 19 November 1970, 47–52. Rpr. in *CW*, 198–213.

1971

'The Rhetoric of Blindness: Jacques Derrida's Reading of Rousseau.' In *BI*, 102–42.

1972

'Roland Barthes and the Limits of Structuralism.' *Yale French Studies* 77 (1990), 177–90. Transcription of unpublished manuscript probably written in 1972. Revised version, based on a later typescript, published in *RCC*, 164–77.

'Genesis and Genealogy in Nietzsche's *Birth of Tragedy*.' *Diacritics* 2:4 (Winter 1972), 44–53. Rpr. as 'Genesis and Genealogy (Nietzsche)' in *AR*, 79–102.

1976

'Political Allegory in Rousseau.' *Critical Inquiry* 2:4 (Summer 1976), 649–75. Rpr. as 'Promises *(Social Contract)*' in *AR*, 246–77.

1977

'The Purloined Ribbon.' *Glyph* 1 (1977), 28–49. Rpr. as 'Excuses *(Confessions)*' in *AR*, 278–301.

1978

Foreword to *The Dissimulating Harmony,* by Carol Jacobs, vii–xiii. Baltimore: Johns Hopkins University Press, 1978. Rpr. in *CW*, 218–23.

1979

Introduction to *Studies in Romanticism* 18:4 (Winter 1979), 495–99.
'Allegory *(Julie).*' In *AR*, 188–220.
'Self *(Pygmalion).*' In *AR*, 160–87.
'Autobiography as De-Facement.' *MLN (Modern Language Notes)* 94:5 (December 1979), 919–30. Rpr. in *RR*, 67–81.
'Shelley Disfigured.' In *Deconstruction and Criticism,* ed. Harold Bloom et al., 399–73. New York: Seabury Press, 1979. Rpr. in *RR*, 93–123.

1980

'Interview with Paul de Man.' *The Yale Review* 73:4 (Summer 1984), 576–602. Conducted by Robert Moynihan, 1980.

1981

'Hypogram and Inscription: Michael Riffaterre's Poetics of Reading.' *Diacritics* 11:4 (Winter 1981), 17–35. Rpr. in *RT*, 27–53.
'Murray Krieger: A Commentary.' In *RCC*, 239–62. Response at a 1981 conference at Northwestern University.

1982

'The Resistance to Theory.' *Yale French Studies* vol. 63 (1982), 3–20. Rpr. in *RT*, 3–20.
'Sign and Symbol in Hegel's *Aesthetics.*' *Critical Inquiry* 8:4 (Summer 1982), 761–75.

1983

Foreword to rev., 2d ed. of *BI*, XI–XII.
'Dialogue and Dialogism.' *Poetics Today* 4:1 (Spring 1983), 99–107. Rpr. in *RT*, 106–14.
'Anthropomorphism and Trope in the Lyric.' In *RR*, 239–62.
'"Conclusions": Walter Benjamin's *Task of the Translator.*' *Yale French Studies* 69 (1985), 25–46. Edited transcript of the last of six Messenger Lectures, Cornell University, 4 March 1983. Rpr. with question and answer session in *RT*, 73–105.
'Phenomenality and Materiality in Kant.' In *Hermeneutics: Questions and*

Prospects, ed. Gary Shapiro and Alan Sica, 121–44. Amherst: University of Massachussets Press, 1984.

'An Interview with Paul de Man.' *Nuova Corrente* 93 (1984), 303–13. Conducted by Stefano Rosso, 4 March 1983. Rpr. in RT, 115–21.

Preface to RR, vii–ix.

Secondary Sources

Arac, Jonathan. 1983. 'Afterword.' In *The Yale Critics: Deconstruction in America,* ed. Jonathan Arac et al., 176–99. Minneapolis: University of Minnesota Press.

Assouline, Pierre. 1990. *L'Epuration des intellectuels.* 2d ed., rev. Brussels: Editions Complexe.

Attridge, Derek. 1987. 'Language as History / History as Language: Saussure and the Romance of Etymology.' In *Post-Structuralism and the Question of History,* ed. Derek Attridge, Geoff Bennington, & Robert Young, 183–211. Cambridge: Cambridge University Press.

Bahti, Timothy. 1989. 'Lessons of Remembering and Forgetting.' In *Reading de Man Reading,* ed. Lindsay Waters & Wlad Godzich, 244–58. Minneapolis: University of Minnesota Press.

Balfour, Ian. 1989. '"Difficult Reading": De Man's Itineraries.' In *Responses: On Paul de Man's Wartime Journalism,* ed. Werner Hamacher, Neil Hertz, & Thomas Keenan, 6–20. Lincoln: University of Nebraska Press.

Barny, Roger. 1991. 'Robespierre, Rousseau et le problème réligieux: De la "réligion civile" à l'époque révolutionnaire.' In *Rousseau, die Revolution und der junge Hegel,* ed. Hans Friedrich Fulda & Rolf-Peter Horstmann, 176–202. Stuttgart: Klett-Cotta.

Benjamin, Walter. 1977a. 'Die Bedeutung der Sprache im Trauerspiel und Tragödie.' In *Gesammelte Schriften.* Vol. 2, bk. 1, *Aufsätze, Essays, Vorträge,* ed. Rolf Tiedemann & Herman Schweppenhäuser, 137–40. Frankfurt am Main: Suhrkamp.

———. 1977b. *Illuminationen: Ausgewählte Schriften.* Frankfurt am Main: Suhrkamp.

———. 1978. *Ursprung des deutschen Trauerspiels,* ed. Rolf Tiedemann. Frankfurt am Main: Suhrkamp.

Bialostosky, Don H. 1992. *Wordsworth, Dialogics, and the Practice of Criticism.* Cambridge: Cambridge University Press.

Blanchot, Maurice. 1949. 'La littérature et le droit à la mort.' In *La part du feu,* 305–45. Paris: Gallimard.

———. 1955. *L'espace littéraire*. Paris: Gallimard.
Bloom, Allan. 1988. *The Closing of the American Mind*. New York: Simon and Schuster.
Bové, Paul. 1983. 'Variations on Authority: Some Deconstructive Transformations of the New Criticism.' In *The Yale Critics: Deconstruction in America*, ed. Jonathan Arac et al., 3–19. Minneapolis: University of Minnesota Press.
Bretzius, Stephen. 1987. '"By Heaven, Thou Echoest Me": Lentricchia, *Othello*, de Man.' *Diacritics* 17:2 (Spring), 21–32.
Camus, Albert. 1952. 'Lettre au directeur des *Temps modernes*.' *Les Temps modernes* 8:82 (August), 317–33.
———. 1977. *Essais*, ed. R. Quilliot and L. Faucon, introduction by R. Quilliot. Paris: Gallimard (Bibliothèque de la Pléiade).
Carroll, David. 1980. 'Representation or the End(s) of History: Dialectics and Fiction.' *Yale French Studies* 59, 201–22.
Cebulla, Michael. 1992. *Wahrheit und Authentizität: Zur Entwicklung der Literaturtheorie Paul de Mans*. Stuttgart: M-&-P.
Chambers, E. K. [1903] 1963. *The Medieval Stage*. 2 vols. Oxford: Oxford University Press.
Chase, Cynthia. 1986. 'Giving a Face to a Name: De Man's Figures.' In *Decomposing Figures: Rhetorical Readings in the Romantic Tradition*, 82–112. Baltimore: Johns Hopkins University Press.
———. 1989. 'Trappings of an Education.' In *Responses: On Paul de Man's Wartime Journalism*, ed. Werner Hamacher, Neil Hertz, & Thomas Keenan, 44–79. Lincoln: University of Nebraska Press.
———. 1991. 'Translating Romanticism: Literary Theory as the Criticism of Aesthetics in the Work of Paul de Man.' *Textual Practice* 4:3 (Winter), 349–75.
Chebel d' Appollonia, Ariane. 1991a. *Histoire politique des intellectuels en France, 1944–1954*. Vol. 1, *Des lendemains qui déchantent*. Bruxelles: Editions Complexe.
———. 1991b. *Histoire politique des intellectuels en France, 1944–1954*. Vol. 2, *Le temps de l'engagement*. Bruxelles: Editions Complexe.
Christensen, Jerome. 1990. 'From Rhetoric to Corporate Populism: A Romantic Critique of the Academy in an Age of High Gossip.' *Critical Inquiry* 16 (Winter), 438–65.
Culler, Jonathan. 1971. 'Frontiers of Criticism.' *The Yale Review* 61:2 (December), 259–71.

———. 1990. 'The Future of Paul de Man.' *Colloquium Helveticum* 11/12, 259–74.

De Graef, Ortwin. 1990. 'A Stereotype of Aesthetic Ideology: Paul de Man, Ernst Jünger.' *Colloquium Helveticum* 11/12, 39–70.

———. 1992. 'De zelfbepaling van het Amerikaanse subject.' *Tmesis* 2, 114–19.

———. 1993a. *Serenity in Crisis: A Preface to Paul de Man, 1939–1960*. Lincoln: University of Nebraska Press.

———. 1993b. 'de Mania.' Letter to the Editor. *London Review of Books*, 16 December, 4.

De Man, Hendrik. 1944. *Cahiers de ma montagne*. Brussels: Toison d'Or.

Derrida, Jacques. 1967. 'La structure, le signe et le jeu dans le discours des sciences humaines.' In *L'ecriture et la différence*, 409–28. Paris: Seuil.

———. 1972. 'La mythologie blanche: la métaphore dans le texte philosophique.' In *Marges de la philosophie*, 247–324. Paris: Minuit.

———. 1978. *Eperons: Les styles de Nietzsche*. Paris: Flammarion.

———. 1980. 'Le facteur de la vérité.' In *La carte postale de Socrate à Freud et au delà*, 440–524. Paris: Flammarion.

———. 1985. 'In Memoriam.' *Yale French Studies (The Lesson of Paul de Man)* vol. 69, 13–16.

———. 1986. *Mémoires: For Paul de Man*. Trans. Cecile Lindsay, Jonathan Culler, and Eduardo Cadava. New York: Columbia University Press.

———. 1988. 'Otobiographies: The Teaching of Nietzsche and the Politics of the Proper Name.' Trans. Avital Ronnell. In *The Ear of the Other: Otobiography, Transference, Translation*, ed. Christie McDonald, 1–38. Lincoln: University of Nebraska Press.

———. 1989. 'Like the Sound of the Sea Deep Within a Shell: Paul de Man's War.' Trans. Peggy Kamuf. In *Responses: On Paul de Man's Wartime Journalism*, ed. Werner Hamacher, Neil Hertz, & Thomas Keenan, 127–64. Lincoln: University of Nebraska Press.

De Schutter, Dirk. 1988. 'Heideggers filosofie van de transcendentie.' *Tijdschrift voor Filosofie* 50:3 (September), 453–91.

De Waelhens, Alphonse. [1942] 1971. *La philosophie de Martin Heidegger*. Louvain: Nauwelaerts.

D'Hondt, Jacques. 1991. 'Le vieil Hegel et la critique des idées abstraites de Rousseau.' In *Rousseau, die Revolution und der junge Hegel*, ed. Hans Friedrich Fulda & Rolf-Peter Horstmann, 74–93. Stuttgart: Klett-Cotta.

Esch, Deborah. 1990. 'The Work to Come.' *Diacritics* 20:3 (Fall), 28–49.

Felman, Shoshana, and Dori Laub, M.D. 1992. *Testimony: Crises of Witnessing in Literature, Psychoanalysis, and History.* New York: Routledge.
Felperin, Howard. 1985. *Beyond Deconstruction: The Uses and Abuses of Literary Theory.* Oxford: Clarendon Press.
Fletcher, Angus. 1972. 'The Perpetual Error.' *Diacritics* 2:4, 14–20.
Gabriel, Norbert. 1989. 'Paul de Man on Hölderlin.' In *(Dis)continuities: Essays on Paul de Man,* ed. Luc Herman, Kris Humbeeck, & Geert Lernout, 111–32. Amsterdam: Rodopi.
Gadamer, Hans-Georg. 1965. *Wahrheit und Methode: Grundzüge einer philosophischen Hermeneutik.* 2d ed., enlarged. Tübingen: Mohr.
Gasché, Rodolphe. 1986. *The Tain of the Mirror: Derrida and the Philosophy of Reflection.* Cambridge: Harvard University Press.
——— . 1989. 'In-Difference to Philosophy: de Man on Kant, Hegel, and Nietzsche.' In *Reading de Man Reading,* ed. Lindsay Waters & Wlad Godzich, 259–94. Minneapolis: University of Minnesota Press.
Geldof, Koenraad. 1992. *La voix et l'évenement: Pour une analytique du discours métalittéraire.* Diss., Louvain.
Gelley, Alexander. 1962. 'Staiger, Heidegger, and the Task of Criticism.' *Modern Language Quarterly* 23:3 (September), 195–216.
Godzich, Wlad. 1986. 'Foreword: The Tiger on the Paper Mat.' In Paul de Man, *The Resistance to Theory,* ix–xviii. Minneapolis: University of Minnesota Press.
Goodhart, Sandor. 1989. 'Disfiguring de Man: Literature, History, and Collaboration.' In *Responses: On Paul de Man's Wartime Journalism,* ed. Werner Hamacher, Neil Hertz, & Thomas Keenan, 226–45. Lincoln: University of Nebraska Press.
Hamacher, Werner. 1979. 'Hermeneutische Ellipsen: Schrift und Zirkel bei Schleiermacher.' In *Texthermeutik: Aktualitat, Geschichte, Kritik,* ed. Ulrich Nassen, 113–48. Paderborn: Schöningh.
——— . 1989. 'LECTIO: de Man's Imperative.' Trans. Susan Bernstein. In *Reading de Man Reading,* ed. Lindsay Waters & Wlad Godzich, 171–202. Minneapolis: University of Minnesota Press.
Hamlin, Cyrus. 1989. 'Literary History Beyond New Criticism: De Man's Essays on Romanticism and Modernism.' In *(Dis)continuities: Essays on Paul de Man,* ed. Luc Herman, Kris Humbeeck, & Geert Lernout, 133–48. Amsterdam: Rodopi.
Harrier, Richard. 1993. 'de Mania.' Letter to the Editor. *London Review of Books,* 18 November, 4.

Hartman, Geoffrey H. 1980. *Criticism in the Wilderness: The Study of Literature Today*. New Haven: Yale University Press.

Hart Nibbrig, Christiaan L. 1990. 'La Musique de la théorie ou: Que veut dire "représenter."' Trans. from German by Marc S. Abbühl. *Colloquium Helveticum* 11/12, 109–24.

Haverkamp, Anselm. 1985. 'Error in Mourning—A Crux in Hölderlin: "dem gleich fehlet die Trauer" ("Mnemosyne").' *Yale French Studies (The Lesson of Paul de Man)* vol. 69, 238–53.

Hegel, G. W. F. 1941. *La phénoménologie de l'esprit*. Trans. into French by Jean Hyppolite. 2 vols. Paris: Aubier.

———. 1967. *Einleitung in die Ästhetik*, ed. Wolfhart Henckmann, foreword by Heinrich Gustav Hotho. Munich: Fink.

———. 1970. *Werke in zwanzig Banden*. Vol. 12, *Vorlesungen über die Philosophie der Geschichte*. Frankfurt: Suhrkamp.

———. 1977. *Phenomenology of Spirit*. Trans. A. V. Miller, analysis of text and foreword by J. N. Findlay. Oxford: Clarendon Press.

———. 1988. *Phänomenologie des Geistes*. Ed. Hans-Friedrich Wessels & Heinrich Clairmont, introduction by Wolfgang Beusiepen. Hamburg: Meiner.

Heidegger, Martin. 1959. *Gelassenheit*. Pfullingen: Neske.

———. [1926] 1977. *Gesamtausgabe*, 1. Abteilung, Vol. 2, *Sein und Zeit*. Frankfurt am Main: Klostermann.

———. 1978. *Being and Time*. Trans. John Macquarrie and Edward Robinson. Oxford: Blackwell.

———. [1950] 1981. 'Vorwort zur Zweiten Auflage.' In *Gesamtausgabe*, 1. Abteilung, Vol. 4, *Erläuterungen zu Hölderlins Dichtung*, 8–9. Frankfurt am Main: Klostermann.

Hölderlin, Friedrich. 1951. *Sämtliche Werke: Grosse Stuttgarter Ausgabe*. Vol. 2, *Gedichte nach 1800*. Ed. Friedrich Beißner. Stuttgart: Kohlhammer.

———. 1969a. *Werke und Briefe*. Vol. 2, *Der Tod des Empedokles—Aufsätze—Übersetzungen—Briefe*. Ed. Friedrich Beißner & Jochen Schmidt. Frankfurt am Main: Insel.

———. 1969b. *Werke und Briefe*. Vol. 3, *Erläuterungen*. Ed. Friedrich Beißner & Jochen Schmidt. Frankfurt am Main: Insel.

———. 1979. *Sämtliche Werke: Frankfurter Ausgabe*. Vol. 14, *Entwürfe zur Poetik*. Ed. Wolfram Grodeck & D. E. Sattler. Frankfurt am Main: Roter Stern.

———. 1982a. *Sämtliche Werke: Frankfurter Ausgabe*. Vol. 10, *Hyperion I*.

Ed. Michael Knaupp & D. E. Sattler. Frankfurt am Main: Roter Stern.

———. 1982b. *Sämtliche Werke: Frankfurter Ausgabe.* Vol. 11, *Hyperion II.* Ed. Michael Knaupp & D. E. Sattler. Frankfurt am Main: Roter Stern.

———. 1984. *Sämtliche Werke: Frankfurter Ausgabe.* Vol. 5, *Oden II.* Ed. Michael Knaupp & D. E. Sattler. Frankfurt am Main: Roter Stern.

———. 1988. *Essays and Letters on Theory.* Ed. and trans. Thomas Pfau. Albany: State University of New York Press.

Hoy, David Couzens. 1978. 'Hermeneutic Circularity, Indeterminacy, and Incommensurability.' *New Literary History* 10:1 (Autumn), 161–73.

Husserl, Edmund. [1935] 1976. 'Die Krisis des europäischen Menschentums und die Philosophie.' In *Gesammelte Werke.* Vol. 6, *Die Krisis der europäischen Wissenschaften und die transzendentale Phänomenologie,* ed. Walter Biemel, 314–48. The Hague: Martinus Nijhoff.

Hyppolite, Jean. 1946. *Genèse et structure de la 'Phénoménologie de l'Esprit' de Hegel.* Paris: Aubier.

———. 1974. *Genesis and Structure of Hegel's 'Phenomenology of Spirit.'* Trans. Samuel Cherniak and John Heckman. Evanston: Northwestern University Press.

Jacobs, Carol. 1989. 'Allegories of Reading Paul de Man.' In *Reading de Man Reading,* ed. Lindsay Waters & Wlad Godzich, 105–20. Minneapolis: University of Minnesota Press.

Jameson, Fredric. 1992. *Postmodernism; or, The Cultural Logic of Late Capitalism.* London: Verso.

Jeanson, Francis. 1951. *Montaigne par lui-même.* Paris: Seuil.

———. 1952a. 'Albert Camus ou l'âme révoltée.' *Les Temps modernes* 7:79 (May), 2070–90.

———. 1952b. 'Pour tout vous dire...' *Les Temps modernes* 8:82 (August), 354–83.

Johnson, Barbara. 1990. 'Poison or Remedy? Paul de Man as Pharmakon.' *Colloquium Helveticum* 11/12, 7–20.

Judt, Tony. 1992. *Un passé imparfait: les intellectuels en France 1944–1956.* Trans. into French by Pierre-Emmanuel Dauzat. Paris: Fayard.

Kaplan, Alice. 1993. *French Lessons: A Memoir.* Chicago: University of Chicago Press.

Kennedy, Alan. 1990. *Reading Resistance Value: Deconstructive Practice and the Politics of Literary Critical Practice.* London: Macmillan.

Klein, Richard. 1973. 'The Blindness of Hyperboles: The Ellipses of Insight.' *Diacritics* 3:2 (Summer), 33–43.

———. 1989. 'De Man's Resistances: A Contribution to the Future Science of DeManology.' In *Responses: On Paul de Man's Wartime Journalism*, ed. Werner Hamacher, Neil Hertz, & Thomas Keenan, 283–97. Lincoln: University of Nebraska Press.

Kojève, Alexandre. [1947] 1985. *Introduction à la lecture de Hegel: Leçons sur la 'Phénoménologie de l'Esprit.'* Lectures taught from 1933 to 1939 at the Ecole des Hautes Etudes, assembled by Raymond Queneau. Paris: Gallimard.

Lacoue-Labarthe, Philippe. 1987. *La fiction du politique: Heidegger, l'art et la politique*. Paris: Bourgois.

Legros, Robert. 1991. 'De la réligion du coeur à la réligion du peuple.' In *Rousseau, die Revolution und der junge Hegel*, ed. Hans Friedrich Fulda & Rolf-Peter Horstmann, 94–110. Stuttgart: Klett-Cotta.

Lehman, David. 1991. *Signs of the Times: Deconstruction and the Fall of Paul de Man*. New York: Poseidon Press.

Lemmens, Willem. 1994. 'Zelf en gemeenschap: de paradox van de moderne identiteit volgens Charles Taylor.' *Tijdschrift voor Filosofie* 56:1, 117–33.

Lentricchia, Frank. 1983. *Criticism and Social Change*. Chicago: University of Chicago Press.

Lepenies, Wolf. 1988. *Between Literature and Science: The Rise of Sociology*. Trans. R. J. Hollingdale. Cambridge: Cambridge University Press.

Levinas, Emmanuel. [1956] 1975. 'Le regard du poète.' In *Sur Maurice Blanchot*, 7–26. Fata Morgana.

Loesberg, Jonathan. 1991. *Aestheticism and Deconstruction: Pater, Derrida, and de Man*. Princeton: Princeton University Press.

Lottman, Herbert. 1981. *La rive gauche: du Front populaire à la guerre froide*. Trans. into French by Marianne Véron. Paris: Seuil.

McCarthy, Patrick. 1982. *Camus: A Critical Study of His Life and Work*. London: Hamish Hamilton.

McGann, Jerome. 1988. *Social Values and Poetic Acts*. Cambridge: Harvard University Press.

Merleau-Ponty, Maurice. 1947. 'Lecture de Montaigne.' *Les Temps modernes* 3:27 (December), 1044–60.

———. 1960. *Signes*. Paris: Gallimard.

———. 1964. *Signs*. Trans. and introduction by Richard C. McCleary. Evanston: Northwestern University Press.

———. [1947] 1980. *Humanisme et terreur: Essai sur le problème communiste*. Introduction by Claude Lefort. Paris: Gallimard.

Mizumura, Minae. 1985. 'Renunciation.' *Yale French Studies (The Lesson of Paul de Man)* vol. 69, 81–97.

Montaigne. 1988. *Les essais*. Ed. Pierre Villey. 3 vols. Paris: Quadrige/ P.U.F.

Nägele, Rainer. 1985. *Texte, Geschichte und Subjektivität in Hölderlins Dichtung: 'Uneßbarer Schrift gleich.'* Stuttgart: Metzler.

Nancy, Jean-Luc. 1982. *Le partage des voix*. Paris: Galilée.

———. 1990. *La Communauté désoeuvrée*. New edition, revised and augmented. Paris: Bourgois.

Negri, Antonio. 1991. *The Savage Anomaly: The Power of Spinoza's Metaphysics and Politics*. Trans. Michael Hardt. Mineapolis: University of Minnesota Press.

Newmark, Kevin. 1988. 'Editor's Preface.' *Yale French Studies (Phantom Proxies: Symbolism and the Rhetoric of History)* vol. 74, iii–vii.

———. 1989. 'Paul de Man's History.' In *Reading de Man Reading*, ed. Lindsay Waters & Wlad Godzich, 121–35. Minneapolis: University of Minnesota Press.

———. 1992. *'L'absolu littéraire:* Friedrich Schlegel and the Myth of Irony.' MLN *(Modern Language Notes)* 107:5, 905–30.

Nietzsche, Friedrich. 1980. *Sämtliche Werke. Kritische Studienausgabe*. Ed. Georgio Colli & Mazzino Montinari. 15 vols. Munich: DTV.

Norris, Christopher. 1982. *Deconstruction: Theory and Practice*. London: Methuen.

———. 1988a. *Paul de Man: Deconstruction and the Critique of Aesthetic Ideology*. New York: Routledge.

———. 1988b. 'Utopian Deconstruction: Ernst Bloch, Paul de Man, and the Politics of Music.' In *Deconstruction and the Interests of Theory*, 29–58. London: Pinter.

Paglia, Camille. 1991. 'Ninnies, Pedants, Tyrants, and Other Academics.' *The New York Times Book Review*, 5 May, 1, 29, 33.

Philipsen, Bart. 1990. 'Herz aus Glas: Hölderlin, Rousseau, und das "blöde" Subjekt der Moderne.' In *Bild-Sprache: Texte zwischen Dichten und Denken. Festschrift für Ludo Verbeeck*, ed. Luc Lambrechts & Johan Nowé, 177–94. Leuven: Universitaire Pers Leuven.

———. 1994. *Die List der Einfalt. Eine NachLese zu Hölderlins spätesten Dichtungen*. München: Fink.

Philonenko, Alexis. 1991. 'Rousseau et Hegel. Droit et Histoire.' In *Rousseau, die Revolution und der junge Hegel*, ed. Hans Friedrich Fulda & Rolf-Peter Horstmann, 23–40. Stuttgart: Klett-Cotta.

Plato. 1937. *The Republic*. Trans. Paul Shorey. 2 vols. Cambridge: Harvard University Press.

———. 1987. *The Republic*. Trans. Desmond Lee. 2d ed., rev. London: Penguin.

Poulet, Georges. [1961] 1979. *Les métamorphoses du cercle*. Preface by Jean Starobinski. Paris: Flammarion.

Putnam, Hilary. 1983. 'Why There Isn't a Ready-made World.' In *Realism and Reason. Philosophical Papers*, vol. 3, 205–28. Cambridge: Cambridge University Press.

Rajan, Tilottama. 1985. 'Displacing Post-Structuralism: Romantic Studies after Paul de Man.' *Studies in Romanticism* 24 (Winter), 451–74.

Rand, Richard. 1986. 'Ozone: An Essay on Keats.' In *Post-Structuralist Readings of English Poetry*, ed. Richard Machin & Christopher Norris, 294–307. Cambridge: Cambridge University Press.

Raval, Suresh. 1981. *Metacriticism*. Athens: University of Georgia Press.

Redfield, Marc W. 1989. 'Humanizing de Man.' *Diacritics* 19:2 (Summer), 35–53.

———. 1990. 'De Man, Schiller, and the Politics of Reception.' *Colloquium Helveticum* 11/12, 139–67.

Rolland, Romain. 1942. *Le Voyage intérieur*. Paris: Albin Michel.

Rorty, Richard. 1993. 'In a Flattened World.' *London Review of Books* 15:7 (8 April), 3.

Rosiek, Jan. 1989. 'Source, Writing, (Dis)Figuration: Martin Heidegger and Paul de Man.' In *(Dis)continuities: Essays on Paul de Man*, ed. Luc Herman, Kris Humbeeck, and Geert Lernout, 85–97. Amsterdam: Rodopi.

———. 1992. *Figures of Failure: Paul de Man's Criticism 1953–1970*. Aarhus: Aarhus University Press.

Rousseau, Jean-Jacques. 1959. *Œuvres Complètes*. Vol. 1, *Les Confessions. Autres Textes Autobiographiques*. Ed. Bernard Gagnebin et al. Paris: Gallimard (Bibliothèque de la Pléiade).

———. 1964. *Œuvres Complètes*. Vol. 2, *La Nouvelle Héloïse. Théatre. Poésies. Essais littéraires*. Ed. Bernard Gagnebin et al. Paris: Gallimard (Bibliothèque de la Pléiade).

Ruskin, John. 1963. 'Of the Pathetic Fallacy.' In *English Literary Criticism: Romantic and Victorian*, ed. Daniel G. Hoffman & Samuel Hynes, 200–217. New York: Appleton-Century-Crofts.

Sartre, Jean-Paul. 'Réponse à Albert Camus.' *Les Temps modernes* 8:82 (August), 334–53.

Schaefer, David Lewis. 1990. *The Political Philosophy of Montaigne*. Ithaca: Cornell University Press.
Servotte, Herman. 1990. 'Paul de Man über Wordsworth.' In *Bild-Sprache: Texte zwischen Dichten und Denken. Festschrift für Ludo Verbeeck*, ed. Luc Lamberechts & Johan Nowé, 259–64. Leuven: Universitaire Pers Leuven.
Shelley, Percy Bysshe. 1963. 'A Defence of Poetry.' In *English Literary Criticism: Romantic and Victorian*, ed. Daniel G. Hoffman & Samuel Hynes, 160–90. New York: Appleton-Century-Crofts.
Shusterman, Ronald. 1988. *Critique et poésie selon I.A. Richards: De la confiance positiviste au relativisme naissant*. Lille: Atelier National de Reproduction des Thèses.
Silverman, Hugh J., and Don Ihde, eds. 1985. *Hermeneutics and Deconstruction*. Albany: State University of New York Press.
Simon, Gerhard. 1991. *Nationalism and Policy toward the Nationalities in the Soviet Union: From Totalitarian Dictatorship to Post-Stalinist Society*. Trans. Karen Forster and Oswald Forster. Boulder: Westview Press.
Spanos, William V. 1976. 'Heidegger, Kierkegaard, and the Hermeneutic Circle: Towards a Post-Modern Theory of Interpretation as Disclosure.' *boundary 2* 4:2 (Winter), 455–88.
———. 1977. 'Breaking the Circle: Hermeneutics as Dis-Closure.' *boundary 2* 5:2 (Winter), 421–57.
Spinoza, Baruch. 1977. *Spinoza's Ethics and On the Correction of the Understanding*. Trans. Andrew Boyle, introduction by T. S. Gregory. London: Dent.
Starobinski, Jean. 1982. *Montaigne en mouvement*. Paris: Gallimard.
Stucky, Willy. 1980. *Friedrich Hölderlin und Albert Camus: Zur Verwandtschaft zentraler Gedanken eines schwäbischen 'Theologen' des ausgehenden 18. Jh. und eines franco-algerischen Agnostikers des 20. Jh*. Zürich: ADAG.
Taylor, Charles. 1975. *Hegel*. Cambridge: Cambridge University Press.
———. 1989. *Sources of The Self: The Making of the Modern Identity*. Cambridge: Harvard University Press.
———. 1991. *The Malaise of Modernity [The Ethics of Authenticity]*. Concord: Anansi.
Terada, Rei. 1993. Review of Paul de Man, *Romanticism and Contemporary Criticism. Studies in Romanticism* 23:3 (Fall), 457–63.

Toulmin, Stephen. 1990. *Cosmopolis: The Hidden Agenda of Modernity.* New York: The Free Press.
Van Beers, Jan. 1921. *Gedichten: Eeuwfeestuitgave.* Antwerp: Opdebeek.
Verene, Donald Phillip. 1985. *Hegel's Recollection: A Study of Images in Hegel's 'Phenomenology of Spirit.'* Albany: State University of New York Press.
Wahl, Jean. 1962. *Tableau de la philosophie française.* Rev. ed. Paris: Gallimard.
Warminski, Andrzej. 1984. 'Missed Crossing: Wordsworth's Apocalypses.' *MLN (Modern Language Notes)* 99:5 (December), 983–1006.
———. Forthcoming. 'Ending Up / Taking Back (with two postscripts on Paul de Man's historical materialism).' Typescript.
Waters, Lindsay. 1989. 'Introduction. Paul de Man: Life and Works.' In Paul de Man, *Critical Writings, 1953–78,* ix–lxxiv. Minneapolis: University of Minnesota Press.
Weber, Samuel. 1989. 'The Monument Disfigured.' In *Responses: On Paul de Man's Wartime Journalism,* ed. Werner Hamacher, Neil Hertz, and Thomas Keenan, 404–25. Lincoln: University of Nebraska Press.
Wordsworth, William. 1959. *The Prelude; or, Growth of a Poet's Mind,* ed. Ernest de Selincourt. 2d ed., rev. by Helen Derbishire. Oxford: Clarendon Press.
———. 1974. 'Preface to the Edition of 1815.' In *The Prose Works of William Wordsworth,* vol. 3, ed. W. J. B. Owen & Jane Worthington Smyser, 21–52. Oxford: Clarendon Press.
———. 1989. *William Wordsworth* (The Oxford Authors). Ed. Stephen Gill. Oxford: Oxford University Press.
Wright, T. R. 1988. *Theology and Literature.* Oxford: Blackwell.

Index

Abrams, Meyer, 248n.17
Absolute Spirit. *See* Hegel: Absolute Spirit in
'"Achill" by Friedrich Hölderlin,' 218n.8
Action. *See* Consciousness: and action
Action française, 170
Adorno, Theodor W., 246n.8
Algeria, as French colony, 233n.68
Allegories of Reading (AR), 211, 213–14, 223n.6, 238n.27; Preface to ('PAR'), 72, 214
Allegory, 201–2, 211–12
'Allegory (*Julie*)' ('RJ'), 51, 237n.24
'Allegory and Irony in Baudelaire' ('AIB'), 142, 163–64, 175, 208, 252n.3, 253n.12, 327n.24, 328n.29
Analogism: and Romanticism, 58–59, 80–81, 122–23, 176, 248n.17; Wordsworth and, 82–88. *See also* Hölderlin: and analogism
Anthropology: and intersubjective interpretation, 129–30; and literature, 128, 138, 176
'Anthropomorphism and Trope in the Lyric' ('AT'), 212, 252n.4, 253n.12
Apocalypse: Hölderlin and, 98–100; and language, 79; and memory, 81–82, 99–101, 111; and Romanticism, 79–81, 98–99, 121–23, 176–77. *See also* History: fulfillment of
Arac, Jonathan, 248n.15
Aristotle, 141
Arnold, Matthew, 238n.28
Assouline, Pierre, 232n.64, 233n.67
Attridge, Derek, 252n.6
Authenticity: and empiricism, 141–45, 162–63, 174–75, 185, 203, 238n.29; and hermeneutics, 197, 200; and literature, 136, 137; and nothingness, 141–42, 144, 168–69, 175, 185–89, 203, 207–9; and reading, 186; and Romanticism, 114–15, 122, 140, 141–43 (*see also* Beautiful Soul: as figure of lucidity)

Bachelard, Gaston, 155–58, 159, 160, 162, 241n.47; and Sartre,

Bachelard, Gaston (*continued*) 175; and Taine, 156–58
'Bachelard and Burke' ('BB'), 155–61, 218n.8, 241n.47
Bahti, Timothy, 221n.28, 228n.17, 251n.25
Balfour, Ian, 224n.21
Barnabas, 253n.10
Barny, Roger, 234n.5
Barrès, Maurice, 170
Barthes, Roland, 127, 232n.64
Baudelaire, Charles: and Benjamin, 201; and Camus, 106; and Mallarmé, 80–81, 154, 162; and Romanticism, 239n.29; and Sartre, 175; and Taine, 152, 154–55; 'Le Cygne,' 201–2; 'Obsession,' 253n.12
Baudrillard, Jean, 232n.64
Beautiful Soul, 244n.67; and Absolute Spirit, 333n.53; as figure of delusion, 105–7, 111, 132–33, 165; as figure of lucidity, 132–33, 137, 140, 142–44, 164–66, 176, 178, 208, 211; and Spiritual Animal, 242n.53. *See also* Hegel: Beautiful Soul in
Beauty, as mediation, 88–90
Being: and history, 78–79; and ideology, 78–79; and language, 79, 186, 187–88, 196, 251n.25; and memory, 84
Beißner, Friedrich, 219n.11, 225n.32, 228n.20
Benjamin, Walter, 201, 251n.30, 252n.31; 'Die Bedeutung der Sprache,' 33; 'Über den Begriff der Geschichte,' 95; *Ursprung des deutschen Trauerspiels*, 201, 251nn.30,31
Bialostosky, Don, 226n.1, 233n.72
Blake, William, xii, 161
Blanchot, Maurice: and Heidegger, 187–88; *L'espace littéraire*, 186, 247n.9; 'La littérature et le droit à la mort,' 93, 242n.53
Blindness and Insight (*BI*), xiii–xiv, 127, 234n.3, 235n.11, 236n.14, 247n.11, 248n.15. *See also* 'Foreword'
Bloom, Allan, 241n.43
Bloom, Harold, 218n.7
Bonaparte, Napoleon, 35; and Hegel, 166; and Rousseau, 35, 168
Böschenstein, Bernard, 224n.23
Bourdieu, Pierre, 232n.64
Bové, Paul, 248n.15
Bretzius, Stephen, 241n.47
Brown, T. E.: 'Dartmoor: Sunset at Chagford,' 29
Burke, Kenneth, 159–61, 162, 241n.48; *Permanence and Change*, 159; *A Rhetoric of Motives*, 241n.47

Camus, Albert: and Baudelaire, 106; and *épuration*, 232n.67; and fascism, 104, 109; and French Resistance, 106; and Gide, 106; and Hegel, 104; and Heidegger, 229n.24; Hellenism of, 124–25; and history, 104, 105, 106–8, 109, 124; and

Hölderlin, 105; and Jeanson, 105–8, 109, 147; and Marxism, 107; and Merleau-Ponty, 232n.62; and nihilism, 104–5, 108; revolt and revolution in, 103–9, 124, 232–33n.67; and Sartre, 105–8, 147, 231–32n.62; and Stalinism, 107; 'Autocritique,' 101; *Carnets (Notebooks)*, 103, 124; *L'homme révolté*, 103–9; 'Lettres à un ami allemand' ('Letters to a German Friend'), 106; 'Le temps du mépris,' 232n.67
Carroll, David, 251n.27
Cebulla, Michael, 235n.11, 327n.22
Cercle du Libre Examen (student organization), 232n.62
Chambers, E. K.: *The Medieval Stage*, 203, 252n.7
Chase, Cynthia, 234n.2, 239n.30, 244n.67, 247n.13
Chebel d'Appollonia, Ariane, 229n.36, 230n.52, 233n.67
Christ, 206, 253n.10
Christensen, Jerome, 226n.4
'Circularité de l'interprétation dans l'œuvre de Maurice Blanchot, La.' See 'Impersonality in the Criticism of Maurice Blanchot'
Coleridge, S. T., 248n.17
Combat, 232n.67
Comments, 236n.12
Communism, 107–8, 231n.62, 241n.48
'"Conclusions": Walter Benjamin's *Task of the Translator*' ('WB'), 176, 245n.69
Consciousness: and action, 17–18, 34–41, 167, 219n.15; circularity of, 188–89; and *Dasein*, 188, 220n.22, 247n.12, 250n.24; and earth, 25–28, 46–47, 48, 125; and form, 152–58, 160–63, 190–95, 198–200; and history, 33–43; intentional structure of, 26–28, 162, 190–95; ontological priority of, 5, 9, 25–28, 32, 45–46, 48, 58, 78, 85, 89, 95, 125, 188, 220n.22, 242n.53, 247n.12, 250n.24 (*see also* Literature: as language of privileged consciousness); relation to object, 15, 16, 23–28, 45–47, 152–54, 160 (*see also* Analogism)
'Contemporary Criticism of Romanticism, The' ('CCR'), 123, 124, 133, 134, 236n.14, 237n.20, 246n.8
Corngold, Stanley, 237n.22
Crisis: and criticism, 115, 128, 134, 175; and literature, 9, 78, 113, 114–15; and phenomenology, 134–35, 238n.29; and structuralism, 136; structure of, 134–36
Critical Writings, 217n.3
Criticism: and crisis, 115, 128, 134, 175
'Criticism and Crisis' ('CC'), 115, 127–39, 143, 145–46, 163, 164, 165, 166–67, 174, 175, 177, 184, 190, 207, 235n.12, 236n.14,

Index | 275

'Criticism and Crisis' (*continued*) 237n.24, 245n.71, 247n.15, 253n.15
Culler, Jonathan, 223n.4, 248n.15
Cuypers, Stefaan E., 245n.72

Dasein, 188, 220n.22, 247n.12, 250n.24
'Dead-End of Formalist Criticism, The' ('DF'), 220nn.17,20, 223n.2, 241n.48, 248n.16
De Man, Hendrik: *Cahiers de ma montagne*, 232n.66
De Man, Paul, interviews with ('INT 1980,' 'INT 1983'), 70, 236n.14. See also titles of specific works
Demystification: and literature, 133–34, 137–40, 188; and Romanticism, 117, 119, 132–34, 137–40
De Quincey, Thomas, 226n.4
Derrida, Jacques, 223n.1, 226n.39, 232n.64, 234n.5, 252n.6; and Heidegger, 249n.19; and structuralism, 131, 236n.14; *La carte postale*, 203; *De la grammatologie*, 222n.36, 236n.14; 'Like the Sound of the Sea,' 109, 228n.22, 233n.67; *Mémoires*, 203, 236n.14; 'La structure, le signe et le jeu,' 130, 236n.14, 237n.21
Descartes, René, 31, 141, 221n.25
De Schutter, Dirk, 249n.19, 253n.12
Desire, 137, 142–43
Destiny, 12–19, 71, 96–97

De Waelhens, Alphonse: *La philosophie de Martin Heidegger*, 13
D'Hondt, Jacques, 234n.5
Dialectic: final term of, 28 (*see also* Hegel: synthesis in); of inwardness and action (*see* Consciousness: and action)
'Dialogue and Dialogism' ('DD'), 206, 218n.8
Dissumulating Harmony, The (Carol Jacobs): de Man's foreword to, 212
'Double Aspect of Symbolism, The' ('DA'), xii, 21, 28, 154, 165, 175, 184, 202, 217n.4, 233–34n.1
Doubrovsky, Serge, 200–201, 251n.29
Dualism, 26–28, 221n.25

Earth: as equivalent of consciousness, 25–28, 46–47, 48, 125; as *In-der-Welt-sein*, 25, 221n.26; in pastoral convention, 18–19
Empiricism: and authenticity, 141–45, 162–63, 174–75, 185, 203, 238n.29; and fiction, 136–39, 187, 207; and history, 177, 187
Empson, William, 220n.17, 241n.47
Epuration, 110, 232n.64, 232–33n.67
Esch, Deborah, 236n.15
Ethics: and literature, 151, 181–83; and science, 151–52
Excess: and recollection, 40–43,

276 | Index

78, 111. *See also* Apocalypse; Romanticism: and Titanism
Existentialism, 107–8

Fascism, 104, 109
Faust, as Romantic prototype, 114, 124
Felman, Shoshana, 228n.23, 229n.36
Felperin, Howard, 251n.28
Fiction: and empiricism, 136–39, 187, 207; and history, 177, 187; and politics, 172–73
Fifth Gauss Lecture, fragment of, 145, 147, 163, 236n.15, 252n.3
Fletcher, Angus, 248n.15
'Foreword [to *Blindness and Insight*]' ('FBI' 1970), 209, 234n.3, 247n.11
'Foreword [to second edition of *Blindness and Insight*]' ('FBI' 1983), 203–4, 211, 213
Foreword to *The Dissumulating Harmony* ('CJ'), 212
Form: and consciousness, 152–58, 160–63, 190–95, 198–200; as essence of art, 152–53; as essence of literature, 156–58, 161, 173, 185–86; as evasion, 106; as transcendence, 112
Formalism, 209, 247–48n.15; and intentionality, 190–91
'Form and Intent in the American New Criticism' ('FI'), 190–98, 200–201, 208, 237n.24, 247n.15, 248nn.16,17, 249nn.21,23, 250n.25
Foucault, Michel, 232n.64; *Les mots et les choses*, 238n.29

Frank, Joseph, 224n.22
Freud, Sigmund, 140
Front populaire, 231n.62
Frye, Northrop, 248n.15

Gabriel, Norbert, 221n.26
Gadamer, Hans-Georg, 249n.19
Gasché, Rodolphe, 221n.25, 254nn.17,18
Geldof, Koenraad, 251n.27
Gelley, Alexander, 248n.19
'Genesis and Genealogy (Nietzsche)' ('NG'), 214, 222n.1
George, Stefan, xi, 169, 170, 171–74, 217n.4, 245n.69; and Hölderlin, 173; politics and historical ideology in, 161, 173
'Georg Lukács's *Theory of the Novel*' ('GL'), 198–200
Gide, André, 172; and Camus, 106
Girard, René, 246n.8; *Le Mensonge romantique*, 124
Godzich, Wlad, 221n.31, 234n.3, 241n.47
Goebbels, Paul Joseph, 244n.67
Goethe, J. W. von, 13, 18; *Wilhelm Meisters Lehrjahre*, 133
Goodhart, Sandor, 252n.3
Greece, as historical type, 15–16, 34, 37, 40, 118–19, 124–25, 243n.62
Gregory, T. S., 140, 240n.40
Gulag, 108
Guyon, Bernard, 219n.8

Hamacher, Werner, 225n.34, 249n.19, 253nn.11,12
Hamburger, Michael, 68

Hamlet, as Romantic prototype, 114
Hamlin, Cyrus, 247n.15
Harrier, Richard, 244n.63
Hartman, Geoffrey, 238n.28
Hart-Nibbrig, Christian, 223n.1
Haverkamp, Anselm, 220n.22, 225n.31, 228n.20
'Heaven and Earth in Wordsworth and Hölderlin' ('HEW'), 80–89, 91, 95, 99, 175, 226n.4, 227n.5
Hegel, G. W. F., 21; Absolute Spirit in, 111, 142, 165, 199, 242n.53; Beautiful Soul in, 105–6, 111, 133, 164–65, 233n.69, 242n.53; and Camus, 104; and Heidegger, 81–82, 169; and Hölderlin, 243n.61; and Kant, 81–82; and Napoleon, 166; and Merleau-Ponty, 243n.61; and pastness of art, 71–72; politics and historical ideology in, 34–36, 64–65, 72, 166, 168; and Romanticism, 81–82, 169; and Rousseau, 28, 34–36, 72–73, 104, 168, 219n.8, 234n.5, 242n.52; and Spinoza, 155; Spiritual Animal in, 242n.53; synthesis in, 28, 34–36, 42, 71–72; and Taine, 155; *Phänomenologie des Geistes (Phenomenology of Spirit)*, 42, 104, 105–6, 111, 133, 142, 165–66, 199, 223n.3; *Vorlesungen über die Philosophie der Geschichte*, 72–73
'Hegel on the Sublime,' 244n.67
Heidegger, Martin, 13, 25, 220n.22, 238n.29; and experience of Being, 185; and Blanchot, 187–88; and Camus, 229n.24; and Derrida, 249n.19; and dualism, 221n.25; and Hegel, 81–82, 169; and hermeneutics, 65–66, 193–94, 196–97, 225n.30, 248n.19, 249n.23, 250nn.24,25; and Hölderlin, 65–66, 169, 220n.23, 221n.26, 246n.8, 250–51n.25; and Kant, 81; and Levinas, 247n.14; and literature, 128; *Erläuterungen zu Hölderlins Dichtung*, 188, 194, 250n.25; 'Rectoral Address,' 169; *Sein und Zeit*, 65, 188, 193–94, 225n.30, 247n.12, 248n.19, 249n.23, 250n.24, 250–51n.25
'Heidegger's Exegeses of Hölderlin' ('HE'), 65, 217n.4, 220n.23, 246n.8, 248n.19, 251n.25
Heller, Erich: *The Artist's Journey into the Interior*, 114, 123, 124
Hermeneutics: and authenticity, 197, 200; circle of, 65–66, 185, 186–89, 193, 225n.30, 248–49n.19, 250–51n.25; and fulfillment, 65–67, 70, 177–78, 185, 188–89, 192–96, 197–98, 199–200, 207–9; and history, 187–89; and reading (*see* Reading: and understanding); and rhetoric, 204–9; and science, 193, 249–50n.23; and temporality, 199
History: and Being, 78–79; and consciousness, 33–43; and destiny, 12–19, 71, 96–97; and

empiricism, 177, 187; exemplary periods in, 15–16, 117–18 (*see also* Greece, as historical type; Romanticism: as privileged historical concern); and fiction, 177, 187; fulfillment of, 41, 56–57, 78–79, 96–97 (*see also* Apocalypse); and hermeneutics, 187–89; and ideology, 34–36, 78–79 (*see also* Politics); and literature, 33–34, 37–38, 80–81, 97, 233n.72; and nihilism, 104, 109; as noematic correlative, 33–34, 36; and science, 145–47; and technology, 229n.24. See also Temporality: historical law of
Hitler, Adolf, 109, 167; and Nietzsche, 122, 168
Hobbes, Thomas, 141
Hölderlin, Friedrich, xi, 4, 171, 218n.1; and Adorno, 246n.8; and analogism, 59–61, 62–63, 84–85, 88–92, 97; and apocalypse, 98–100; and Camus, 105; notion of demi-gods in, 13–14; and destiny, 12–19, 105; and George, 173; and Hegel, 243n.61; and Heidegger, 65–66, 169, 220n.23, 221n.26, 246n.8, 250–51n.25; *idealisch* in, 12, 219nn.11,12; and Merleau-Ponty, 243n.61; politics and historical ideology in, 35, 64–65, 161; and recollection, 47, 52–54, 55, 69–70; and Rousseau, 11, 18–20, 24–25, 26–27, 32, 35, 40–41, 47, 52, 61–62, 67, 69–70, 79–81, 94, 100, 115, 116, 185; notion of source in, 13–14; and temporality, 54–56, 89–90; *vaterländische Umkehr* in, 105, 144, 173; and Wordsworth, 79–82, 84, 91, 94–95, 97, 98, 100, 113, 115, 116, 117, 122, 123, 185; 'An die Stille,' 12, 70; 'Feiertags-Hymne,' 246n.8; 'Der Gesichtspunkt, aus dem wir das Altertum anzusehen haben' ('The Viewpoint from Which We Must Look at Antiquity'), 116; 'Grund zum Empedokles,' 228n.19; 'Hymne an die Menschheit,' 12, 64; *Hyperion*, 12, 54–56, 59–61, 70, 85, 88–91, 133, 225n.27, 226n.40; 'Mnemosyne,' 41–42, 69–70, 72–73, 98–100, 103, 113, 115, 125, 148, 221n.33, 228n.20; 'Palingenesie,' 77; 'Der Rhein,' 12–28, 34, 40, 52–53, 55, 68–69, 91, 220n.23; 'Rousseau,' 12, 61–64, 67–69; 'Über den Unterschied der Dichtarten,' 219n.11
'Hölderlin and the Romantic Tradition' ('HRT'), xii, 11–12, 219nn.14,16, 220n.17, 229n.24
Howard, Richard, 217n.3, 228n.21
Hoy, David Couzens, 249n.19
Husserl, Edmund, 102, 238n.29; and Mallarmé, 245n.71; 'Die Krisis des europäischen Menschentums,' 134–36, 140, 236–37n.19
'Hypogram and Inscription' ('MR'), 237n.25, 245n.73

Index | 279

Hyppolite, Jean, 230n.41; *Genesis and Structure of Hegel's 'Phenomenology,'* 35–36, 165, 233n.69

Ideality (*Idealisch*), 12, 34, 41, 47, 56–57, 67, 78, 96, 170, 219n.12
Ideology: and Being, 78–79; as confusion, 237n.23; and history, 34–36, 78–79 (*see also under individual authors and movements:* politics and historial ideology in); and science, 149–52, 161
Ihde, Don, 249n.19
'Image and Emblem in Yeats' ('WBY'), xiii, 125, 217n.1. *See also* 'Mallarmé, Yeats and the Post-Romantic Predicament'
'Image of Rousseau in the Poetry of Hölderlin, The' ('IR'), 9–10, 11–32, 33–37, 40–42, 44, 46, 47, 61–65, 68–70, 71, 78, 79, 88, 95, 100, 115, 116, 122, 164, 168, 175, 219n.15, 220n.19, 222n.1, 223n.6, 226n.1, 247n.12, 248n.19, 250n.25
Imagination, self-sufficiency of, 3–9, 21, 23, 25–26, 28, 46–47, 125; in Wordsworth, 85–87, 227n.9, 234n.6. *See also* Consciousness
'Impersonality in the Criticism of Maurice Blanchot' ('MB'), 174, 185–88, 208, 214, 245n.71, 247nn.9,11
In-der-Welt-sein, 25, 221n.26
Intentional structure: of consciousness, 26–28, 162, 190–95; and formalism, 190–91
'Intentional Structure of the Romantic Image' ('IS'), xi, 3–9, 11, 21, 22, 23, 25, 27, 39, 46, 62, 78, 79, 125, 163, 175, 207, 211, 217n.1, 218nn.1,5, 221n.32, 226n.1
Interpretation: anthropology and, 129–30; linguistics and, 129, 131; and Romanticism, 117–20; as sheltering act, 99, 115, 117, 125. *See also* Hermeneutics
'Introduction [to *Studies in Romanticism*]' ('SR'), 190, 212, 253–54n.15
'Introduction to the Poetry of John Keats' ('JK'), 37
'Inward Generation, The' ('IG'), 3, 56, 57, 162, 163, 164, 244n.65
Irony: as disruption, 192, 198–200, 201, 211; as totalization, 192, 199–200, 211–12

Jacobs, Carol, 253n.14
Jameson, Fredric: *Postmodernism*, 211
Jeanson, Francis: and Camus, 105–8, 109, 147; and Montaigne, 233n.68
John, Gospel according to, 252n.9, 253n.10
Johnson, Barbara, 244n.67
Judt, Tony, 229n.36, 230n.52, 232n.64, 233n.67
Jünger, Ernst, 3, 241n.45

Kant, Immanuel, 237n.23; and Hegel, 81–82; and Heidegger,

280 | *Index*

81; and Nietzsche, 223n.3; and Romanticism, 81–82
'Kant and Schiller,' 244n.67
Kaplan, Alice, 244n.63
Keats, John, 37, 225n.24; and Mallarmé, 218n.8, 241n.49; 'Ode on a Grecian Urn,' 241n.49; *Selected Poetry* (introduction by de Man), 37
'[Keats]' ('K'), 218n.8, 241n.49
'Keats and Hölderlin' ('KH'), 225nn.24,26
Kennedy, Alan, 241n.47
Kirghize, 230n.56
Klein, Richard, 129, 245n.69
Knaup, Michael, 225n.23
Koestler, Arthur, 231n.58
Kojève, Alexandre: *Introduction à la lecture de Hegel*, 81, 165–66
Kravchenko-affair, 107

Lacan, Jacques, 232n.64, 252n.2
Lacoue-Labarthe, Philippe: *La fiction du politique*, 173, 244n.67
Language: and apocalypse, 79; and Being, 79, 186, 187–88, 196, 251n.25
Languages of Criticism and the Sciences of Man, The (1966 Johns Hopkins colloquium), 130, 175–76, 235–36n.12
Lee, Desmond, 245n.68
Legros, Robert, 219n.8
Lehman, David, 235n.11
Lemmens, Willem, 243n.60
Lentricchia, Frank, 241n.47
Lepenies, Wolfgang, 241n.44, 244n.66
Levin, Harry, xi, 231n.62, 233n.68; de Man letter to, xi, 231n.62, 233n.68
Levinas, Emmanuel: and Heidegger, 247n.14; 'Le regard du poète,' 181, 247n.10
Lévi-Strauss, Claude, 129–31, 156, 174, 235n.11
Linguistics: and intersubjective interpretation, 129, 131; and literature, 128, 138
'Literary History and Literary Modernity' ('LH'), 96, 177
'Literary Self as Origin, The' ('GP'), 237n.24, 246n.8
Literature: and anthropology, 128, 138, 176; and authenticity, 136, 137; and crisis, 9, 78, 113, 114–15; and demystification, 133–34, 137–40, 188; and ethics, 151, 181–83; fictional essence of, 136–39, 187, 207; and form, 156–58, 161, 173, 185–86; and history, 33–34, 37–38, 80–81, 97, 233n.72; and knowledge, 156–57; as language of privileged consciousness, 128–29, 131–32, 133–34, 184–86; and linguistics, 128, 138; and nationalism, 169–70, 172–73, 243–44n.62; and nihilism, 168; and nothingness, 137–40; ontological priority of, 185; and philosophy, 128; and politics, 160–61 (*see also under individual authors and movements:* politics and historical ideology in); and psychoanalysis, 128, 138, 176; and science, 121, 146, 151–52,

Index | 281

Literature (*continued*)
237n.22; and sensory perception, 157; and sociology, 128, 146, 152, 159–61, 176; and temporality, 84, 186–89
'Literature of Nihilism, The' ('LN'), 114–15, 122, 123, 124, 165, 166, 167–68, 172, 174, 251n.30
Loesberg, Jonathan, 222n.36, 236n.14
Lottman, Herbert, 229n.36, 230n.52, 233n.67
Lovejoy, Arthur O., 233n.1
'Ludwig Binswanger and the Sublimation of the Self' ('Ludwig Binswanger et le problème du moi poétique') ('LB'), 139, 141–42, 144, 174, 238n.29, 251n.29
Lukács, Georg: *Theorie des Romans (The Theory of the Novel)*, 198–200
Luke, Gospel according to, 252n.9, 253n.10
Lyotard, Jean-François, 232n.64
'Lyric and Modernity' ('LM'), 204

Macquarrie, John, 249–50n.23
Madagascar, as French colony, 107, 230n.56
'Madame de Staël and Jean-Jacques Rousseau' ('RDS'), 164
Mallarmé, Stéphane, xi, 174; and Baudelaire, 80–81, 154, 162; and crisis, 134, 184; and Husserl, 245n.71; and Keats, 218n.8, 241n.49; politics and historical ideology in, 38, 96, 122, 241n.48; and Rousseau, 39; and Yeats, xiii; *Un coup de dés*, 186
'Mallarmé, Yeats and the Post-Romantic Predicament' ('PHDI,' 'PHDM,' 'PHDY'), xi–xiii, 38–39, 96, 122, 163, 173–74, 217nn.3,4, 241n.48. *See also* 'Image and Emblem in Yeats'
Malraux, André, 56, 62
Mark, Gospel according to, 252n.9, 253n.10
Marx, Karl, 140
Marxism: and existentialism, 107–8, 231n.62; and nihilism, 107–8; as pastoral, 241n.48; and Stalinism, 107–8
'Mask of Albert Camus, The' ('AC'), 103, 124, 125, 148
Mathematics, 210, 253n.12
Matthew, Gospel according to, 252n.9, 253n.10
McCarthy, Joseph, 111
McCarthy, Patrick, 229n.36, 231n.58
McGann, Jerome, 237n.22
'Médiation poétique dans l'œuvre de Mallarmé, Stefan George et W.-B. Yeats, La.' *See* 'Mallarmé, Yeats and the Post-Romantic Predicament'
Memory: and apocalypse, 81–82, 99–101, 111; and Being, 84; and mourning, 99, 113, 115; and temporality, 84
Mendès-France, Pierre, 233n.68

Merleau-Ponty, Maurice, 231n.58, 231n.62, 232n.62, 243n.61; *Les aventures de la dialectique*, 231n.62; *Humanisme et terreur*, 231n.58; 'Lecture de Montaigne,' 231n.58; *Signes (Signs)*, 101

Miller, J. Hillis, 242n.22

Milton, John, 86

Mizumura, Minae, 223n.9

'Modern Poetics: French and German' ('MP'), 169, 172–73, 174, 175

Montaigne, Michel de, 37–38, 240–41n.43; conservatism in, 102–3, 108, 233n.68; and Jeanson, 233n.68; and memory, 101; and Merleau-Ponty, 231n.58; revolt in, 102–3, 108, 109–10, 228n.23, 232n.65, 233n.68; and Rousseau, 115; serenity in, 3, 113; transcendence in, 111–13, 115; and wars of religion, 102–3, 109–10, 232n.64; 'Apologie de Raimond Sebond,' 3, 228n.21; 'On Custom,' 102, 110, 228n.21

'Montaigne and Transcendence' ('MT'), 3, 101–3, 108, 109–13, 203, 232n.62, 233n.68

Moscow Trials, 108, 232n.64

Mosley, Nicholas: *Hopeful Monsters*, 174

Mourning, 99, 113, 115

Moynihan, Robert, 225n.32

'Murray Krieger: A Commentary' ('MK'), 248n.18

Music, 222n.1

Nägele, Rainer, 220n.19, 225nn.28,32

Nancy, Jean-Luc, 245n.68, 249n.19, 250n.24

Napoleon, 35; and Hegel, 166; and Rousseau, 35, 168

Nationalism: and literature, 169–70, 172–73, 243–44n.62; and Stalinism, 108

Natural being. *See* Object

Nazism: and German Romanticism, 124, 166–67

'Néant poétique, Le' ('PN'), xi, 217n.3

Negri, Antonio, 153, 240–41n.43

Neoplatonism, 89

Nerval, Gérard de, xii

Newmark, Kevin, xiv, 218nn.6,8, 253nn.12,14, 254n.16

'A New Vitalism' ('HB'), 218n.7

Newton, Isaac, 155, 156, 158, 160

Nietzsche, Friedrich, 140, 172, 234n.5; and Hitler, 122, 168; and Kant, 223n.3; *Fröhliche Wissenschaft*, 223n.3; *Die Gebürt der Tragödie (Birth of Tragedy)*, 222n.1

Nihilism, 163, 172; and communism, 107–8; and existentialism, 107–8; as fascism, 104, 109; as historicism, 104, 109; literature of, 168; and revolution, 104; as Stalinism, 104, 109

Noematic correlative, 33–34, 36, 64, 78

Index | 283

Norris, Christopher, 36, 38, 223n.1, 223n.6, 236n.14
Nothingness: and authenticity, 141–42, 144, 168–69, 175, 185–89, 203, 207–9; and literature, 137–40; as nihilism, 163; Rousseau and, 137–38, 140, 201
Novalis, xii

Object: and consciousness (*see* Consciousness: relation to object); and form (*see* Consciousness: and form); ontological priority of, 5, 22–23, 45–46, 162, 220nn.21,22. See also Rousseau: and sensory perception; Sensory perception: transcendence of
Ontological priority: of literature, 185. *See also under* Consciousness; Object
'Oldest System-Program of German Idealism, The,' 44, 58

Paglia, Camille, 240–41n.43
Pastoral, 18–19, 56, 175, 220nn.17,20, 241n.48
Pater, Walter, 222n.36
'Patterns of Temporality in Hölderlin' ('PT'), 56, 79, 122, 140, 166, 169, 175, 185–86, 194, 208, 237n.24, 238n.27, 246n.8, 250–51n.25
Paul, Saint, 253n.10
Péguy, Charles, 151
Pfau, Thomas, 219n.12
'Phenomenality and Materiality in Kant' ('PMK'), 212, 237n.23
Phenomenology, and crisis, 134–35, 238n.29
Philipsen, Bart, 224n.23, 226n.40
Philonenko, Alexis, 234n.5, 242n.51
Philosophy, and literature, 128
Plato, 166; and Rousseau, 245n.68; *The Republic*, 244–45n.68
'Poetic Nothingness' ('PN'), xi, 217n.3
Politics: and fiction, 173; in George, 161, 173; and Romanticism and post-Romanticism, 35, 36–40, 120–23, 167–69, 172–73 (*see also under individual authors:* politics and historical ideology in); in Wordsworth, 93–97
Post-Romanticism. See Romanticism: and post-Romanticism
Poulet, Georges, 30, 248n.17; *Les métamorphoses du cercle*, 184
'Preface [to *Allegories of Reading*]' ('PAR'), 72, 214
'Preface [to *The Rhetoric of Romanticism*]' ('PRR'), xiii, 177, 213, 246n.8
Preuves, 247n.15
'Process and Poetry' ('PP'), 3, 72, 81
Prometheus, as figure of excess, 15, 124
Psychoanalysis, and literature, 128, 138, 176
Putnam, Hilary, 245n.72

Quilliot, Roger, 229n.36

Racism, and Soviet anti-Semitism, 108, 230–31n.57
Rajan, Tilottama, 226n.1
Rand, Richard, 252n.6
Raval, Suresh, 248n.15
Reading: and authenticity, 186; and understanding, 52, 68–69, 72–73, 192, 196, 202, 208–10
Recollection, and excess, 40–43, 78, 111. *See also* Hölderlin: and recollection; Rousseau: excess and recollection in
Redfield, Mark, 36, 223n.4, 244n.67, 254n.18
Relativism, 130, 138–39, 235n.11
Renunciation, 122, 264, 208
'Resistance to Theory, The' ('RT'), 237n.23, 245n.73
Revolt: in Camus, 103–9, 124, 233n.67; and *Gelassenheit*, 229n.24; and revolution, 103–9, 113. *See also* Montaigne: revolt in
Revolution: French, 40, 122, 168, 230n.43, 324n.5; July 1830, 95; and nihilism, 104; and revolt, 103–9, 113; and Romanticism (*see* Romanticism: and apocalypse; Romanticism: politics and historical ideology in)
Rhetoric, and hermeneutics, 204–9. *See also* Trope
'Rhetoric of Blindness, The' ('ROB'), 214, 222n.1, 236n.14, 237n.24
Rhetoric of Romanticism, The (RR), xii; Preface to ('PRR'), xiii, 177, 213, 246n.8

'Rhetoric of Temporality, The' ('ROT'), 59, 203–4, 211, 212, 239n.29, 252n.3
Richards, I. A., 235n.11, 248n.16
'Riddle of Hölderlin, The' ('RH'), 68, 121, 124, 161
Rilke, Rainer Maria, xii, 170
Robespierre, Maximilien de, 232n.64, 245n.2
Robinson, Edward, 249–50n.23
Rolland, Romain: and Spinoza, 150; *Voyage intérieur*, 147, 148–51, 239–40n.38
'Roland Barthes and the Limits of Structuralism' ('RB'), 127
Romanticism: and analogism, 58–59, 80–81, 122–23, 176, 248n.17; and apocalypse, 79–81, 98–99, 121–23, 176–77; and authenticity, 114–15, 122, 140, 141–43 (*see also* Beautiful Soul: as figure of lucidity); celebration of, 121–23, 125; and demystification, 177, 199, 132–34, 137–40; and desire, 137, 142–43; German tradition in, 124, 166–67, 170 73; and interpretation, 116–20; as interruption of history, 82–83; misreading of, 58–59, 125–26; and Napoleon, 130, 168; politics and historical ideology in, 35, 36–40, 120–23, 167–69, 172–73; and post-Romanticism, xi–xiii, 39, 114, 133–34, 139–40, 141–45, 146–47, 163, 168, 173, 176–78, 184, 207–8, 254n.15; as privi-

Index | 285

Romanticism (*continued*)
leged historical concern, xiii,
11, 80, 103, 116–20, 139–40,
141–45, 147, 176–78, 213–15,
234n.3; rejection of, 123–25;
and renunciation, 122, 164;
and structuralism, 128–35,
137–40, 238–40n.29; and Symbolism, xi–xii, 184, 218n.8,
241–42n.49; and temporality,
224n.22; and Titanism, 98–99,
117–20, 121, 123, 142, 176–77
Romanticism and Contemporary Criticism (*RCC*), xiii, 227n.5,
235n.7, 252n.3
Rorty, Richard, 243n.60
Rosiek, Jan, 37, 220n.22, 220–21n.25, 221n.26
Rousseau, Jean-Jacques, xi, 5,
127, 138, 175, 223n.6; and
Benjamin, 252n.31; excess and
recollection in, 40–43, 47–48,
49, 91, 96; and French Revolution, 40, 122, 168, 234n.5; and
Hegel, 28, 34–46, 72–73, 104,
168, 219n.8, 234n.5, 242n.52;
and Hölderlin, 11, 18–20, 24–25, 26–27, 32, 35, 40–41, 47,
52, 61–64, 67, 69–70, 79–81, 94, 100, 115, 116, 185; and
Mallarmé, 39; and Montaigne,
115; and Napoleon, 35, 168;
and nothingness, 137–38, 140,
201; and Plato, 244–45n.68;
politics and historical ideology
in, 34–35, 96, 100, 121–22; and
Schiller, 223n.6; and sensory
perception, 7–8, 20–21, 23–25, 28–32, 45, 47, 48, 87, 125,
221–22nn.34,36; and temporality, 48–52; as turning
point in history, 27, 33, 42, 44,
242n.53; vice and virtue in,
181–83, 252n.31; and Wordsworth, 79–81, 94–96, 100, 117,
122, 185; and writing, 182–85; *Confessions*, 37; *Contrat
social (Social Contract)*, 36, 37;
Emile, 104; *Essai sur l'origine des
langues (Essay on the Origin of
Languages)*, 222n.1; *Julie, ou La
Nouvelle Héloïse*, 4, 6–9, 36, 37,
133, 211; *Narcisse*, 166, 181–83;
Pygmalion, 238n.27; *Rêveries du
promeneur solitaire*, 4, 9, 20–21,
24, 29–32, 44, 48–52, 53, 69,
148, 221–22nn.32,33,34,36,
224n.19
'Rousseau and the Transcendence
of the Self' ('RTS'), 50, 115,
121, 126, 140, 141, 143, 144,
166, 184–85, 222n.6, 237n.20,
238n.27
Rousset, David, 107
Ruskin, John: 'Of the Pathetic
Fallacy,' 83, 227n.7

Saint-Just, Louis Antoine Léon
de, 232n.64
Sartre, Jean-Paul, 201, 239n.32,
251n.29; and Bachelard, 175;
and Baudelaire, 175; and
Camus, 105–8, 147, 231n.62;
and Merleau-Ponty, 231n.62;
Les mots, 37
'Sartre's Confessions' ('JPS'), 37–38, 39, 122, 145, 207, 239n.32
Sattler, D. E., 225n.32

Saussure, Ferdinand de, 129
Schaefer, David Lewis, 228n.21, 232n.65
Schelling, F. W. J. von, 35, 89
Scherer, Jacques, 246n.6
Schiller, Friedrich, 223n.6
Schleiermacher, Friedrich E. D., 225n.34, 248n.19
Science: and ethics, 151–52; and hermeneutics, 193, 249–50n.23; and history, 145–47; as ideology of realism, 149–52, 161; and literature, 121, 146, 151–52, 237n.22; and sociology, 146; and structuralism, 127, 130–32, 190, 236n.14
'Self (*Pygmalion*)' ('RNP'), 238n.27
Sensory perception: and literature, 157; and music, 222n.1; and temporality, 87; transcendence of, 7–9, 20–21, 29–32, 35, 44–45, 71, 78, 87, 113, 124, 125
Serenity: as evasion, 3–4, 8, 163, 164, 212, 224n.64; as lucidity, 9, 57, 72, 164, 177, 208, 212
Servotte, Herman, 226n.4
Shakespeare, William, 86
Shelley, Percy Bysshe, 168, 243n.60; *A Defence of Poetry*, 63
'Shelley Disfigured' ('SD'), 212, 214, 215, 218n.8, 226n.4
Shorey, Paul, 244–45n.68
Shusterman, Ronald, 225n.11
'Sign and Symbol in Hegel's *Aesthetics*' ('SS'), 212
Silverman, Hugh J., 249n.19
Simon, Gerhard, 230n.56, 230–31n.57

Slansky-trial, 108
Sociology: and literature, 128, 146, 152, 159–61, 176; and science, 146
Soviet concentration camps, 108
'Spacecritics' ('SC'), 224n.22, 248n.15, 251n.30
Spanos, Vincent W., 249n.19
Spinoza, Baruch, 139, 151–52, 158, 163, 175, 239–40n.38, 240n.43; and Hegel, 155; and Rolland, 150; and Taine, 153–54, 156; *Ethics*, 153, 240n.42; *Treatise on the Correction of the Understanding*, 150
Spiritual Animal, 242n.53
Stalinism, 104, 107–9, 230n.56, 230–31n.57, 231n.58
Starobinski, Jean: *Montaigne en mouvement*, 101, 228n.21
Structuralism, 209; crisis of, 136; and Romanticism, 128–35, 137–40, 238–40n.29; and science, 127, 130–32, 190, 236n.14
'Structure intentionnelle de l'Image romantique.' See 'Intentional Structure of the Romantic Image'
Stucky, Willy, 229n.35
Studies in Romanticism, Introduction to, 190, 212, 253–54n.15
'Symbolic Landscape in Wordsworth and Yeats' ('SL'), 234n.6
Symbolism, and Romanticism, xi–xiii, 184, 218n.8, 241–42n.49

Taine, Hyppolite, 152–55, 161, 240n.43, 241n.44; and Bache-

Index | 287

Taine, Hyppolite (*continued*)
lard, 156–58; and Baudelaire, 152, 154–55; and Hegel, 155; and Spinoza, 153–54, 156
'Taine and Baudelaire' ('TB'), 152–55, 156, 158, 161–63, 218n.8, 247n.9
Taylor, Charles, 233n.69, 241n.43, 243n.60
Temporality: of action vs. interpretation, 99; and hermeneutics, 199; historical law of, 16, 17, 54, 70, 187; and literature, 84, 186–89; and memory, 84; and natural time, 49–52, 54–55, 224n.22; and sensory perception, 87
Temps modernes, Les, 105, 107, 231n.58
'Temptation of Permanence, The' ('TP'), 56, 63, 81, 220n.21, 229n.24, 241n.43, 251n.25
Terada, Rei, 219n.10
Terror: in French Revolution, 230n.43, 232n.64, 234n.5; ideology of, 92, 103, 144
'Thematic Criticism and the Theme of Faust' ('F'), 70, 217n.4, 234n.1
'Time and History in Wordsworth' ('THW'), 127, 177, 186, 187, 226n.4, 227n.5, 234n.6, 246n.8, 252n.3
Titanism. *See* Romanticism: and Titanism.
Tito, Marshal, 233n.68
Totality: and allegory, 201–2, 211–12; and irony, 192, 199–200, 211–12. *See also* Hermeneutics: and fulfillment
Toulmin, Stephen, 240–41n.43
Trope, 204–9
Tunisia, as French colony, 107

Ullmann, Stephen, 248n.15
Understanding. *See* Reading: and understanding

Valéry, Paul, xii, 3
Van Beers, Jan: 'Aan mijne Jongens,' 243–44n.62
Vaterländische Umkehr, 105, 144, 173
Verene, Donald Phillip, 165, 242n.51
Vietnam, as French colony, 107
Virgil, 86
Voltaire, 129, 133

Wagner, Richard, 172
Wahl, Jean: *Tableau de la philosophie française,* 31–32
Warminski, Andrzej, xiv, 234n.1, 237n.23, 244n.64, 254n.17
Wartime Journalism, 3, 110, 114, 146, 147, 148–52, 149, 164, 239–40nn.37, 38
Wasserman, Earl, 241n.49, 243n.60
Waters, Lindsay, 231n.62, 233n.68
Weber, Samuel, 236n.15
'Whatever Happened to André Gide?' ('AG'), 172
'What Is Modern?' ('WM'), 145, 169, 175

288 | *Index*

'White Shirts' ('Doctors' Plot'), 108, 230–31n.57
Wimsatt, William, 247n.15
Wordsworth, William, xi; and analogism, 82–88; and De Quincey, 226n.4; and Hölderlin, 79–82, 84, 91, 94–95, 97, 98, 100, 113, 115, 116, 117, 122, 123, 185; Imagination and Fancy in, 85–87, 227n.9, 234n.6; origin and tendency in, 246n.8; politics and historical ideology in, 93–97; and recollection, 96–97; and Rousseau, 79–81, 94–96, 100, 117, 122, 185; and sensory perception, 87, 234n.6; 'Composed after a Journey across the Hamilton Hills,' 11; 'A Poet's Epitaph,' 45, 174; Preface to *Lyrical Ballads* (1802), 83, 85, 227n.5; Preface to *Poems,* 83, 86, 87, 204, 227nn.8,9; *The Prelude,* 4, 21, 77–78, 93, 94, 98, 148; *River Duddon* cycle, 234n.6; '[There was a Boy],' 54, 83–84, 85, 87, 93, 226n.4, 234n.6; 'These words were uttered in a pensive mood,' 5; 'Tintern Abbey,' 33
'Wordsworth and Hölderlin' ('WWH'), 80, 83, 87, 93–100, 116–19, 123, 125, 177, 226n.4, 227n.5, 228n.17, 234n.1
'Work of Georges Poulet, The' ('GP'), 237n.24, 246n.8
Wright, T. R., 252n.7, 253n.8

Yeats, William Butler, xi, xii, 125, 169–70, 172, 173, 217n.1; image and emblem in, 235n.6; and Mallarmé, xiii; serenity in, 224n.64
'Yeats and the German Romantic Tradition' ('YRT'), xii, 169–72, 218n.8, 218n.1

Index | 289

In the *Texts and Contexts* series:

VOLUME 1
Inscribing the Other
By Sander L. Gilman

VOLUME 2
Crack Wars
Literature,
Addiction, Mania
By Avital Ronell

VOLUME 3
Madness and Art
The Life and Works of Adolf Wölfli
By Walter Morgenthaler
Translated by
Aaron H. Esman

VOLUME 4
Serenity in Crisis
A Preface to Paul de Man,
1939–1960
By Ortwin de Graef

VOLUME 5
The Mirror and the Word
Modernism, Literary Theory,
and Georg Trakl
By Eric B. Williams

VOLUME 6
Undertones of Insurrection
Music, Politics, and the Social Sphere
in the Modern German Narrative
By Marc A. Weiner

VOLUME 7
Herbarium, Verbarium
The Discourse of Flowers
By Claudette Sartiliot

VOLUME 8
Finitude's Score
Essays for the End of the Millennium
By Avital Ronell

VOLUME 9
The Imaginary Jew
By Alain Finkielkraut
Translated by Kevin O'Neill
and David Suchoff

VOLUME 10
*Antisemitism, Misogyny, and the Logic
of Cultural Difference
Cesare Lombroso and Matilde Serao*
By Nancy A. Harrowitz

VOLUME 11
*Organic Memory
History and the Body in
the Late Nineteenth and Early
Twentieth Centuries*
By Laura Otis

VOLUME 12
*Richard Wagner and the Anti-Semitic
Imagination*
By Marc A. Weiner

VOLUME 13
*Titanic Light
Paul de Man's Post-Romanticism,
1960–1969*
By Ortwin de Graef

OHIO UNIVERSITY LIBRARY

Please return this book as soon as you have finished with it. In order to avoid a fine it must be returned by the latest date stamped below. All books are subject to recall after two weeks or immediately if needed for reserve.

QUARTER LOAN

JAN 1 0 1996

JAN 0 4 1996

JUN 1 4 1995